a.j.

WITHDRAWN

The Autobiography of James Monroe

James Monroe Law Office in Fredericksburg, Virginia,
in which James Monroe practiced law from 1786
to 1789. This building, now a museum, houses
numerous articles belonging to Monroe.

The Autobiography of
James Monroe

Edited, and with an Introduction by
Stuart Gerry Brown

With the assistance of
Donald G. Baker

SYRACUSE
UNIVERSITY
PRESS

SYRACUSE UNIVERSITY PRESS

*This work has been published with
the assistance of a Ford Foundation grant.*

Preface

The Monroe Papers in the New York Public Library contain two long fragments of an unfinished autobiography left by President Monroe. Previously known only to a handful of scholars, the manuscript is here printed in its entirety by the kind permission of the Library. It is my hope that not only students of Monroe and his age but the general reader with an interest in American politics and American presidents will find it valuable.

The autobiography is the work of Monroe's last years. It is possible to date the period of its composition fairly closely. He retired to "Oak Hill," Loudoun County, Virginia, on leaving the Presidency in March, 1825. On December 5, 1827 he raised with his old friend, Judge John McKean, a question about publishing "a memoir, remarks, and documents, in a pamphlet" as a method of impressing Congress with the importance and the cost of his two European missions. He refers in the manuscript to the publication in 1828 of the journals of the Confederation Congress. On May 2, 1829 he wrote to Lafayette, "My mind is not inactive, and in the employment given to it, a review of past occurrences in which I have acted, and of which I have been a witness, occupies a large portion of my time. I do not know that anything will appear to the public during my life." Finally, he speaks of his wife in the present tense. She died on September 23, 1830. Thus it appears that Monroe drafted these pages at intervals between the end of 1827 and the end of 1830. His feeble condition makes it unlikely that he wrote anything after his removal to New York in November, 1830. He died July 4, 1831.

The manuscript consists of some 105–110 sheets, or roughly 400 pages. Monroe folded each sheet in half so that there were four pages on which to write. He followed the practice of writing on the right-hand

v

side of each page, leaving a left-hand column blank for any corrections, comments, or revisions that he wished to make later.

A combination of factors—the effect of the years in darkening the paper, the fading of the brown ink used by Monroe, the use of a rather poor quality of paper that contributed to the blurring of the ink, plus Monroe's cramped style of writing—results in words and sometimes entire lines or paragraphs being almost illegible. An added difficulty is Monroe's habit of spelling words phonetically if he did not know their correct spelling.

The reader should understand that the manuscript is a draft. There are only occasional corrections, suggesting that for the most part Monroe went over it only once. This will account for a certain amount of repetition and for the uneven manner of treating certain incidents. The punctuation has been corrected and modernized here, so far as Monroe's heavily parenthetical and periodic style permits. An occasional excessively long paragraph has been broken up. Otherwise the text is transcribed as Monroe left it.

Monroe's notes, incomplete and unsystematic, have been removed from the text. Most of these are references to the original edition of his *A View of the Conduct of the Executive, etc.* I have altered them to correspond with the page numbers in Hamilton's edition of Monroe's writings. I have also transferred, as far as possible, references to letters to the pages of this edition. The annotation I have supplied is intended to show any important contrasts between Monroe's views contemporary with an incident related here, and his views of the same incident in retrospect; to supplement Monroe's account where important additional material is available; and to correct errors he himself would have caught had he revised his manuscript. A few obviously careless errors in dates have been corrected in the text. I should like here to record my gratitude to my friend and colleague, Professor Edwin H. Cady, for valuable advice on the problem of annotation.

My research assistant, Mr. Donald G. Baker, struggled so heroically (and successfully!) with Monroe's handwriting in transcribing the manuscript, and proved so helpful in many other ways, that I have thought it proper for his name to appear on the title page. I alone am responsible, of course, for any errors.

My friend and former student, Professor Ralph Ketcham of the University of Chicago, now editing the Madison papers, has provided me with important leads to unpublished Monroe letters, some of which are used here in the notes. I am grateful to him for this and much other assistance. My secretary, Mrs. Pat Tamborini, prepared the printer's copy not only meticulously but cheerfully.

Mr. Laurence Gouverneur Hoes, President of the Monroe Memorial Foundation, has been exceedingly generous in providing appropriate illustrative materials. His cooperation has been an inspiration both to me and to the editors of the Syracuse University Press.

I am grateful to the American Philosophical Society and to the Rockefeller Foundation for grants supporting my research on Monroe, and other presidents, undertaken in the course of an extensive study of presidential leadership. This book is a kind of offshoot of that study.

S. G. B.

Maxwell Graduate School of Citizenship and Public Affairs,
Syracuse University
July, 1959

Contents

List of Illustrations

All of the photographs in this book (except the reproduction of Monroe's manuscript) have been reproduced through the courtesy of the James Monroe Law Office Museum, Fredericksburg, Virginia. Most of the articles illustrated are on view in the Law Office Museum.

James Monroe:
The Political Education of a President

These massive fragments of an autobiography left by President Monroe, though ponderous in style, have about them other and more valuable weightinesses. They are instructive both to the student of biography and to the student of American presidential politics. As biographical materials they do not need an introduction. But some comment on their political significance may be in order.

I

James Monroe may fairly be called the first important professional politician of the United States: that is, he was the first of our prominent men who chose politics as his career, clearly preferring public to private life despite occasional perfunctory disclaimers. Monroe's vocational objective over forty years, though never directly stated, was to hold responsible public office. No American ever succeeded better. Before the Revolution was over he had been elected to the Virginia Assembly and the Virginia Executive Council. Thereafter, he served in the Congress of the Confederation, the Virginia Ratifying Convention, the Senate in the First Congress, as Minister to France, Governor of Virginia, Minister again to France and also to Spain and to Britain, Governor of Virginia again, Secretary of State, Secretary of War, and President for two terms. In 1820 Monroe reached a peak of political success never again to be sighted by anyone: he was re-elected to the Presidency without opposition. During all the years he was out of office only at brief intervals.

Monroe made few political mistakes, and each time quickly recovered. On his first mission to France in the 1790's he behaved naively, and by modern standards, improperly, but he exploited his "misconduct" so skillfully that his return in disgrace looked more like the

1

return of a martyred hero of the democratic cause and soon brought him the Governorship of Virginia. Again, in 1807, disappointed at the failure of President Jefferson and Secretary of State Madison to accept and applaud his treaty with Great Britain, Monroe allowed himself to be drawn away from his long-standing alliance with the Republican giants. Indeed, he was cajoled by John Randolph to such an extent that he did not forbid the use of his name against Madison for the Presidency in 1808. But he did not actually seek the nomination and he did not openly break with his friends. Shortly he could return to the Governor's chair and, by 1811, his political skills and his important following were sorely needed in Washington. He rejoined Madison as Secretary of State almost on terms of Presidential capitulation. His final political mistake cost him nothing, though it cost his party its unchallenged hold on the government. In his second term as President, Monroe not only spoke frequently of his unalterable decision to retire, but refused utterly to maintain party leadership and to use his power to project his successor. The result was the appearance of several warring candidates in the midst of his official family, and the eventual splitting of the Republican Party. Thus the statesman whose career was born in revolution and advanced in partisan conflict lived to see a full cycle of his own making. Under Monroe's leadership the Republicans wrought the total electoral destruction of their Federalist opponents, yet during his Presidency the Republican Party collapsed into feuding factions and precipitated the return of the two party system.

The two extended autobiographical fragments which form this book are evidently the work of a politician. Even the circumstances of the writing have their political significance. While the tone of the book is designedly dispassionate and the third person is used (with some inconsistency) to create an impression of objective review at a period when ambition is long since satiated, service completed, and accounts rendered, nevertheless Monroe was deeply engaged at the time of composition in trying to obtain money from Congress in satisfaction of claims dating back to the 1790's. After his retirement from the Presidency in 1825 he found his financial situation increasingly difficult. He had pressing debts and very inadequate income from his lands. In the fall of 1830, coincident with his wife's death, he despaired of ever reaching financial stability in view of the obligations he faced, gave up his home in Virginia, and went to live with his son-in-law, Samuel Gouverneur, in New York. There is no doubt that the autobiography was intended in part to raise money through sales and in part to help persuade the Congress to act. The book, of course, was never finished, and the eventual appropriation by Congress of $30,000 (May, 1831) was far less than Monroe needed or felt he was owed.

But these circumstances of Monroe's financial straits account in some measure for the moralizing which characterizes the book and the defensive manner in which both his European missions are presented. Little is left of the bitter political polemics which set the tone of his contemporary accounts of the 1794–1796 mission, and the hurt he suffered when Jefferson and Madison did not support his treaty with Britain in 1807 is omitted, yet the whole is aimed to show the public a devoted, if long suffering, public servant, not the least of whose woes is that his ungrateful government owes him substantial money. The strategy is sound, though the execution is not always successful.

These are the reminiscences of an aging statesman who had, in some ways, passed beyond politics by the very fullness of his political success. But they deal with periods in his long career when he was serving his personal political apprenticeship, helping to build his party, and reaching his political maturity. The first section recounts his adventures from boyhood to his forty-first year in a reasonably continuous narrative. It is instructive to see which events, which turnings, and which persons Monroe chose to select for special emphasis as he looked back from the vantage point of his great final eminence.

Monroe was a *bona fide* military hero of the Revolution—a fact which stood well to his advantage in his political career. In his autobiography he seems to have intended to give just enough account of his role as soldier to remind his reader, but to be very careful lest he seem to be boasting like a professional veteran. As he recounts the events leading up to and including the battle of Trenton, he slips occasionally from the third to the first person. But he makes no more than necessary of his wound, and contemporary accounts of the Delaware crossing assign him a larger role than he assigns himself. Indeed, Monroe seems embarrassed to speak of his exploits in the same breath with his mention of General Washington. At this point in the manuscript there is a paragraph which interrupts the narrative abruptly to make a homily on how unimportant Monroe was—"a mere youth"—and how mighty were Washington and the other Revolutionary leaders. Yet when, after three years of service, there is no appropriate command for the young major and he returns to Virginia, he does not hesitate to obtain from Washington a letter of recommendation that would serve him well in civil life. With the letter from Washington and the influence of his uncle, the eminent Judge Joseph Jones, Monroe was in a good position to build a public career onto his war record.

Politics begins in earnest at this point. While Monroe was, of course, concerned to obtain the best training possible for a career in the law, he weighed carefully the relative advantages of study with George Wythe or Thomas Jefferson. Judge Jones, to whom he confided his meditations, could place him with either man. Wythe, Chancellor of the Virginia high court and professor of law at William and Mary, had been Jefferson's teacher and was recognized then, as later, as perhaps the finest legal mind of his era in America. Jefferson had practiced but little and was at the time engrossed in his duties as Governor of Virginia. In choosing to go to Jefferson, young Monroe consulted his interest in pursuing a political rather than a legal career. Preferment in public office was more likely to be forthcoming to a protegé of Mr. Jefferson than to a protegé even of Chancellor Wythe.

Back at Williamsburg, Monroe tells us, he resumed his studies at the College in addition to reading law under Jefferson and acting as aid to the Governor. But scholarship, the record indicates, was not the young man's chief concern. Before the end of 1779 the seat of government was moved from Williamsburg to Richmond, and Monroe had to decide once more whether to continue as a student, taking Wythe's course, or go to Richmond with Jefferson. He went with Jefferson.

When opportunity came for another brief excursion into the military side of the war, Monroe took it and again acquitted himself with distinction. By the time of Yorktown, at the age of twenty-three, he had established himself among the leadership to stay. At the Peace Ball in Fredericksburg, November 11, 1781, honoring Washington, contemporary accounts list "Colonel James Monroe" just after George Mason and daughter and before R. H. Lee, General Harry Lee, Baron Von Steuben, Admiral De Grasse, and others.

As Jefferson's protegé he entered politics. His election to the Assembly was owing to several components of his public character: he was a landed gentleman of modest holdings; he had served well in the war and was recommended by Washington; he was a nephew of Joseph Jones; and he was an assistant to Jefferson, who warmly commended him. These components added up to a very promising whole.

In the Assembly Monroe became acquainted with Madison, Mason, Henry, R. H. Lee, and others. He behaved modestly and cultivated an aspect of sober good sense and reliability, an aspect with which he was always thereafter identified. Soon he was elected to the Executive Council. He attached himself still closer to Jefferson, and began a regular correspondence with nearly all of the leaders, but especially with Jefferson and Madison.

The pages in his autobiography given to the sessions of Congress between 1783 and 1786 show that Monroe's attachment to politics was serious and intelligent. He was a willing student of important problems and did not form a judgment until he had good mastery of the details. But he had a knack of selecting for specialization the issues which could help him to appeal to the broadest segments of the population and to appear as a forward looking young legislator. In particular, his attention to the issue with Spain over the navigation of the Mississippi and his concern for liberal legislation to open up the western lands identified him as a spokesman for the "common man," rather than for the eastern planter, or banker, or man of commerce. He collaborated with Jefferson as a junior partner in drafting the so-called "Ordinance of 1784" which underlies the Northwest Ordinance of 1787 and, most notably, forbids slavery in the new lands. In the summer of 1784, after the session of Congress was concluded and Jefferson had departed on his mission to France, Monroe made his first long journey into the West. It was an adventurous journey as his memoir recounts it. But he omits the interesting fact that he bought a large tract of land in central New York State, just south of Fort Stanwix (Rome), with a plan to settle there and farm with free labor—hired hands, not slaves. He interested Madison in the project. But it failed for lack of money to hold the land and because of the pressure of public service. This abortive venture is important, nevertheless, for what it reveals about the young politician. He had, in fact, a real feeling for the "West." His support of the western farmer in Congress was not an easy, calculating policy, but a matter of conviction. His hatred of slavery was genuine. He had made Jefferson's democratic and agrarian principles very much his own, and his appeal to the common man throughout his career was a *bona fide* appeal. Political expediency and conviction were, in Monroe's case, fortunately identified during this early term in Congress, as they were to be most of the time in the future.

II

At the close of his term in Congress in 1786, Monroe supported and attended the Annapolis Convention, thereby identifying himself with the growing movement for a stronger central government. But his conduct during 1787–1789 shows how careful he was to take the best political soundings before committing himself to specific positions on constitutional principles and proposals. In the Virginia Assembly, to which he returned in 1787, he found a majority, led by Mason and Henry, highly sceptical of the Philadelphia document. He set forth his own views with caution, advocating stronger central power but also fuller protection of states' rights and individual liberties.

Upon his election to the Virginia Ratifying Convention he took his assignment with the utmost seriousness. Few delegates to the state conventions prepared themselves for their responsibilities as well as did Monroe. He devoted months to the study of political history. Like Madison before him, he familiarized himself with all of the important republican constitutions and pondered long and deeply on the principles of representative government. He then applied what he had learned to the draft document from Philadelphia. The results of this study he wrote into a long essay ("Some Observations on the Constitution") which, like most of his writing, tends to be turgid in style but remains, nevertheless, one of the most thoughtful early studies of the Constitution. He had it printed, intending to circulate it among his constituents, but, as he tells us, he was dissatisfied with the "printing" and had it withdrawn before many people had seen it. Since the printing is at least as good as in most pamphlets of the time, it is safe to conclude that it was actually Monroe's caution that led him to think a second time about circulating it. At other times he spoke of it as "too loosely drawn." At any rate, the essay contains substantial support for many of the provisions of the draft constitution, so many that Washington and Madison were by no means displeased with it. Yet it concludes with a tentative rejection of the whole document because it seemed insufficiently democratic. Monroe thought that the Senate would be a meeting of ambassadors negotiating treaties, rather than a legislative body, and that the President, in the provisions for his election, was too far removed from the people. Like many others he objected to the absence of a bill of rights. For these reasons he seemed to be saying that he would vote against adoption. At the same time he writes always as a nationalist and pleads for stronger central government. The whole study contains some remarkable insights and some excellent forecasts, while its political impact is a skillful example of "strategic obfuscation." This is not to say, again, that the ambivalence is merely calculated. The tone of the document is sincere and there is no reason to doubt that Monroe's dilemma was genuine.

At the Convention Monroe played his part with great political sagacity. He was not aggressive enough to be counted among the leaders of either the Federalists, led by Madison and Marshall, or the Anti-Federalists, led by Mason and Henry. Yet he was by no means inconspicuous. Instead, he carved out a place for himself distinct from all others, appealing in important ways to both sides of the great controversy. However the struggle might turn out, Monroe would not be attainted in the eyes of either side.

In the debates Monroe expressed three main views, each at some length, but with modesty and proper deference to those with whom he might for the moment disagree. First, he sided vigorously with those who objected to the absence of a bill of rights; second, he sided with the Federalists against the states'-righters on the need for strong national government; third, and most significantly, he reiterated his view that the Senate would be a body of diplomats and not a proper democratic legislature. He hammered home his third point by reverting to the question of the navigation of the Mississippi. On this issue he commanded great respect, since he had fought for the West against New England in the old Congress where the westerners had lost. Now in the Convention where he was called upon as an authority, Monroe warned that a coalition of northeastern states interested in fisheries and commerce could use the Senate to realize their own interests at the expense of the West. In the end, Monroe voted against ratification. But his stand for civil liberties and for the common man of the West built on to his base of popularity much more effectively than a narrow states'-rights stand would have done; and his plea for strong central government enabled him to stay in the good graces of Washington, Madison, and the other victors.

In the autobiography Monroe makes it appear that after the Convention he retired from public life as a matter of deep inclination to practice law. The fact is, however, that he immediately contested a seat in the election to the first House of Representatives, and lost to Madison. His "retirement" was thus forced and temporary. He tells us that his selection to succeed Grayson in the Senate in 1790 came without any effort on his part. But his correspondence with Jefferson and others shows that he maneuvered quietly to line up support in the legislature. At any rate, his own account shows him entering into the new national government with a gusto he cannot produce for us when he talks about his "attendance at the bar."

* ### III

Nearly half of Monroe's unfinished autobiography is given to an account of his first mission to France, 1794–1796. On any showing, this was one of the most remarkable diplomatic ventures ever undertaken by a modern government. Its naive and paradoxical character can only be explained by the innocence of the American Administration of the ways of the world. The manner in which it was executed, whatever it may tell us about James Monroe, serves to show how green was the Revolution in the minds of at least some Americans, and how curiously contradictory revolutionary ardor and national self interest may sometimes appear to be. At any rate, in all the long years afterward Monroe never managed to press the traumatic experience of this ill-fated mission into the background of his consciousness. There is even point to the notion that his whole later career was conducted with a view to vindicating his conduct then, and fixing his reputation for wise statesmanship, to heal the spiritual wounds he had suffered.

It is instructive to compare the massive pamphlet he published in 1797—*A View of the Conduct of the Executive in the Foreign Affairs of the United States*—with his handling of the same material in his old age. The querulous and polemical elements are gone, at the end, but the defensive posture remains. He was betrayed, he believed, by an Administration which was itself betraying the spirit and principles of the Revolution, while he strove to keep that spirit and those principles alive. "The principle on which that contest turned [war between France and Britain] was that on which our governments were founded, and it was believed, by those who formed the Anti-Federal party, that the result in favor of either side would produce a corresponding effect with us."

Thus an "Anti-Federalist" was dispatched to shore up a "Federalist" policy. In the Senate Monroe had voted against the confirmation of Jay to go to London, as he had earlier voted against Morris for Paris. Once the Jay mission was under way, Monroe was chosen for the French mission precisely because he was well known, from his association with Jefferson and Madison as well as his conduct in the Senate, to be an ardent partisan of France and an opponent of Jay's mission. The simple strategy of Washington and Randolph was to send an Anglophile to London and a Francophile to Paris to counteract each other. The intended guile, however, lay in the fact that Jay was to negotiate a treaty and Monroe was not. The Administration had taken a decision effectively ranging the United States on the side of Britain. Monroe's function was to persuade the French it was not so. How well he succeeded the reader may judge from Monroe's own account and from the documents he cites.

The consequences of this first mission served to advance Monroe's political education in several important ways. Most immediately, the effect of his recall was to harden his opposition to the Federalists and steer him toward more formal organization with his fellow oppositionists. Gallatin, writing to his wife, leaves us a useful account of the political context in which Monroe acted after his return to the United States:

> Mr. Monroe arrived last night . . . I spent two hours with him, during which he gave us (Jefferson and Burr, who is also in town) much interesting information, chiefly in relation to his own conduct and to that of the Administration respecting himself and France. . . . The time they chose to recall Monroe was when from his correspondence they had reason to believe that he had succeeded in allaying the resentment of the French. Then, thinking they had nothing to fear from France, and that they had used Monroe so as to obtain every service that he could render, they recalled him, with the double view of giving to another person the merit of terminating the differences and of throwing upon him (Monroe) the blame of any that had existed before. I am happy to tell you that from my conversation with Monroe, from his manner and everything about him (things which are more easily felt than expressed), I have the strongest impression upon my mind that he is possessed of integrity superior to all the attacks of malignity, and that he had conducted [himself] with irreproachable honour and the most dignified sense of duty. Sorry am I to be obliged to add that I am also pretty well convinced that the American Administration have acted with a degree of meanness only exceeded by their folly, and that they have degraded the American name throughout Europe.

Three days later Gallatin announced, again to his wife, that "We give tomorrow a splendid dinner to Monroe at Oeller's hotel, in order to testify our approbation of his conduct and our opinion of his integrity. Jefferson, Judge McKean, the governor, and about fifty members of Congress will be there; for which I expect the Administration, Porcupine & Co. will soundly abuse us." The Republican Party, as a national organization, had its origins in dinners such as this. Monroe from this moment was deeply involved in both the national party and the Virginia branch. His partisanship was confirmed by events and toughened by experience.

Another consequence of Monroe's mission and recall was to enhance his reputation among the farmers of the West as the spokesman not only for Republican liberalism, but for their interests as against the interests of the moneyed men on the eastern seaboard. "Republics should approach near to each other," he told the French National Convention in his unprecedented address. Monroe appeared thereafter as the symbol of that revolutionary unity among common men everywhere against monarchy and privilege which had been stirred by Jefferson and Paine in 1776 and by the French in 1789, and which could be usefully advanced by the American Republicans in their bitter fight with the Federalists. But the unity of the Republicans arose from great diversity. The planters of Virginia's tidewater had little in common with the new men of the West except their fears of eastern capital and of the British. Monroe, a member of the planter class though a minor planter, made his appeal to the Virginia aristocrats chiefly by what he was against. They were conservative and devoted to tradition, and the French Revolution, though it deeply moved a few like Jefferson, could not arouse their sympathies. But in the West, and among the workers of the eastern cities, there was no fear of the French, and the revival of the Revolutionary slogans sounded good. Thus Monroe had it both ways. There were, of course, three ways. But since the third was irreconcilable with the other two, Monroe's lot was cast with the Republicans until they or the Federalists should triumph.

Finally, the French mission opened Monroe's eyes to the world as Jefferson's vision had been broadened by his years in Paris. When he set out for Europe, Monroe was less well read, less perceptive, less cultivated than Jefferson had been. And his native gifts were not comparable. But he was, nevertheless, an intelligent and observant man. The political lessons he drew from his experience were sound. Thereafter, he shared with Jefferson, indeed with most Americans, the earnest wish to keep aloof from the troubles of the Old World, to have good commercial relations with everyone, political connections with none. But unlike most of his friends and colleagues, he seems to have assumed that such a condition was more desirable than probable. The safest course for the United States, he thought, was extension of the sphere of freedom. One can draw a straight line from the Address to the French National Convention in 1794 to the Monroe Doctrine.

IV

In his memoirs Monroe hastens over his first term as Governor of Virginia (1799–1802) in the most perfunctory manner. Perhaps he intended to go back to it, but at any rate the fragment which he did write took him almost immediately into his second European mission and enabled him to deal consecutively with the development of his views on foreign affairs. This account of his second French mission, his mission to England, and his unsuccessful efforts to negotiate a treaty with Spain, comprises the final one-third of these autobiographical fragments. But the account is not complete, breaking off before he had negotiated his unhappy treaty with Britain.

Monroe's account of the Louisiana Purchase negotiations is rather more modest than might have been expected. He makes a good deal of the importance of his status as a plenipotentiary minister outranking Livingston, and the deference paid to him by the French government, but he does not make a direct claim to credit for the cession. He is careful to state categorically that Marbois made his announcement of Napoleon's decision to Livingston privately, thus protecting the pride of the Livingston family and giving his own role at the crucial moment a secondary status. On the other hand, he points out that Livingston's correspondence with Talleyrand up to the time of Monroe's arrival gave no hint of the impending offer, and that Livingston himself was of the opinion that they would do well even to get the port at New Orleans. Only after Monroe's arrival with full powers did the First Consul shift his position. Monroe leaves the matter of credit at this point, asking the reader to make up his own mind. Later, while he was in London, Monroe found that Livingston was opposed to his agreement to advance the French two million francs before the treaties were ratified. Again Monroe is scrupulously careful not to offend the Livingstons, though making it appear that the decision to advance the money was probably crucial to keeping Napoleon from changing his mind. Finally, he gives an account of his last conversation with Napoleon in which he stood firmly on the ground that France should intercede with Spain to help the United States secure the Floridas. The whole account is written with great political skill, uncorrected draft though it is. No reader was likely to be offended by it; no reader was likely to receive the impression that Monroe was at all arrogant; yet any reader would see that Monroe's mission was of the first importance to his country, and that his role had been central in acquiring both of the great recent additions of territory. The clarity with which he assessed Napoleon's motives in ceding Louisiana, again, shows how Monroe had grown in political sophistication.

Monroe's observations on the French Revolution, included at the end of the account of his second mission, are fully in keeping with his status as an ex-President of the American Republic, the last of the Revolutionary fathers, and an unswerving friend of liberty throughout a long life. But it is perhaps proper to point out that the contrast he draws between the libertarian condition of the French government during his first mission and the authoritarian character it had taken on by the time he returned is somewhat specious. His contemporary account of his first mission shows that he overlooked the authoritarian aspects of France under the Committee of Public Safety and the Directory almost entirely, in favor of emphasis upon revolutionary slogans. The slogans corresponded with his own views and with his hopes regarding France, and they were important in the political controversy with the pro-British Federalists. But the posture he assumed in 1794–1797 makes the foresight which he claims in his memoirs something less than fully convincing. It may be that, as he says, he anticipated a drift backwards toward the ancient tyranny. But Monroe was no Burke to look upon the Terror and predict Napoleon.

In London and in Madrid Monroe learned to distrust professional diplomats, including the French whose duplicity regarding Florida he discovered only while trying to get Spain to cede that province. But his language is restrained, indeed it is "diplomatic." A stilted and somewhat pompous style is even helpful in these passages describing his interminable and fruitless negotiations with various British ministers and with Cevallos of Spain. The impression is of a sincere and devoted American patriot who would persevere to achieve justice for his country, despite his certainty that his counterparts in the diplomatic game will not play fair.

Monroe's meditations on sovereignty which precede his unfinished account of the Spanish mission contain a revealing passage:

> In those of the first class [governments with sovereignty in the people], at a period of revolution and convulsion, although the government which may be formed is that with which you have to treat, yet as the people in that state move in mass and form in reality the government, a course of conduct may be necessary to gain their good will, to prevent the most serious injury.

Here is a final apology for his behavior in France in 1794, his address to the Convention, his hailing the ceremonial placing together of the American and European republican flags, his overt partisanship for the French Revolution. At the end of his career he still thought it good and proper diplomacy. It is instructive to observe that these were the thoughts running through his mind as he set about reconstructing his unhappy experience with the despotic government of Spain. The chief ingredients of Monroe's education for the Presidency, for his role as maker of foreign policy, are to be found in these vividly recollected experiences of his middle years. It is not necessary to search further for an understanding of his goals as President—acquisition of the Floridas, exclusion of further European colonization from the Americas, recognition of and fraternal relations with the Latin American revolutionary republics, even the deeply self-interested understanding with Britain which enabled him to succeed so well.

One cannot help wishing that Monroe had either begun to write his autobiography earlier, or had lived long enough to finish it. But these substantial fragments are enormously useful in reconstructing the education of a President. We can see how his political mind and character were formed and tested, how he adjusted his ambitions to reality, how well his principles were attuned to the hopes of the people. And we can see how, with much pain and some blundering, he added the dimension of diplomat to that of politician. This is much indeed; so perhaps it is idle to regret that the President "of all the people" did not finish his story and tell us how it felt to preside over the "Era of Good Feelings."

Chronology of Events During Period of Monroe's Autobiography

April 28, 1758

Born in Westmoreland County, Virginia, the son of Spence Monroe and of Elizabeth, the sister of Judge Joseph Jones. Early education was under the direction of the Reverend Archibald Campbell. Matriculated to the College of William and Mary at the age of 16.

1776

A Cadet in the Third Virginia Regiment, under Colonel Hugh Mercer. Promoted to a Lieutenancy and ordered to the main army under General Washington. Participated in the battles of Harlem Heights (September 16) and White Plains (October 28), retreated with the army through New Jersey, and was wounded at the battle of Trenton (December 26). Later promoted to the rank of Captain for his efforts at Trenton.

1777

Appointed aide-de-camp to Lord Stirling in July. Engaged in the battles at Brandywine (September 11) and Germantown (October 4).

1778–9

With Washington and Stirling at Valley Forge; at the battle of Monmouth (June 28). Desiring a command of his own, he returned to Virginia with a letter of recommendation from Washington. Appointed a Lieutenant-Colonel of a command to be raised in the State of Virginia, but the state's exhausted finances prevented the raising of such a group. Re-entered College of William and Mary.

1780

Studied law under Governor Jefferson. Appointed military commissioner to the Southern army to obtain knowledge concerning the state of military affairs in that quarter. Returned to complete his study of law.

1782

Elected to the House of Delegates; selected by the Assembly as a Member of the Executive Council.

June 6, 1783

Elected as a delegate from Virginia to Congress for a three-year term beginning November 3, 1783.

December 13, 1783

Congress assembled at Annapolis; ratification of a definitive treaty of peace with Great Britain.

June, 1784

During adjournment of Congress in summer, toured the northwest frontier to determine what type of government Congress should establish for frontier lands.

November, 1784

Congress reassembled at Trenton.

November, 1786

Attended Annapolis Convention. Upon completion of his three-year term in Congress, married Elizabeth Kortright and returned to Richmond to take up the practice of law.

1787

Elected again to the Virginia Assembly.

1788

Selected as a member to the Virginia Convention to ratify the Federal Constitution. Published his essay, "Observations Upon the Proposed Plan of Federal Government," but then withheld it from circulation. After ratification defeated by Madison for the House of Representatives in the First Congress under the new Constitution.

1789

Returned to the practice of law.

November, 1790

Elected by state legislature as United States Senator from Virginia to fill vacancy caused by death of William Grayson.

March 3, 1791

Re-appointed as Senator from Virginia.

May, 1794

Nominated and confirmed as Minister Plenipotentiary of the United States to the Republic of France.

August, 1794

Arrived in Paris and received by the National Convention.

November, 1794

Jay signed Treaty of Amity, Commerce, and Navigation with Great Britain.

1795

Treaty of Amity, Commerce, and Navigation with Great Britain received by Secretary of State (March 7); given to Senate for consideration (June 8) and approved (June 24). Treaty ratified by President (August 18).

August 19, 1795

Resignation of Edmund Randolph from office of Secretary of State.

December 10, 1795

Timothy Pickering nominated and confirmed as Secretary of State.

February 29, 1796

Proclamation by the President of the Treaty with Great Britain.

June, 1796

Criticized by Secretary of State in letter (June 13) for not taking all possible steps that might lead to a termination of French criticisms of the Jay Treaty.

September, 1796

Recalled from his mission to France.

December, 1796

Charles Cotesworth Pinckney nominated to replace Monroe as Minister Plenipotentiary to France; Monroe takes leave of French government.

February 8, 1797

Congress counts electoral vote of 1796; Adams elected President.

June, 1797

Monroe arrives in Philadelphia after his trip from France.

December 2, 1797
Publication of *A View of the Conduct of the Executive, &c.*

December 6, 1799
Monroe elected Governor of Virginia.

November, 1800
Presidential election; Jefferson and Burr each receive 73 electoral votes for the Presidency.

February, 1801
Jefferson elected President.

January, 1803
Nominated and appointed Envoy Extraordinary and Minister Plenipotentiary to treat with France for the purchase of New Orleans and the lands eastward of the Mississippi.

April 18, 1803
Commissioned Minister Plenipotentiary to Great Britain.

April 30, 1803
Official texts of the treaty for cession of Louisiana Territory signed by American Ministers and the French.

July, 1803
Monroe leaves France to assume his duties as Minister to Great Britain.

October, 1803
Senate advises President to approve Treaty for purchase of Louisiana.

1803–6
Monroe fulfills his duties as Minister to Great Britain and Envoy Extraordinary to Spain.

May 12, 1806
Monroe and William Pinkney jointly appointed as Commissioners for the settlement of differences between the United States and Great Britain.

December 31, 1806
Signs with Pinkney a Treaty of Amity, Commerce, and Navigation with Great Britain.

March, 1807
Jefferson refuses to send Treaty to Senate for consideration.

December, 1807
Monroe arrives at Norfolk and returns home.

The Autobiography of James Monroe

Articles owned by James Monroe. He drilled with the gun
on the palace green in Williamsburg as a young student
before he left to join the forces of General Washington
in New York. Carved on the butt of the gun is
"JM. W-M 76," standing for James Monroe,
William and Mary College, 1776. Monroe
used the sword in the
Revolutionary War.

1

Soldier in the Revolution

James Monroe, late President of the United States, was born in Westmoreland County in 1758 on Monroe's creek, which empties into the Potomac River, between Mattox and Mosier's creeks. His ancestor, Andrew Monroe, emigrated from Scotland, Fowlis, in 1650. He belonged to an ancient highland clan, was a captain in the service of Charles the First, and came over immediately after he was beheaded.[1] In 1650, a tract of land was granted to him on that creek, which was then in Northumberland County. He returned to Scotland on the restoration of Charles the Second and brought over with him some of his relatives, on which account another tract was granted to him. At the period of Mr. Monroe's birth, almost all the land bordering on each side of that creek belonged to the family in its several branches, which had become numerous. His father, Spence Monroe, a name derived from a family in that quarter with which he had become connected, was a very worthy and respectable citizen possessed of good landed and other property. His mother, Elizabeth Jones, was a very amiable and respectable woman, possessing the best domestic qualities, a good wife and good parent. Her father emigrated from Wales and died possessed of considerable property, a portion of which descended to her. Her brother, Joseph Jones, took the degree of barrister of law in England, and was a distinguished revolutionary patriot, honored by his country with the highest offices and at the most difficult period. On the establishment of the General Court in 1776, on the adoption of the State Constitution, he was appointed the presiding judge in that court. In 1777, he was elected to Congress, in which he served until 1783, and then retired in compliance with an Article of the Confederation which was adopted in 1781 and limited the service of its members to three years. He was not long afterwards replaced on the bench of the General Court in which he served till his death, in 1805. Few men possessed in a higher degree the confidence and esteem of his fellow citizens, or merited it more, for soundness of intellect, perfect integrity, and devotion to his country.

Of his father's family there were none, though numerous, who had held any office of note except Andrew Monroe, his father's uncle, who had held a command in the militia of Westmoreland County, with the rank of Colonel or of Lieutenant Colonel, under Richard H. Lee. John Monroe, son of the latter, had visited Scotland, and in an interview at Edinburgh with the celebrated Dr. Monro, traced the connection between the branches in a common origin to the clan adverted to.

The last academy or school in Westmoreland County was managed by the Reverend Archibald Campbell, a Scotchman, the clergyman of the parish, a man of profound learning, and who had the best connections in Scotland.[2] Twenty-five students only were admitted into his academy, but so high was its character that youths were sent to it from the more distant parts of the then colony. Mr. Monroe was placed in that academy, when a boy, by his father, and he remained in it more than four years, until his father's death in 1774, when he was removed by his uncle, Mr. Jones, the executor of his father's will, to William and Mary College, in which he was placed on due examinations, his classical acquirements permitting it, in the philosophical school, in the class of students. The opportunities afforded for instruction in that college, considering the early epoch at which it was founded, were great. The grammar school comprised the ancient languages. The philosophical school was divided into several professorships: one of natural philosophy, including mathematics, astronomy, and all the experimental branches, with an excellent apparatus; one of moral philosophy, including belles-lettres, logic, and rhetoric; and likewise a school of divinity. He pursued his studies in this college until January 1776, when it being essentially shut up by the procession of the war, he left it in his eighteenth year, and entered with John Francis Mercer and several other youths of great merit as a cadet in the Third Virginia Regiment, which was raised and commanded by Colonel Hugh Mercer, who was soon afterwards appointed a brigadier general and who fell fighting gallantly at the head of his brigade in the battle of Princeton. Mr. Monroe was appointed a lieutenant in that regiment soon after he joined it, in Captain John Thornton's company, and in which grade he served the whole of that campaign.

As Mr. Monroe had been employed, with little intermission, from the time that he entered into the army until his retirement in 1825 from the high office which he then held, and from a very early period, in the most important trusts abroad and at home, he was necessarily a party, in the stations which he held, to the great events which occurred in them, so far as they related to his own country; a spectator of many others on the interesting theater on which he moved; and well acquainted with almost all which mastered that very interesting epoch. In this work I shall present his view of those events, noticing those of each class and referring to the records and other documents which support them in every instance. The sketch will be partly historical and partly biographical, commencing with his entrance into the army, and pursuing it in all the most interesting details through his whole career.

As the war then pressed on New York and there were few regular regiments in the army, the Third Virginia Regiment, commanded by Colonel Weedon, was ordered there, which it reached by rapid marches immediately after the battle of Long Island, in which Smallwood's and Haslet's regiments were nearly cut to pieces. Weedon's regiment was posted on Harlem Heights, where the troops that were drawn together in that quarter, to oppose the enemy who soon afterwards landed on York Island, took possession of the city, and menaced Fort Washington. Three companies of that Regiment, Thornton's in which Mr. Monroe was a lieutenant, Chilton's, and Ashby's, under the command of Major Leitch, and a like number of troops from Connecticut, under Colonel Knolton, were detached in advance of the army, across the valley, at Harlem, to meet them. This small corps met the head of a column of the enemy at the edge of a wood, through which it passed bordering on the valley, and fighting gallantly, checked its career. Knolton and Leitch both fell, and their wounds being mortal, died, the first on that day, the other a fortnight afterwards. Such was the good conduct of this small detachment in that encounter that the commander, in reviewing the occurrence in the general orders of the succeeding day, bestowed on it the highest commendation. Checked at that point, the enemy passed up the Sound, with intention to fall in the rear of the troops which were collected around Fort Washington. This movement drew our army to the White Plains, where something like a general action ensued, in which the enemy gained the advantage. They then moved down towards the fort, and in the disposition which was made of our force, the Third Regiment was ordered into Jersey, to support Fort Lee, which was erected on the south side of the Hudson, opposite to Fort Washington. That Regiment took its position at Newark. Both those forts fell, and immediately afterwards General Washington drew the few remaining troops back in that quarter, to the same point. The enemy, knowing how inconsiderable his forces were, pressed on him, and thus commenced through Jersey a retreat which will be for ever celebrated in the annals of our country for the patient suffering, the unshaken firmness, and gallantry of this small band when brought to action, of which the army consisted, and of the great and good qualities of its commander. We passed the Delaware at Trenton and occupied the commanding ground contiguous to it on the opposite shore. Soon after this, the winter having commenced, the enemy retired to winter quarters, stationing their troops in the different towns through Jersey, from the Delaware to New York.

As Mr. Monroe was in that retreat, it may not be improper to insert here a notice which he took of it in a message to Congress, May 2d 1822, in which, in tracing the origin of our institutions, his attention was drawn to those who bore the most distinguished part in their establishment. "On the 15th of June 1775 (says he), a commander-in-chief of all the forces, raised and to be raised for the defense of American liberty, was appointed by unanimous vote of Congress, and his conduct in the discharge of the duties of that high trust, which he held through the whole of the war, has given an example to the world for talents as a military commander, for integrity, fortitude, and firmness under the severest trials, for respect to the civil authority and devotion to the rights and liberties of his country, of which neither Rome nor Greece have exhibited the equal. I saw him in my earliest youth, in the retreat through Jersey, at the head of a small band, or rather, in its rear, for he was always near the enemy, and his countenance and manner made an impression on me which time can never efface. A lieutenant then in the Third Virginia Regiment, I happened to be on the rear guard at Newark, and I counted the force under his immediate command by platoons as it passed me, which amounted to less than 3,000 men. A deportment so firm, so dignified, so exalted, but yet so modest and composed, I have never seen in any other person."

The success of the enemy in the battles of Long Island and the White Plains, with the capture of Forts Washington and Lee, and the retreat of our army through Jersey, put fairly at issue with the nation the great question whether they were competent and resolved to support their independence, or would sink under the pressure. The councils of the union exhibited a firmness which showed that they were equal to the crisis. The Congress of the United States and the legislatures of all the states were in session, and not the slightest symptom of hesitation was seen in either of those public bodies. The most active efforts were made by all, and with the most faithful cooperation between them, each performing its appropriate duties, to raise and support a force which would meet and defy the enemy in the field the next campaign. General Washington was equally attentive to his duties. He perceived that the British Commander, by the disposition which he had made of his troops, had estimated his success beyond their merit: that he considered the country as essentially conquered. The opportunity for profiting of that error, of depressing the British power, and elevating the hopes and spirits of his country, was favorable, and he resolved to take advantage of it. The force at Trenton was small, but believed by the British commander to be superior to any that he could bring to bear on it. His other troops in Jersey were dispersed through the towns in a line from the Delaware to the Hudson, at Princeton, New Brunswick, Elizabethtown, and Newark.

The first attack was to be made on Trenton, on the result of which everything would depend. This was arranged in a general council, on great consideration, and with consummate judgment. The command of the vanguard, consisting of 50 men, was given to Captain William Washington, of the Third Virginia Regiment, an officer whose good conduct had already been noticed. This appointment having been communicated to the other officers by Colonel Weedon, Lieutenant Monroe promptly offered his services to act as a subaltern under him, which was promptly accepted. On the 25th of December, 1776, they passed the Delaware in front of the army, in the dusk of the evening, at Coryell's ferry, 10 miles above Trenton, and hastened to a point, about one and one-half miles from it, at which the road by which they descended intersected that which led from Trenton to Princeton, for the purpose, in obedience to orders, of cutting off all communication between them and from the country to Trenton. The night was tempestuous, as was the succeeding day, and made more severe by a heavy fall of snow. Captain Washington executed his orders faithfully. He soon took possession of the point to which he was ordered, and holding it through the night, intercepted and made prisoners of many who were passing in directions to and from Trenton.[3] At the dawn of the day, our army approached, with the Commander-in-chief at its head. Captain Washington then moved forward with the vanguard in front, attacked the enemy's picket, shot down the commanding officer, and drove it before him. A general alarm then took place among the troops in town. The drums were beat to arms, and two cannon were placed in the main street to bear on the head of our column as it entered. Captain Washington rushed forward, attacked, and put the troops around the cannon to flight, and took possession of them.

Moving on afterwards, he received a severe wound and was taken from
the field. The command then devolved on Lieutenant Monroe, who
advanced in like manner at the head of the corps, and was shot down
by a musket ball which passed through his breast and shoulder. He
also was carried from the field. Our troops, then entering the town
in several columns and attacking the enemy as they formed, soon over-
came and made prisoners of them. Lieutenant Monroe was taken to the
same room to which Captain Washington had been carried, and their
wounds were dressed by Dr. Cochrane, the Surgeon General of the
army, and Dr. Riker, who had quartered with them in the country and
accompanied them in the vanguard in the attack on the picket and
advance in the city.

In the great events of which I have spoken Mr. Monroe, being a
mere youth, counted for nothing in comparison with those distinguished
citizens who had the direction of public affairs. In adverting to the
epoch of his commencement, I have thought it proper, and have taken
delight in noticing in appropriate terms, the high character of that
epoch and of those into whose hands its destiny fell. Taken together,
they formed a school of practical instruction, for many successful purposes, of which it is believed that history has furnished no equal
example. It was a school of instruction in the knowledge of mankind, in the science of government, and what is of still great importance, for inculcating on the youthful mind those sound moral and
political principles on which the success of our system depends.[4]

Lieutenant Monroe was carried, on the night after the action, back
to Mr. Coryell's, where he was confined to his bed about ten days,
treated with great kindness, and thence moved by Headquarters to
Mr. Henry Wyncoop's, a very respectable magistrate of Bucks county,
who was afterwards a member of Congress, and where he was confined by his wound nine weeks and treated with like kindness. While at
Mr. Coryell's his wound was dressed daily by Dr. Riker. At Mr.
Wyncoop's, it was dressed in like manner by Dr. King, a physician
who resided in Newtown, a neighboring village, until his health was
restored. It may not be improper to state that for this service compensation was made him by Mr. Monroe himself, who never asked a
remuneration of it or received any pension on account of his wound,
although it was such as to have entitled him to it.

After the battle of Trenton, Captain Washington was promoted to
a Major in the cavalry and Lieutenant Monroe to a Captaincy in the
infantry as a reward for their service, the latter in a regiment to
be raised, the command of which was given to Colonel Thruston. The
attempt to raise the corps failed, and in consequence, Major General

Lord Stirling, under whom Colonel Weedon had acted in the preceding campaign and to whom Mr. Monroe was known, invited him into his family as an aide-de-camp, which invitation he accepted and joined him in that character in July, 1777, at the crossroads in Bucks county, 20 miles above Philadelphia, the army being then on the march to meet the enemy, who had ascended the Chesapeake and were approaching the head of the Elk, at which place they debarked. It was at the same point and at the same time that General LaFayette joined the army, and it was at that period, their ages being nearly equal —the general being a few years older only and moving in the same circle, although their rank was essentially different—that an acquaintance was formed between them which was preserved ever afterwards with the most sincere reciprocal attachment, and attended in their progress through life, in their respective stations, with the most interesting occurrences.

Mr. Monroe acted as aide-de-camp to Major General Lord Stirling through the campaigns of 1777–78, and was present with him in the battles of Brandywine, Germantown and Monmouth, in which his conduct was approved by the Commander-in-chief as well as by his general. A brief notice of those interesting events of which he was a witness and in which, in the station, he held a party, will not, it is presumed, be deemed improper. Lord Stirling's division consisted during the campaign of 1777 of the Jersey Brigade, commanded by General Maxwell, and of the Pennsylvania Brigade, under General Conway, in both of which there were many officers of great merit. He recollects now, with particular interest, in the former the Colonels Ogden, Dayton, Barbeur and Debarts, and in the latter Colonels Craig, Harmer and the Andersons, the elder of whom is now the first comptroller of public accounts at Washington.

As soon as it was known that the enemy was debarking at the head of the Elk, the Commander-in-chief moved by a rapid march through Philadelphia and Wilmington to meet him, and took a position beyond the latter in advance of New Port, in the expectation that the conflict would commence there. General Howe made an attempt to turn his right by moving into the interior towards Lancaster, with intention to place General Washington between him and the coast, in the expectation that if he should succeed in the action which would follow, he would destroy or make prisoners of our whole army. General Washington, aware of his design and resolved to defeat it, recrossed the Brandywine near Wilmington and advanced up the river to meet and give him battle at any point at which he might attempt to pass it. The two armies approached within sight at Shadford, and occupying the opposite heights, annoyed each other by heavy discharge of cannon and light detached parties who skirmished in the valley between them. Intelligence was given to General Washington by Major Jameson of the cavalry, who commanded a reconnoitering party on the approach side, that a large column of the enemy was moving, under Lord Cornwallis, from the rear of General Howe's army up the river with intention to pass it above him and to fall on his right by surprise. General Washington immediately detached two divisions of his army, under Generals Sullivan and Lord Stirling, to meet this column, who took a position near Birmingham meeting house, where the action commenced and was maintained on both sides with great gallantry nearly an hour. The enemy at length succeeded, and in consequence three divisions retired, but in tolerable order. The pursuit was slow, and General Washington having drawn a portion of his other force to that quarter, checked the enemy and covered the retreat without sustaining other loss than of the gallant men who had fallen in the action. In this action, General LaFayette, who stood by the side of Lord Stirling, received a severe wound in the leg and was taken from the field. Many others of Mr. Monroe's personal friends and of the Third Virginia Regiment were wounded and some of them killed in that action. Among the wounded were Colonel Thomas Marshall, the father of the present Chief Justice, and Lieutenant John Francis Mercer, with whom he had become acquainted and intimately connected at William and Mary College, having lodged and studied together in the same rooms and entered with him at the same time as a cadet in that regiment.

Our army, on the night after the battle of Brandywine, retired to Chester, and on the next day crossed the Schuylkill and occupied the plain contiguous to Philadelphia. Soon afterwards it moved up the river, recrossed it, and took post on the high ground between the river and Lancaster. The attitude assumed by it was that of defiance, indicating a willingness to meet the enemy in action, where and when he pleased. General Howe took possession of Philadelphia and seemed inclined to repose. His army occupied the ground near the city, including the neighboring village of Germantown. General Washington was attentive to the conduct of the enemy. He perceived that the British force extended over a large surface and that the body which was at Germantown was not well supported by that at the city and below it. He resolved to attack it, and with that view made secretly the necessary preparations. Having formed his army into columns, with a suitable commander at the head of each, he advanced on them and commenced the attack on the troops that were encamped near German-town, who were taken by surprise and driven before him.

Mr. Monroe had now served through three campaigns, those of 1776, 1777 and 1778; in the first as a lieutenant in the Third Virginia Regiment, and in the two latter as an aide-de-camp to Major General Lord Stirling, and in which he had been a party, in those grades, to the most interesting occurrences of our revolutionary conflict. Having entered the army with enthusiastic zeal in support of our cause in his eighteenth year, he was anxious to pursue the same career until it should be accomplished. His object now was to obtain a command in the army. The duties of an aide-de-camp gave him none, being, when in action, to bear the orders of his general to the troops under him, and when in camp, or on the march, to take those of the Com-mander-in-chief, daily, from the adjutant general of the army to report them to his own general and issue them with such, in addition to the divisions under his command, as he might direct. Those duties he had performed in the two last campaigns to the entire satisfaction of his own general and of the Commander-in-chief, of which they gave him the most ample testimony. In the line of the army, no commission could be granted to him, for no new regiments were to be raised and many officers of merit were deranged in consequence of the loss of troops, inactive and otherwise, the inability to supply their place by recruits, and the want of command. Thus circumstanced, he conceived the idea of applying to his native state for authority to raise a corps and to take it to the South, in which quarter the war then pressed with great force. General Washington and Lord Stirling approved this project and gave him strong letters of recommendation to the legislature of the state in support of it.[5] The legislature adopted the plan and passed an act for raising a force, with a view to the southern war, to the command of one regiment of which he was appointed, with the rank of lieutenant colonel. Of this favorable opinion enter-tained of his previous conduct, a just idea may be formed when it is recollected that this appointment was conferred on him before he had attained the full age of twenty-one. He made the most active efforts to raise the regiment, but failed, and was in consequence thrown out of the service. The disposition to serve his country in any line in which he might be useful remained in full force, but no opportunity presenting itself in that in which he had before acted, and being too young for civil employment, he was left at liberty, without any im-peachment of his patriotism, to pursue the object for which he had been originally destined. Indeed the obligation to do it under existing circumstances was imperative.

Earliest known portrait of James Monroe, painted after
he had served in the American Revolution, probably
during the time he was studying law under
Thomas Jefferson. The artist is unknown.

2

Lawyer and Legislator

His father and uncle had intended him for the bar, to which his mind had by preference been directed. To raise the regiment to which he had been recently appointed, he was now replaced in Williamsburg, near the college which he had left three and a half years before. Mr. Jefferson, a very enlightened and distinguished revolutionary patriot and one of the most eminent lawyers in the state, was then its governor, and John Francis Mercer, Mr. Monroe's friend who had left the college and entered the Third Regiment with him, had, by accepting the office of aide-de-camp to Major General Charles Lee, lost also his rank in the line and in consequence retired from the army, was then engaged with several other distinguished youths in the study of law under Mr. Jefferson, among whom was William Short and Archibald Stuart, who were likewise students at the college. Mr. Monroe immediately re-entered the college, resumed his study of general science in it, and on the introduction by Judge Jones to Mr. Jefferson, to whom he was already well known by the letter above referred to, he engaged in the study of the law under him and persevered in it until he obtained a license to practice in the courts of the state.[6]

A good foundation had been laid by Mr. Monroe of a classical and philosophical education, for his age, before he entered the army. Commencing in that great theater with advantage at the earliest moment at which the mind is capable of expanded exertion, the opportunity afforded to him for practical instruction, aided by the society in which he moved, could not fail to have been eminently useful to him. Young as he was, he became acquainted with all the general officers of the army, with their aides, and with all the other officers in that circle who were most distinguished for their talents and merit.

31

Their society gave him lessons of practical instruction, the most interesting that can be conceived, the tendency of which must have been, as the members who composed it came from all the states, to break down local prejudices and attach the mind and feeling to the union. Possessing the confidence of his general, he knew all the springs of action and the principles on which every movement turned. This mind must thus have been trained to the habit of calm deliberation of those interesting subjects and with all the advantages stated. On his retirement from those active services and resuming his studies at the place at which he had before prosecuted them, it was natural that he should review with deep interest the past, and look forward with great solicitude to the success of the cause, in defense of which he had already made such exertions, and in one instance, nearly fallen a victim. His mind was, nevertheless, now devoted to his studies, which he pursued with the utmost zeal and perseverance. It is fair to remark that, if his previous education had enabled him to discharge with advantage his duties in the army and to profit in like degree of the excellent opportunity afforded him by the society in which he moved, to improve his knowledge of mankind and of public affairs, those acquirements must have been equally useful to him on his retirement, in his renewed application to the study of elementary and abstract science.

Two opportunities occurred, while Mr. Monroe was engaged in the study of the law, of rendering service to his country, of which he availed himself. On the fall of Charlestown and the loss of our army in it in 1780 the Executive of the state was desirous of obtaining a correct knowledge of the actual state of affairs in that quarter; of the amount of our force; of that of the enemy; and of the resources and measures adopted by the southern states for their defense. An invitation was given to Mr. Monroe by the Executive to perform that service, which he promptly accepted and executed to the satisfaction of the government.[7] Soon after his return, a detachment of the enemy landed at Norfolk, under General Lesslie, in sufficient force to menace a more general invasion of the state. A large body of militia was called immediately into service and the command of one of the regiments given to him, in which his friend Colonel Mercer was appointed with him, with the rank of lieutenant colonel and Robert Goode, with that of major. The force [which] was promptly collected, assuming under the command of General Muhlenberg an imposing attitude, had the desired effect. The army abandoned the idea of penetrating into the interior and soon withdrew.

In 1781 Mr. Monroe, after he had concluded his study of the law, sold his tract of land on Monroe creek, in Westmoreland County, to Mr. James Corbin of Caroline, with intention to establish himself in Richmond to prosecute his profession in the superior courts of the Commonwealth. In this he was checked by the invasion of the state by Arnold and the suspension of all legal proceedings. He was at that period invited by his fellow citizens in King George County, to whom he was generally known and among whom he had many friends, it being the residence of his uncle, Judge Jones, to represent them in the General Assembly, and with which he most willingly complied. In April, 1782, he, with Mr. George Fitzhugh, was elected to the House of Delegates.[8] Soon after the Assembly met, there being several vacancies in the Council, he was elected to a seat in that body by the General Assembly, and from which he was transferred by a like vote in the ensuing year—his conduct being approved and the confidence of his fellow citizens throughout the state increasing—to the Congress of the United States. In the latter station, he served the constitutional term of three years, which terminated in November, 1786.

Being taken from the bar by his election to the Council and afterwards to Congress, and the fund arising from the sale of his land in Westmoreland County lying inactive, he invested the greater part of it in western lands, by the purchase of persons to whom such lands had been granted, and of warrants from the state, under which surveys were made and patents granted to himself. A portion also he invested in lots in Richmond with a view to his establishment there. His western acquisition was increased by his grant for military service, 5,333 acres, and the application of the sum allowed for the depreciation of his pay while in the army, which was thus disposed of. His election to Congress having been made in the spring session of 1783, to take effect in December, he was invited by Mr. Jefferson to pass the interval with him at his residence in Albemarle, with which he complied. Mr. Jefferson urged him to establish himself in that county, assuring him that it would connect him with the western counties, from which he could throw into his hands much business, which he should be happy to do. Having formed a strong attachment to Mr. Jefferson by the relation which had before existed between them, and having become acquainted with many respectable families and citizens in the county during the visit, he resolved to make the establishment suggested, and with that view, to purchase a tract of land then for sale in the neighborhood, belonging to Mr. Marks, who had intended to move to Georgia, which tract now belongs to Mr. Rogers and Dr. Everett. To accomplish this object he gave a power to his friend Colonel Harvie, who made the purchase and offered to convey it to him, with an intimation that if he had no anxiety respecting it, he would retain it himself. Inferring from what passed that Colonel Harvie wished to own the tract and having received other proofs of kindness from him before this occurrence, he promptly yielded his claim in accommodation with the desire of the Colonel. He still, however, retained the disposition to make his permanent settlement in that county and to purchase some other tract when he should retire from Congress and take his station at the bar.

The first session, under his first appointment to Congress, was held at Annapolis and commenced in December, 1783. The Virginia delegation consisted of Mr. Jefferson, Mr. Hardy, Mr. Arthur Lee, John Francis Mercer and himself. The contest for our liberties had succeeded by the complete establishment of our independence. A definitive treaty to that effect had been concluded, and its ratification was among the first acts of that session. The resignation of the Commander-in-chief of all our forces of the commission under which he had acted through the whole war, was a necessary consequence of its termination, and which occurred in an early stage of that session. The scene was highly interesting. The manner in which he took his leave and the sentiment expressed in the audience given him by Congress of the conduct through that arduous struggle was such as evinced the high sense entertained of his merit and became the dignity of the body under whom he had so served. It could not fail to excite the sensibility of Mr. Monroe to reflect that he had served as a lieutenant under him only a few years before. Nor could it otherwise than be gratifying to him to recollect that his promotion had been the result of the free suffrage of his fellow citizens, founded in part, at least, on the favorable opinion entertained and expressed of his conduct in that service, unsolicited and unsought by himself.

The interval between the ratification of the definitive treaty of peace with Great Britain and the adoption of our present constitution forms a very interesting epoch in our political career. The sovereignty was vested in the people. There was no privileged order in any of the states and never had been. Every state had formed its government in the progress of the revolution, generally at its commencement, and the union of the states, which had been formed by joint effort and cooperation and which rested on a love of liberty and patriotism only at that early period, had been cemented by a regular bond, by the Articles of Confederation, which were proposed in 1776, almost at the same moment with the act declaring of our independence, and which had been carried into complete effect in 1781. Our system was in full operation as to both governments, those of the states individually and that of the United States, and the power in the hands of the people, unrestrained, to give to each in their respective spheres the form and endowment which experience might dictate. The theater on which Mr. Monroe was now placed was a very important one. It was important not only to his fellow citizens, but to the whole civilized world, because the people were called on to make a fair experiment of the practicability of free government and under circumstances more favorable to their success than were ever enjoyed by any other people. I shall notice the proceedings of each session in the order in which they occurred, connecting in the digest which I shall present the several subjects together, so as to give a distinct idea of the progress made in each instance, and especially in those which had for their object the improvement of the government and the permanent welfare of the nation.

In this session the state of Virginia, by virtue of a power vested in her delegates, sold to the United States her right and title, derived from her charter, to the territory northwest of the river Ohio, for the purposes and on the conditions specified in the deed, which bears date on the 1st of March, 1784. Mr. Jay, who had been the President of Congress in 1779, afterwards Minister to Spain, and one of the negotiators who had signed the treaty of peace with Great Britain, was appointed Secretary of Foreign Affairs. Mr. Jefferson, who had been a member of Congress in 1776, who drew the Declaration of Independence, was afterwards Governor of the State of Virginia and then a member of Congress, was appointed a Minister Plenipotentiary, and associated with Doctor Franklin and Mr. Adams, with authority to form a commercial treaty with all the principal powers of Europe with whom such treaties had not already been concluded. Mr. Morris, the Minister of Finance, who had also rendered very important service, had resigned and in consequence a Board of Treasury, consisting of three members, was instituted. The claims of our revolutionary officers and troops demanded attention and were provided for. Greater gallantry and patriotism were never displayed by any band before. The claims of the foreign officers who had served in our army were likewise attended to, among which we find noted in the Journal particularly those of Baron Steuben, of Generals Du Portail and Armand, of Colonels Kosciusko and Fleury. The Baron DeKalb had fallen gallantly fighting on the plains of Camden, under General Gates. General Pulaski had fallen before, fighting with like gallantry, in the attack on Savannah.

The measures above specified were incidental to the termination of the war, and among those first adopted. Others of high importance claimed attention, a part of which were disposed of during the session, the residue put in train for further consideration. Peace had not yet been concluded with the Indians who had taken part against us in the late war. Commissions were appointed and invested with power to treat with the tribes of our northwestern, western, and southern frontiers. A requisition was made on the states for the funds necessary to enable the government to fulfill the engagements entered into respecting the public debt, and to support the government in its foreign and internal relations. In this act, a detailed view was given of the debt, so far as it had then been liquidated of the calls which had been previously made on the states for their respective quotas and of their payments under them. A notice was also taken of the recommendation of the 18th of April, 1783, to grant to the United States an impost on the commerce of the several states for the term of fifteen years, and of those who had complied with it. The establishment of a temporary government over the territory northwest of the river Ohio, ceded by Virginia, was taken up but not decided on. A recommendation to the other states who held vacant territory to make like cessions was adopted, and measures were likewise taken for the settlement of all controversies between the states individually, respecting their territorial claims and boundaries arising under their original charters.

Our relations with foreign powers even at this early period became an object of the highest importance. The interests which were wounded and put in peril by the commercial regulations of other powers called in question the competency of Congress, under the powers granted to it by the Articles of Confederation, to protect ourselves from prostration and utter ruin. Other powers took care of themselves and sought to turn their intercourse with us to their particular advantage. The trade with the British colonies was claimed as a monopoly by the parent country, although their existence for their supplies and the sale of their produce essentially depended on us. The states individually could accomplish no object for themselves. Many of them made countervailing regulations against those of a foreign power. They were sure to throw the commerce of such powers into the adjoining states, from which it would be smuggled into the states who had made such regulations. A temptation would thus be given to each state to watch the measures of the others and to endeavor to turn those to its particular advantage. A commercial war would ensue, and in consequence, the union so much weakened, if not broken. The condition of all would be less favorable than it was in their colonial state under the general, through monopolizing and oppressive, regulations of the parent country. These considerations urged Congress to call on the states for an enlargement of the power of the general govern- ment to enable it to manage the whole concern, for local as well as the general interest. The subject, however, in this stage and in this view was new, and in consequence a comprehensive and well-digested system could not be pressed . . . [part of page missing] . . . [on the] 30th of April, 1784, [a] report of a committee consisting of Mr. Gerry, Mr. Read, Mr. Williamson, Mr. Chase, and Mr. Jefferson contains a marked feature of the policy which it was then deemed necessary to pursue and of the power to give effect to it. The measure recommended to the states was the investment of Congress with power for the term of fifteen years to prohibit absolutely the importation into any of the states, or exportation from them, of goods, wares and merchandise in any vessels belonging to or navigated by the subjects of powers with whom the United States should not have formed treaties of commerce; and likewise to prohibit the subjects of a foreign state from importing into the United States any goods, wares or merchandise not the produce or manufacture of such states, unless authorized by treaty. The right of prohibition called for, al- though confined to special objects, would by the exercise of it cut off the whole commerce of the United States with any power to whom it might be applied, and the reasons assigned for it comprised every interior concern of the whole union on the principle that every section had a common interest in every other most minute circumstance to whom a complete regulation might be extended. As motive for the grant, it was urged that the value of our produce and land and the fortune of every citizen depended on the success of our commerce, and that unless Congress should be vested with complete power to secure reciprocal advantages in our intercourse with other nations, it would be annihilated.

The United States had already formed treaties of commerce with France and Holland, with the one on the 6th of February, 1778, and with the other on the 8th of October, 1782. A letter had also been received through Mr. Morris, the Superintendent of Finance, from General LaFayette in May, 1783, with one to him from the Count De Vergennes and likewise one from Mr. De Colonne, in which as- surance was given to him that L'Orient, Bayonne, Dunkirk and Mar- seilles—the latter with the exception of a single article—should be made free ports for our commerce and every accommodation and encouragement to it which their government might be able. It may fairly be inferred, therefore, that the power called for was intended to be applied to other nations and not to them. The communication thus received furnished a new and strong proof of the interest which General LaFayette took in the welfare and prosperity of our country. Of this sentiment the President was authorized to be organ, by a letter which should address to him the high sense which Congress entertained of his service relative to our commerce with France.

A petition from the state of Massachusetts, praying that a federal court might be appointed to decide a controversy between that state and the state of New York respecting their territorial rights, was among the last subjects which were brought before Congress in this session. An invitation to both states to appear by their lawful agents on the first Monday in December ensuing, at the place at which Congress might then sit, to proceed in the affairs in the manner prescribed by the Articles of Confederation was the measure adopted.

On the 3d of June, 1784, Congress adjourned to meet at Trenton on the 30th of October following, having previously appointed a committee of the states to remain in session during the recess.

During this session Mr. Jefferson and Mr. Monroe, having taken a house and lived together, had agreed to visit in the recess our northwestern frontier, passing by Pittsburgh to Detroit, thence by Lakes Erie and Ontario, taking a view of the falls of Niagara between them, to the St. Lawrence and back through Vermont and New York to Trenton, to which place Congress would adjourn. High interests were connected with the territory which had been ceded by Virginia to the United States, lying between the Ohio, the lakes and the Mississippi. It was to be formed into new states not less than 100 nor more than 150 miles square, which were to be admitted with the same rights as the original states. The vacant land within that territory was to be sold for the benefit of the union. The relation also which the northwestern portion of our union bore to Canada was in itself an important circumstance. They knew that the more thoroughly they became acquainted with the condition of every part of the union, the better able they would be to perform their duties in Congress.[9] Mr. Jefferson's appointment to Europe prevented their proposed excursion together. Mr. Monroe, however, resolved to execute the plan himself, so far as he might be able, and in which he apprehended no difficulty, the Indians having sued for peace, and the whole route, when on land, being within our limits.

Hearing that Governor Clinton intended to treat with the tribes within the state of New York at the head of the Mohawk river, he resolved to change the projected route and to join the Governor and his party, and ascend the river with them to the theater of negotiation, with intentions to proceed thence through the Lakes Oneida, Ontario and Erie, to Detroit and thence by Pittsburgh home. With this view, he proceeded to Albany, where he found the Governor and commissioners, and went with them to Wood Creek, at the head of the Mohawk river,[10] where the tribes were assembled and prepared to treat. He met then many of the chiefs of the Six Nations, and among them Colonel Brandt of the Mohawk tribe, who had held that rank in the British army; and they, knowing that he was a member of Congress, were attentive to him.

An opportunity soon offered itself for proceeding by journey with a fair prospect of completing it in the manner contemplated. A party under the direction of Mr. Taylor of Schenectady, who had been engaged in commerce with the remote western tribes before the Revolutionary War, had prepared to proceed by the route stated to Detroit in batteaux. Mr. Monroe embarked with them, entered the Ontario at Fort Oswego, and passing along the eastern coast, reached the Fort Niagara at the mouth of the river of that name, which formed the communication over the falls between the Lakes Erie and Ontario. Colonel Depeyster, who then commanded that fort, which was still in the possession of the British, although under the treaty it belonged to us, received Mr. Monroe with attention and treated him with kindness. To remove the batteaux up the river beyond the falls required a delay of several days, during which Mr. Monroe associated with the British officers, dined daily with the Colonel, who in many conversations dissuaded him from the prosecution of his journey, but without effect.

As soon as the batteaux were removed and ready to pursue the voyage, Mr. Monroe called on Colonel Depeyster for a passport, as they would be found, in ascending the lake to Detroit, to adhere to the Canada shore. The Colonel then renewed his advice, and with new lights, which gave it more force. He stated that Major Day, who was then Governor of Detroit, had been taken prisoner with Governors Hamilton and Rocheblave, by General G. R. Clark at Fort St. Vincennes, and sent by him to Williamsburg, where they were imprisoned by Governor Jefferson in retaliation for the treatment of some of our citizens who had been made prisoners in that quarter during the war, and that he thought the resentment of Governor Day was such that it would be unsafe for Mr. Monroe to attempt to pass through the Indian country from Detroit to Pittsburgh unprotected by a strong guard. He advised him to take the route by the eastern side of Lake Erie to the river Allegheny and thence by that river to Pittsburgh, and offered to procure for him, under the direction and responsible to the British agent, Mr. Dean, a guard of Indians

who should conduct him in safety to that point. Mr. Monroe yielded
to his advice and in consequence a guard of six Mohawk chiefs was
procured, and proceeding by the Falls, which he viewed from both
sides of the river, he advanced to Lake Erie, and leaving the Indian
chiefs on the American side of the river at its junction with the lake,
passed over to Fort Erie on the British side, which was commanded
by Major Warren. The Major met him at the landing place and after
the first salutation asked him if he had heard of the fate of his party.
Mr. Monroe inquired what party? The party who came with him
from the States. He had not. The Major then informed him that,
having landed about 50 miles up the lake to prepare and take their
dinner, a party of Indians who saw them approached under cover,
fired on and killed several, including Mr. Taylor, two only having
escaped, who had returned in a batteaux which had just passed on the
fort on their right by Niagara to New York. He advised him likewise
to return, believing it to be unsafe, after that occurrence, to confide
in the protection of those chiefs, since they might apprehend a renewal of the war on our part in resentment for it; he was fearful they
would destroy him in the passage. Mr. Monroe was unwilling to return,
but seeing great force in the reasons urged, agreed to remain with the
Major that night, to weigh more fully the subject before he decided on
it. About midnight an Express arrived from Colonel Depeyster who,
having heard of the disaster, sent him with a letter to urge Mr.
Monroe's return, for like reasons with those which had been given
by Major Warren. Mr. Monroe adopted their counsel and returned
on the next day to Fort Niagara, where he remained a week and then
descended Lake Ontario in a British sloop of war to Fort Carlton, at
the entrance of the St. Lawrence, and thence in a batteaux down that
river to Montreal, from whence he proceeded by the Lake Champlain
through Vermont, by Albany, to New York. This narrow escape from
destruction, forming an interesting incident in Mr. Monroe's life, it is
thought not improper to notice it.[11]

It happened by a singular casualty, which would not otherwise
excite his surprise, that in passing from Niagara in the British sloop
of war to Fort Carlton he should find among the passengers Colonel
Brandt, the Indian chief, a connection of Sir J. |sic| Johnson, whom
he had seen at Wood Creek, and that in descending the St. Lawrence
from the latter Fort to Montreal, it should be in a batteaux under
the direction with the family of Governor Rocheblave, who had been
taken prisoner at Fort St. Vincennes and was confined in Williamsburg.

The Congress met in Trenton on the 1st of November, 1784, and

Mr. Monroe arrived there in time to take his seat on the first day of the session. It was natural that his return to that town should recall to his recollections, and with great sensibility, the important incident of the action which had occurred there on the 26th of December, 1776, both in relation to his country and himself, since it formed a very interesting epoch in our revolutionary struggle, being the first step to the new and imposing attitude which was assumed immediately afterwards by our Commander-in-chief towards the enemy, and which he sustained in every subsequent stage of the contest. It was not until the 30th of that month that a sufficient number of members were collected to form a House competent to proceed to business. R. H. Lee of Virginia was elected the President.

On the first Monday in December the agents of Massachusetts and New York appeared in compliance with the resolution which had been passed at Annapolis on the 3d of June preceding and solicited the appointment of a court to decide the controversy between those states with respect to their territorial rights. Their credentials were approved and authority given to them to appoint judges who should constitute the court. On the 24th they reported the following persons to whom they had agreed to confide that trust: H. Harrison and Thomas Johnson of Maryland; John Rutledge of South Carolina; George Wythe, William Grayson, and James Monroe of Virginia; George Read of Delaware; and Isaac Smith and William Patterson of New Jersey. The selection of so young a citizen as Mr. Monroe and association of him on so important a court with the very distinguished Revolutionary characters named, was a strong proof of the favorable opinion entertained of him at that early period. The controversy was afterwards adjusted amicably between the states so that the court never met.

Shortly after the capture of Lord Cornwallis with his army at York, General LaFayette, who commanded the troops in Virginia that campaign, returned to France on a furlough; but retaining a warm attachment to our country and to the officers with whom he had served, particularly to the Commander-in-chief, he revisited it after the peace in 1784, and passing through Trenton at this period, Congress seized the opportunity of giving him a strong testimonial of the high sense which they entertained of his very important services and great merit. They had taken leave of the Commander-in-chief at Annapolis in the whole body collected. They could place no one on the same ground with him, but they thought it due to General LaFayette to separate them by a single shade only. A committee consisting of a member from every state was appointed and instructed to receive and take leave of him, and in so doing, to express to him the high sense entertained by Congress of his merit and service, both in the United States and in Europe, and that they should always feel great interest in whatever might concern his honor and prosperity. Of this committee Mr. Jay was the Chairman. The interview took place on the 13th of December, 1784 in which the committee expressed to him, in terms corresponding with its instructions, the sentiment entertained of his services and merit and of the interest which the United States would always take in his affairs. This address was conducted in terms the most grateful and affectionate, with an assurance of the ardent wish which he should always cherish for the success of our system of government and the happiness of the American people. It is proper to remark that for his services in the army he had received no compensation, nor did he ask any, either then or afterwards.

At Trenton the delegates from Virginia presented an instruction from the legislature of that state to urge Congress to use their utmost efforts to obtain of Spain the acknowledgment of the right of the United States to the free navigation of the Mississippi. In obedience to this instruction, a resolution was presented and adopted for the appointment of a Minister to Spain for that special object.

The accommodation at Trenton being found insufficient for Congress and all the departments under it, and for the foreign ministers who might be expected there, it was resolved to adjourn on the 24th of December, to meet at New York on the 11th of January ensuing, which was carried into effect in conformity therewith. All the interesting subjects which had been acted on at Annapolis which were left unfinished now claimed attention and, with augmented force, a provision for the public debt and support of the government was one of those which was most urgent. The establishment of a temporary government over the territory ceded northwest of the river Ohio, with an arrangement for the sale of the vacant lands lying within it, was connected with this object and called for by pressing interests. The adjustment of territorial disputes between the states, with the acquisition of cessions from other states holding vacant lands within their limits, likewise claimed attention. It was found also that additional arrangements had become necessary for the conclusion of peace with the Indian tribes. These several subjects were taken up and disposed of in the best manner that the experience of the day would admit of. On the 18th of July, a report was made by a grand committee stating the sums necessary to enable Congress to fulfill its engagements and support the government in all its necessary expenditures in the current year of 1785, with a call on the states to furnish their respective quotas of the sum. This measure was not adopted until the 27th of September following. Many considerations of a local nature, connected with the claims of the states respectively for services and advances which it was urged they had made in different modes in the late war, contributed to this delay. The ill effect was seriously felt, and great apprehension entertained, if a reliance should be placed on requisitions only, that the sums called for and indispensably necessary would not be furnished, and in consequence the public faith be violated and the government, failing in all its duties, be dishonored and shaken. Attention was, therefore, drawn with great urgency to a resource which should not depend on requisition only, but be under the control of Congress itself. The resource which presented itself was that of the impost, the grant of which had been recommended on the 18th of April, 1783, in a very able report drawn by a committee consisting of Mr. Madison [and others].

With that recommendation, many of the states had complied in full extent, others in part only, and some had declined it altogether. It was resolved to press the measure, and with that view, an act passed on the 15th of July, 1786, on the report of a committee consisting of Mr. King, Mr. Pinckney, Mr. Kean, Mr. Monroe and Mr. Pettit. It may not be improper to observe that the subject was first introduced on the 3d of that month by a committee consisting of Mr. Monroe, Mr. Johnson, Mr. Gorham, Mr. Symmes and Mr. Livermore. Whether that report, which was drawn by Mr. Monroe, threw any light on the subject so as to aid in the measure finally adopted, will be seen by reference to the journal of those dates.

The legislature of New Jersey had refused to comply with the requisition of September, 1785, the ill effect of which, in the then embarrassed state of the public finances, was very sensibly felt. On the 7th of March, 1786, a committee was appointed to attend that assembly which was then in session, and to represent to it the fatal consequences which an adherence to that resolution could not fail to produce, as well to the state as to the union. The committee consisted of Mr. Pinckney, Mr. Gorham, and Mr. Grayson, who performed the service on the 22d and reported that the legislature had rescinded the resolution.

The legislature of Pennsylvania had suspended the act granting the impost to the United States until all the states should have granted the supplementary funds which formed a part of the system, according to the resolution of April 17th, 1783. As the impost was the principal object of that recommendation and there was now a fair prospect of a compliance with it in that extent by all the states, it was now deemed proper to make a special and earnest pressure on the legislature of Pennsylvania to remove that obstacle to its operation, should the calculation on the conduct of the other states be verified. A committee consisting of Mr. King and Mr. Monroe was appointed on the 14th of August, 1786, to attend and make application to the legislature to that effect, which they did, and who reported the result to Congress on the 25th of September.

By the view which Mr. Monroe took in 1784 in his visit to Lake Erie and the information which he acquired in it of the state of the territory lying northerly and westerly of the river Ohio, which had been ceded by Virginia to the United States, he was satisfied that the dimensions which had been agreed on for the new states by the compact between the parties were so contracted that if adhered to, they would produce the most serious injury to the citizens who might purchase lands and settle in that territory, and defeat many of the objects contemplated in regard to it by the United States. Under this conviction he considered it a duty to bring the subject before Congress, to obtain from it a recommendation to the states to alter the act of cession so as to permit an enlargement of the dimensions of the new states, and such other modifications in their favor as the nature of the territory as to rivers, mountains and the comparative fertility of its different parts might require, so as to obviate all the evils that were anticipated. We find in the Journal of July 7, 1786, a resolution to this effect which was adopted by Congress on a motion made by him and which was acceded to by the states. It happened, when the subject was taken up in the legislature of the state, that he was a member of the House of Delegates, which enabled him to explain more fully the ground of the recommendation, and which it may be presumed contributed to its adoption.

The relation between the United States and Spain had been friendly, although there were interfering claims between them, and more especially respecting the free navigation of the Mississippi. A minister had been received then, pending the war with Great Britain, and countenance given by her government to the policy pursued by France in favor of our revolution. On the 28th of June, 1785, Mr. Gardoqui arrived at New York, as the representative of his sovereign, and on the 2d of July, he was received and recognized in that character by Congress. He presented, on his introduction, a commission authorizing him in general terms to treat on subjects of interest to the two nations with an assurance that any compact or convention into which he might enter would be approved by his sovereign. On the reception of Mr. Gardoqui and the presentation of his power to treat, a like authority was given to Mr. Jay, our then Secretary of Foreign Affairs, and who commenced immediately the negotiation. The appointment of a minister to treat on that subject was in consequence suspended. The interest of the whole western country within the United States, from the northern extremity of Lake Erie to the Mississippi, depended on the free navigation of that river. Spain then held Louisiana, comprising all that territory beyond the southeast boundary of the state of Georgia, and in consequence, the entire river from that boundary to the ocean lay within her limits. The state of Virginia had always taken a deep interest in the free navigation of that river and had often instructed her delegates to promote it. We find in the *Journals of Congress* that an instruction was given to our ministers who were appointed to form commercial treaties with foreign powers, bearing date of the 3d of June, 1784, not to relinquish or cede, in any event, in their negotiations with the government of Spain, the right of the United States to the free navigation of the river Mississippi; and on the 17th of December following, a resolution, by which it was decided to send a minister to Spain for the special purpose of adjusting the interfering claims of the two countries respecting the navigation of that river. The instructions given to Mr. Jay extended to other objects, and particularly to the boundaries between the United States and the Spanish territories, which we claimed as established in the treaty with Great Britain, but they were in strict accord with the spirit of the resolutions above recited. The public documents will show the progress and result of that negotiation, which failed, and to which I refer. It is known that a disposition existed to accommodate the difference with Spain respecting the navigation of the river, which was supported by a majority of the states in Congress, and to which Mr. Monroe was opposed. We think it proper to quote here a passage from a memoir published by him in 1828 in which he notices that occurrence in the following terms, "My zeal in favor of the free navigation of the Mississippi had been shown on several important occasions. As far back as the year 1786, when a member of the revolutionary Congress, I had strenuously opposed a projected treaty with Spain by which, had it been concluded, the use of that river would have been suspended for a term, and our right to it, as I thought, impaired. It was known that I wrote the paper which was presented by the delegate of the state in opposition to that project. I mention this occurrence with no unfriendly feeling to Mr. Jay, our then Secretary of Foreign Affairs, for no one thinks more highly than I have done and still do of his talents, revolutionary services, and general merit, which I take this occasion, with pleasure, to declare."

We find in the *Journal* of the 13th of July, 1785, that a report of a committee consisting of Mr. Monroe, Mr. Spaight, Mr. Houston, Mr. Johnson, and Mr. King, to whom a motion of Mr. Monroe for vesting the United States with power to regulate commerce between the United States and foreign nations and between the states themselves had been referred, was taken into consideration by a committee of the whole house. It appears that the report was not decided on, but referred to a like committee on the succeeding day, who took it into consideration and with a like result. The object contemplated was thus brought before Congress and the union, and there it rested. It does not appear that Mr. Monroe ever pressed it. It was manifestly his desire to rest that power in the general government, under a conviction that it would be exercised by it with greater advantage to the states, individually, as well as to the union, than by the states themselves: that it was in truth necessary to the preservation of the union. The policy of the measure was fully explained in the report which was drawn by him and which may be seen in the first volume of the laws of the United States, among the preparatory acts leading to a change of the system.

During the revolutionary struggle the effort had been, by every state and the people of each, to exert their best faculties in support of the great cause in which they were engaged. The marked feature of that epoch consisted in the effort of each to excel the others, and they took a pride in the proof which any of them could adduce that they had succeeded. As soon, however, as the revolution was accomplished, a different spirit seemed to pervade every part. Claims for advances made and services rendered were pressed by every state in relief from the calls made on them for the purposes of the union, and a distrust of the general government was manifested by many. The impost had not been granted, nor had the power to prohibit commerce in the vessels of foreign powers, the grant of which had been recommended at Annapolis under the restrictions therein specified. Those propositions were still depending and attended with serious difficulties in many of the states. Aware of the cause to which they were imputable, Mr. Monroe's object was to shun it and to obtain simply the power under a convention, that the benefits resulting from the exercise of it by the general government would be so sensibly felt that it would increase the confidence of the people in that government and dispose them to avail themselves of its aid in other instances in which it might be equally useful, and of which that example would afford an instructive lesson. If the power to regulate commerce should be granted, it might fairly be inferred that the revenue arising from it, or at least in the extent recommended, would soon follow. The power contemplated was confined to a regulation only, leaving the revenue, with the appointment of the collectors and other officers, to the states respectively. By a recurrence to the report it will be seen that a proposition which accorded with it in many respects was introduced by Mr. Madison in the legislature of Virginia on the 30th of November of the same year, 1785, which terminated in an invitation by that assembly to the several states to meet by their representatives in convention to consider how far a uniform system in their commercial regulations would be necessary for their general interest and permanent harmony, and to report such an act, as, when adopted by all the states, should enable Congress to provide for the same.

In compliance with that recommendation, a convention was held at Annapolis in 1786, but which was partially attended, several of the states having declined to send representatives to it. That body therefore digested no plan from a conviction, as is inferred, that a recommendation of any from a few states would not be attended to by the others, nor produce the desired effect. If the object was of sufficient interest to the whole, of which the proof became daily better established, the whole ought to move in it. The convention at Annapolis contented itself by presenting its view of the importance of the subject and recommending a meeting of all the states, by their representatives, in a convention to be held in Philadelphia the ensuing year, with authority to digest and recommend such a system, on a thorough knowledge and full consideration of the exigencies of the country, as their united talents might dictate. Mr. Monroe, finding that the subject had taken this direction in his own state under the auspices of the very patriotic and enlightened citizen who has been mentioned, suspended his proposition and contributed his humble aid, while he remained in Congress, to promote success in the very interesting and promising course which had thus been given to it. A convention was accordingly held the ensuing year, 1787, in Philadelphia, which was composed of the most enlightened men in the union, to whose labors and talents we owe the Constitution by which the states are now bound together.

This sketch will give a just idea of the agency which Mr. Monroe had in the affairs of the union during his service in the Congress under the Confederation, as it likewise will of the course of proceeding and measures that were adopted at that interesting period. In November,

This portrait of Mrs. James Monroe was painted from life
by Benjamin West, during the period when Monroe
was Minister to France.

1786, his third year expired, beyond which, under the Confederation, he could no longer serve. During his service in New York he formed a connection with Miss E. Kortright, a daughter of Mr. L. Kortright, of an ancient and respectable family of that state. She moved with him to Virginia and has been the partner of all the toils and cares to which he has since been exposed in his public trusts abroad and at home. When the nature of these is considered, and the duties of a family devoted to the honor and interest of their country and bound to cherish economy, it will readily be conceived that her burdens and cares must have been great. It is a remark, which it would be unpardonable to withhold, that it was improbable for any female to have fulfilled all the duties of the partner of such cares, and of a wife and parent, with more attention, delicacy and propriety than she has done.

On leaving Congress after forming this connection, he resolved to take his station at the bar and to adhere to it, and with that view to establish himself at Richmond, convenient to the superior courts in which he should practice. Judge Jones, his uncle, who resided then in King George County and who had a house in Fredericksburg, pressed him to take it and to reside there for a time at least, which might enable him to make such arrangements for his residence at Richmond, while at the bar, and his permanent establishment in Albemarle, as he might desire. In support of this plan he offered many inducements, though the tie between them was so heavy a character that little else was necessary to secure a compliance with it. Mr. Monroe took his residence in that town and house in January, 1787, and having many friends in the town and likewise in the county, was elected in the spring following to the General Assembly of the state, and in the next year to the Assembly, and likewise to the Convention which was called to decide on the Constitution which had been agreed on and recommended to the states by the general Convention which had been held in Philadelphia.

In the legislature of the state, the Constitution of the United States was the subject which attracted most attention. In the first year, the call of a Convention to decide on it, which was indispensable, brought its provisions incidentally into view, and several of the members expressed their sentiments respecting it; among them was Mr. G. Mason and Mr. Henry, both of whom were revolutionary characters of great talents and merit who had great weight in the House and state. They were both opposed to it. Mr. Monroe said nothing on the subject. Its powers transcended the limit which he had contemplated, but still he entertained doubts whether it would contribute most to the interest of the union to adopt it, in the hope of amending any of its defects afterwards, or to suspend a decision on it until those amendments should be previously obtained. When elected to the Convention, he expressed those doubts to his fellow citizens of the county before the poll commenced, but, having formed his opinion in favor of the latter course before the meeting of the Convention, he addressed a letter to them to that effect in which he stated the objections which had occurred to him to the Constitution. This address, being imperfectly printed, was not generally circulated; he communicated, however, copies of it to several distinguished characters and among them to General Washington, Mr. Jefferson, and Mr. Madison, who viewed it with liberality and candor. We see a copy of that which was sent to Mr. Jefferson in the Library among the collection of pamphlets transferred by him to the United States. From General Washington an answer was received which is published in the documents attached to this work.[12] In the Convention, Mr. Monroe took part in the debate and in one of his speeches entered fully into the merits of the subject. We find that he was decidedly for a change and a very important one in the existing system, but that the Constitution reported had, in his opinion, defects which required amendment and which he thought had better be made before it was adopted.

From the time that the Constitution was reported from Philadelphia by the Convention who had formed it, the citizens throughout the country became much divided respecting its merits, those opposed to it contending that it would lead to consolidation and monarchy; those who supported it, that its adoption was indispensable to the preservation of the union and of free government. By degrees the parties became violent, each imputing to the other selfish and improper motives. Those in favor of it were called Federalists; those against it, Anti-Federalists. This division was felt in the state assemblies and conventions to whom it was submitted, and in Congress after its adoption, though the confidence reposed in General Washington, who had been unanimously elected to the office of President, abated considerably its violence.

It being known to Colonel George Nicholas, who resided in Albemarle but who was about to move to Kentucky, that Mr. Monroe was desirous of making an establishment in that county, and that he had extensive possessions in Kentucky, he proposed to him during the session of the Convention of which they were both members, to make an exchange of property, to give him his house and lots in Charlottesville and the tract of land contiguous to it for such a portion of Mr. Monroe's lands in Kentucky as should be of equal value.

For the property in Albemarle he fixed his price, and for the lands in Kentucky he proposed that it should be fixed by several persons whom he named, who were among those best known to Mr. Monroe and the most distinguished in that district. It was arranged that Mr. Monroe should visit Albemarle immediately after the adjournment of the Convention, inspect the property offered to him there, and then decide whether he would accede to the proposed exchange and on what conditions. He made the visit accordingly which terminated in an agreement between them whereby each attained the object which he earnestly desired on fair conditions and which were carried into effect in a manner perfectly satisfactory to both parties. Mr. Monroe moved to that county in 1789 and resided there, when at home, until a late period, and enjoyed during the whole time of his residence the most friendly intercourse with his fellow citizens of the county, who have given him proof of their confidence and regard which he will always recollect with great sensibility.[13]

The Constitution was ratified by all the state conventions and carried into effect in 1789, and the distinguished citizen who had commanded our Revolutionary armies and presided in the late national Convention was elected to the Chief Executive status by the unanimous suffrage of the whole people. He served in that trust the two first terms, making eight years, and although regarding the novelty of the station, the divisions among ourselves, and the convulsed state of the world at that important epoch, with its bearing on us, his situation was eminently difficult, and some of his measures were not approved by the Republican party, yet he had the peculiar felicity to enjoy to the end of his services and of his life the undiminished confidence of his country. In the arrangement of parties he belonged, by the force of circumstances, to the Federal, and was in consequence at its head, but he was nevertheless at the head of the nation, not by his office alone, but by the place which he held in the confidence and affections of his fellow citizens. No one suspected him of a desire to promote the establishment of monarchy. His devotion to the rights and liberties of his country and incorruptible integrity had been too fully proved by his long, very eminent and very faithful services to admit any doubt on that point. Of the political principles, however, of some other of our Revolutionary patriots, a portion of whom had rendered service in council and others in the field, a different sentiment was entertained. It was known that they did not confide in a government founded exclusively on the sovereignty of the people; that they considered the experiment, as they called it, which we were then making, as sure to fail, and looked forward to its failing as leading to a change more favorable to their political views and principles. As many of those to whom those sentiments were imputed were placed in both Houses of Congress and in the Executive, the jealousy of the opposite party of the movement of the government was more particularly excited.

It is believed that no person was ever called to a trust of greater delicacy and difficulty than was our first Chief Magistrate. His greater dread was that of disunion, but it proceeded solely from a disinterested regard for the public welfare. His difficulties arose from the nature of the trust itself: the commencement of a new government with a divided sovereignty respecting which, in some of its powers, a great diversity of sentiment had prevailed and strong parties been formed in the discussions which led to its adoption, which still existed and might be felt in its subsequent movement. No such government had ever existed before because the sovereignty, independent of other peculiarities, had never been divided before, nor can it be divided except where the sovereignty is in the people and the government, a trust created by compact, in which those who discharge its duties have no rights or interests of their own, but are mere agents employed for the purpose. Under such circumstances the government may be modified according to the will of those who formed it. In this instance the great object of the change had been to guard against disunion by the incompetency of the confederated system, to accomplish the purpose of its institution. In seeking that object we hazarded the other extreme, that of consolidation, against which it was equally necessary to guard. It was natural, therefore, that all those whose fear had been most excited by either of those dangers should still regard it as the most eminent and be most solicitous to provide against it. Here, then, there was a serious cause of jealousy between the parties which could not fail to show itself in all the important measures of the government.

It is not my intention to give a view in detail of the several instances in which differences occurred between the parties and of the causes which produced them while the Federal party maintained, with vigor, its opposition to the Republican. Such a detail would necessarily comprise a full view of our relations with foreign powers during a very important epoch and of the occurrences which signalized it, forming in effect, a history of its great events. A brief outline of the occurrences in which the difference of sentiment was most distinctly marked will be sufficient for the present purpose.

A question occurred in the outset of the government, a decision which could not fail to be very sensibly felt by the whole community. Into whose hands should the administration be placed in the several departments, under the Executive, and in every grade in each? Should it be confined to those of the Federal party or be extended to a certain portion of the Anti-Federalists? The argument on each side was forcible. In favor of the first proposition it was urged, as it is understood, that the success of the government would depend on committing it especially in its commencement to its friends: that if it should be committed to its opponents or, as they were called, its enemies, they might by an erroneous construction of its powers, and by the establishment of precedents in conformity therewith, impair its strength, if not destroy it: that to divide the offices between the two parties would have a temporizing aspect and be undignified, unworthy the character of the distinguished individual who had been placed at the head of the government. On the other side, it was urged that the opponents to the Constitution were not opposed to a thorough change of the system by the enlargement of its powers and by the adoption of a Constitution: that they had been opposed to certain branches of power only, and to the want of proper checks, by fundamental declarations, against the abuse of power, and which were necessary in all governments; that the sovereignty belonging to the people, the Constitution could derive its form only from their sanction, and which could be given to it only by a majority of votes in each state; that it was the duty of every citizen to vote either for or against it, and provided he discharged that duty conscientiously, voting according to his best judgment, there was as much merit involving one way as the other; that to mark with favor those who voted for it, and with distrust and censure those who voted against it, would be repugnant to the principles of our system and be attended with pernicious consequences. The reasoning in favor of the first proposition prevailed and, in consequence, the Administration, in every department and in the offices in each, was put into the hands of the Federalists and of such as were distinguished partisans on that side, with the exception of one distinguished citizen, who was employed on a foreign mission and who, although he entertained strong objections to the instrument in its then state, would nevertheless, as was understood, have voted for it had he been present.[14]

For the decision on this question, much allowance ought to be made, and especially to the Chief Magistrate. It cannot be doubted that the leading Federalists were for the exclusion of their opponents. It was, therefore, difficult for him to disregard their council and to separate himself, as it were, from them. He was also one of the last of men to take a course which should subject him to the suspicion of pursuing a temporizing policy for any purpose whatever. The mere possibility of exposing himself to such an imputation, by a decision on one way on a question respecting which honest doubts might be entertained by enlightened men, would tend to give to his mind the opposite direction. It is certain, however, that the decision which he made in this instance separated the parties more completely from each other and bound the members of each more closely together. This consideration explains more fully the cause of the pertinacity with which the members of the Federal party adhered together afterwards in all the vicissitudes and in every state of public affairs which occurred. Much allowance ought to be made for human frailties. Vice, alone, is criminal.

The French Revolution, which commenced about the time that this Constitution was carried into operation, was one of those occurrences which excited in a high degree party feeling. The leaders of that revolution, which manifestly emanated our own, some of whom had served here, were desirous of procuring to it the same result by the abolition of the monarchical form and establishment of the sovereignty of the people. It may truly be said that in the expression of sentiment there was scarcely a citizen of the United States who did not take an interest in the contest. It is equally true that all those of the Federal party who doubted the competency of the people to self-government were manifestly opposed to that revolution, in the direction which it took and, as was inferred, from a knowledge of the obstacle it would present to their view of hereditary right. The whole Republican party, and indeed, the great body of the people, were in its favor, for it is an unquestionable fact that the great body of the people, under whatever name or leaders they might pass, were decided republicans.

The Republican party contented itself with expressing its opinion and wishes for the success of the French Revolution. They never thought of engaging in the war in support of it. This, however, did not satisfy that section of the Federal party above alluded to. It was their policy to give it every discouragement on our part, well knowing that a reproach from us would operate with tenfold greater force than from any other quarter. Everything, therefore, was done with a view to that object which it was possible for them to accomplish. Many proofs of this fact may be adduced from the occurrences of the time, and too many persons of the highest respectability are now living who were active agents on the theater, who can attest to it, to admit any doubt of its truth.

As soon as Mr. Monroe retired from Congress in the autumn of 1786, he attended the superior courts of the state at Richmond and engaged in the practice of the law in those courts; and on the establishment of the district courts and his removal to Albemarle, he extended his practice to those courts, in Charlottesville, Fredericksburg, and Staunton. His success at the bar was gratifying to him, and the prospect of future profit very favorable. During this interval he applied the funds arising from his professional exertions to the enlargement and improvement of his establishment in Albemarle, and in aid of which he disposed of other portions of his lands in Kentucky, by means whereof he had considerably augmented it. He made no injudicious contracts and those which he did make were with his friends, such of high character and honor, which he always fulfilled to their entire satisfaction. Attentive to his own concerns, vigilant and active, his credit was good. His establishment had already become extensive, and the prospect of enlarging it still further very promising. He sought no public employment but rather, shunned it.[15] A disposition was manifested by many of his friends in Albemarle to place him in the legislature, but he did not wish it. He had already devoted a large portion of his life in important trusts, and at difficult periods, with zeal and fidelity to his country, and his object was, now that we were blessed with peace and affairs in a prosperous train, to improve his property and provide for his family. While thus engaged, Colonel William Grayson, his estimable friend and relative, who held a seat in the Senate of the United States, departed this life, and the legislature of the state, at the ensuing session in December, 1790, elected him to the vacant trust, in which he served until his subsequent appointment of Minister Plenipotentiary to France, which was conferred on him by the President of the United States in 1794. While a member of the Senate, Mr. Monroe was always at his station in that body, and the session being in the winter, he was likewise always at his station at the bar in the courts in which he practiced. His duties in the Senate, by taking him from home and from the state for some months each year, diminished somewhat his professional profits, but his devotion to his country would not permit him either to decline the office to which he had been elected, unsought by himself, or to withdraw from it in haste. His own affairs were placed on a good foundation, which he had great confidence would be permanent, especially as he intended to retire and devote himself exclusively to them as soon as he could reconcile his retirement from the office he now held to a just sense of what he owed to his country.[16]

From a miniature of James Monroe, painted by
Jean François Sené in Paris, 1794, during
the period when Monroe was
Minister to France.

3

Minister from America to the French Revolution

Although Mr. Monroe was a member of the party called Anti-Federal, yet his conduct was moderate. He had been an advocate for an essential change of the system, and in the convention of the state, by whom the Constitution was adopted, he had declared that sentiment in decided terms. In the Senate he had opposed in several instances the measures proposed by the President, of which it is proper to notice two examples, the appointment of Mr. Morris to France and of Mr. Jay to England, the latter of which occurred a few weeks, only, before this mission was offered to him. The relation, however, which had been formed between them in his early youth was not shaken. In support of this fact, it may not be improper to mention an incident which occurred before his nomination to the Senate and appointment by the President as Minister Plenipotentiary to the French republic. The government of France had demanded the recall of Mr. G. Morris, who then held that station with that government. They considered him unfriendly to their revolution and were anxious that he should be removed and a successor be appointed to him of different principles. As soon as this demand was made known to the President, he resolved to comply with it and, in consequence, instructed the Secretary of State, Mr. Edmund Randolph, to consult with and take the opinion of Mr. Madison and Mr. Monroe as to the person whom they thought best suited to the trust. They recommended a citizen to whom the appointment was offered, and who declined it. The offer was then made to Mr. Monroe, who declined, that he had never contemplated such a trust, that his views were different, and that the proposition was the more unexpected from the consideration that he had opposed in the Senate some of the most important measures of the President. Mr. Randolph replied that the President was decidedly friendly to the French Revolution, and of which, as Mr. Monroe's principles were well known, he was desirous of his appointment to give to the government and people of France an unequivocal proof. With respect to the part he had acted in the Senate, Mr. Randolph assured him that it formed no obstacle to his appointment, for the President had never ascribed it to other than upright and honorable motives. On due consideration and the advice of his friends and of those generally with whom he harmonized in Congress, he resolved to accept it. Of this he apprised Mr. Randolph and, in consequence, his nomination was made to the Senate, approved by it, and the appointment immediately conferred on him.

Mr. Monroe accepted this appointment with an earnest desire to discharge its duties with advantage to his country, satisfaction to his government, and credit to himself. The trusts which he had before held were very distinguished, and considering his age, proof of the high confidence reposed in him by his native state, from all of which he had retired with the approbation of his fellow citizens. The manner of his appointment to this mission was peculiarly gratifying to him, by the person from whom it emanated and the sentiment which accompanied it from that illustrious person in his favor. The theater on which he was called to act was new, and the trust itself, of a nation, the more difficult and delicate from the state in which he left affairs at home and that which existed in France, where his duties were to be performed. Great Britain and France were engaged in war which menaced the existence of each power, and both pursued it with a spirit which manifested a desire to crush, if not to exterminate, the other. All the other powers of Europe were arranged on the side of Great Britain, but with the same object in view. The principle on which the contest turned was that on which our governments were founded, and it was believed, by those who formed the Anti-Federal party, that the result in favor of either side would produce a corresponding effect with us.

In the fury of the contest, both Great Britain and France had struck at and done us great injury. Both had seized a large number of our vessels at sea, condemned and sold their cargoes, and imprisoned many of our citizens. With the government of France a treaty of commerce had been formed in 1778, on liberal principles which had been violated, and much injury inflicted on us in breach thereof. It was well understood that the French Revolution had taken its origin in that of the United States, and as the success of so great a power as France threatened the overthrow of all the monarchies of Europe, the dread of which had united them against her, it might fairly be concluded that the cause of the two countries in that respect was the same, and that the fate of France might decide that of America. If she should be crushed, there seemed to be no ground on which to rest a reasonable presumption that they would not strike at the source from whence the danger emanated. The naval force of Great Britain predominated at sea, and her government had not adopted with us, in favor of neutral powers, those few principles of maritime right which France had done, so that the French government had injured its character as well as its interest by the breach of the treaty of 1778. Mr. Monroe resolved to present these views to the French government and to urge them with great zeal, in the hope of inducing it to revoke the order for seizing our vessels, to restore the treaty to its full force, obtain an indemnity for injuries already received, and to preserve the best understanding and policy between the two governments and the people of the two countries. He sailed from Baltimore the latter end of June and arrived at Havre de Grace on the 31st of July, and at Paris on the 2d of August following.

On Mr. Monroe's arrival at Paris he found that Mr. Morris was at his residence in the country about 30 miles from the city. He apprised him immediately of his arrival and requested his attendance to present him to the Minister of Foreign Affairs, with which he promptly complied. The interview was short but satisfactory. The Minister assured Mr. Monroe that he should deliver forthwith his letter of credence to the Committee of Public Safety, who would, he presumed, recognize him in his official character without delay. He waited several days but heard nothing from the Minister. Intimations were then given him, through Mr. Skipwith, the Secretary of Legation, and soon afterwards directly to himself by persons of very respectable character, holding stations by which they became acquainted with the secret measures and views of the Committee, that there was good cause to believe that his reception would be long delayed, and to apprehend that it might be refused. With one of the persons alluded to Mr. Monroe had been acquainted and in the habit of friendly and confidential intercourse in the United States, when he had served his country in a respectable grade.

Mr. Monroe deems it proper now to state that Mr. Otto was that person whom he had known as Secretary of Legation to the Chevalier de Lucerne, and afterwards as chargé d'affaires of his government. He knew him to be friendly to a good understanding between the two countries and to the success of his mission in all its great objects. His name has heretofore been withheld, arising from the unsettled state of affairs in France, but there can be no longer any need for suppressing it. He held then the office of Undersecretary of Foreign Affairs. In his communication, therefore, Mr. Monroe reposed the most implicit confidence. He asked him with what motive and on what ground the Committee had assumed an attitude so unfriendly towards his country? His reply was answered, and [was] explicit. He assured Mr. Monroe that the Committee had imbibed the most illiberal, as he contrived, unfounded suspicions of the views of our government towards France: that they believed and acted under the belief that Mr. Jay had been sent to England to make a treaty with her government unfriendly to France, and that he, Mr. Monroe, had been sent to France to cover and support the mission to England. The communication excited equally the surprise and indignation of Mr. Monroe. He could not hear without disdain an imputation which was so dishonorable both to his government and himself. He was satisfied that the mission to England, whatever might be its result, had been adopted with the most upright and pure motive in regard to his country, to France, and the French Revolution and every object contemplated by it. The high-minded, honorable, and manly courage which the President had pursued through life, in all the very important stations which he had filled, and the exalted character which he then sustained throughout the civilized world for all the great qualities of the head and heart, placed him above the suspicion of embarking in such low intrigues as are often practiced by old and corrupt governments. And as to himself, Mr. Monroe could not otherwise than be deeply mortified to find that his zeal in support of the great causes in which the people were engaged, which had been evinced in his stations at home and been a strong motive with the President in appointing him to that mission, should by those whose cause he had then supported and intended still further to support, be thus ungenerously rewarded. He found himself embarked on a theater altogether different from that on which he had before acted, and that to support his own principles, the great object of his mission, and the cause of France, he must adopt his conduct and mission to the theater on which he was placed and to the extraordinary state of affairs which then existed there.

Mr. Monroe arrived in Paris a few days after the fall and execution of Robespierre, the first great event which led to the overthrow of the Mountain party, a party whose career had been marked with much violence and cruelty from an early period of the Revolution. He found affairs in a state the most extraordinary that the modern world had witnessed. The contest was between the members of the Convention itself and those on both sides who were friendly to the Revolution and had risked everything in its support. That they should have yielded to such blind infatuation and to such wild and furious passions is a strong proof of the frailty of man and of the danger to which all struggling for liberty, by a people thus circumstanced, are exposed. Notwithstanding the excitement which Mr. Monroe experienced, his purpose in all its views remained unchanged. His zeal for the success of the French Revolution and for the good order and tranquility of France, as well as for that of all the other objects of his mission, was not abated. He viewed affairs before him in their true light, as he did the causes which produced them. He resolved to take no step without due consideration of all circumstances entitled to attention, and the best information respecting them which those best acquainted with them, and in whom he most confided, could give him. He saw distinctly that the government could not be considered as strictly in the hands of the Convention, that it was wielded by the multitudes, or people in mass, among whom those in Paris took the lead. He saw with equal certainty that however wild and distracted the movement had been or might be, the whole community had liberty for its object. On full consideration, he was satisfied that he should not accomplish any of the great objects of his mission, nor even avert the still more serious injuries which were menaced, if he did not adopt a measure which should act on the whole community and induce the people under the influence of the great object which they had in view and the high motives by which they were governed to take part with him in support of their own causes and to bear on the Convention in a manner to give a proper direction to its course, and through it to that of the Committee of Public Safety. He knew that he had the means of producing this result, and he resolved to avail himself of them.

Every branch of his government had declared the great interest which it took in the welfare of France and in the success of the French Revolution. The Senate and House of Representatives had, respectively, passed a resolution to this effect expressed in strong terms, a short time before Mr. Monroe's appointment, with a request by each that the President would communicate it to the French government. Each House brought to view the struggle in which we had been engaged in the same cause, the aid which we had derived from France in it, and the success with which we had been blessed. In performing this duty, of which the Secretary of State was the organ, he declared in his letter to the Committee of Public Safety that the President concurred in the sentiments expressed by those branches, and in the most forcible terms that he could adopt. These documents were committed to Mr. Monroe with intention to promote the great objects of his mission. It could not be doubted, if the strong manifestation which they afforded of the solicitude of the government and people of the United States for the welfare of those of France and the success of the French Revolution should be laid before the nation, that they would produce the desired effect.

The most direct and effectual mode by which this could be accomplished, and the most free from objections, would be to announce his arrival to the Convention by a letter to the President, and to request that that body would designate the department of the government by whom he should be received and recognized as the minister of their ally and sister-republic. In taking this step, it would be proper not to notice the difficulty which had occurred with the Committee, or even that his arrival had been announced to it. His object was to overcome difficulties and to draw the whole nation together in a correct policy and friendly feeling towards his government and country. The Convention was the highest institutional authority in France and, in addressing it, no offense could be given to any department under it. He presumed, on the contrary, that the influence which the measures would have on the people at large would be decisive with the Convention and likewise with the Committee, and that the latter would say nothing of what had occurred with it. He felt great anxiety as to the effect which the measure might have with Great Britain and the other powers at war with France, and as to the light in which it might be viewed by his own government. We were neutral in the war and intended to remain so. He concluded, however, that as our sentiments were known to all to be as expressed in those documents, and the resolution of the two Houses had been published, they would produce no effect unfavorable to our interest with any power; and that our government, especially when apprised of the considerations which produced the measure, would approve it.[17] He indulged a hope, as the act would indicate decision, that it would have a good effect with the allied powers. Nothing could be expected from them in regard to the cause at issue but what should arise from necessity. Their interest in the result differed from ours, and their measures corresponded with their interest. Those of the French government in regard to us were dictated by folly and passion.

It did not become either his government or himself for him to enter into any negotiation with the Committee to obtain his recognition, and he was fearful it should be refused or delayed on the suspicion stated, and made dependent on the result of the negotiation with England, that it would give to her government great advantage in that negotiation. In any event, the indignity to our government and country would be so great that it could not fail to excite the resentment of the whole nation against France, whereby the two peoples would be put at a great distance from each other, and the cause of her Revolution, and of liberty generally, be much injured. He thought that it would be unpardonable in him to remain a calm spectator of such proceeding and to risk those consequences arising from the folly and passion of the Committee—and which could not be imputed to the nation, who were ignorant of the whole affair—especially as he was satisfied that he had the means, by an appeal to it, of preventing them.

On full consideration of all these circumstances, he resolved to take the course suggested, and in consequence addressed a letter to that effect to the President of the Convention on the 13th of August, with a translation of it in French, which was received and read amidst the acclamations of the whole body. It was immediately decreed that the letter to the President, with the letter of credence which accompanied it, should be sent to the Committee of Public Safety, with direction to report thereon during the session of that day. Some of the members of the Committee were then present, and among them Barrère, of the Mountain party, who had been opposed in the Committee, as Mr. Monroe was informed, to his reception, and who took the papers to the Committee and made a report immediately, in the spirit which had been manifested by the House, on which a decree was passed for his reception by the Convention itself at two o'clock p.m. on the next day. A copy of this decree was sent to him in the evening by Merlin de Douay, the President of the Convention, with a request that he would communicate to him a copy of the address which he should present to the Convention when he should be introduced to it, that he might prepare his answer, which was accordingly done. A short time was thus allowed for the preparation of his address regarding the important interests on which it would bear and the effect it might have on France, on the allied powers, on his own country and, in consequence, on himself. This was the more sensibly felt because, as it formed a part of his plan and was necessary to produce the desired effect to present, at the same time, the resolutions of both Houses of Congress with the letter of the Secretary of State above specified, it would be indispensable to have the whole translated into French in the interim. This, however, was accomplished. The address was prepared and a copy, with a translation of it, sent to Merlin de Douay within the time appointed; and all the other papers were likewise translated in due time, so that everything was prepared for his use when he was introduced into the Convention. The translation was made by Mr. Otto, and the other work was executed by Mr. Skipwith, the Secretary of Legation.

Mr. Monroe was received by the Convention at two o'clock on the 14th of August, the time designated by the decree of the preceding day, and his reception corresponded in all respects with the favorable anticipation which he had formed of it. In his letter to the President which announced his arrival, he had assured him of the great interest which the government and people of the United States took in the liberty and happiness of those of France, and in the success of their republic. This letter had been published in all the papers, and the sentiment being new—for all Europe was against them—and the feeling for us being very friendly—the suspicions of the Committee being known comparatively to few—the galleries of the hall were full and the crowd gathered around the building. His address, with the resolutions of the two Houses of Congress and the letter of the Secretary of State written by order of the President and expressive of like sentiments on his part, were received and read amidst the acclamations of the members and all the people present and who surrounded the Hall.[18] The President, in his reply, reciprocated the sentiments contained in those documents and explicitly declared that the people of France owed their initiation into the cause of liberty to the example set for them by those of the United States: that their warriors caught the spirit in our fields, fighting by our side, and brought it home with them and infused it into the mass of the people. He added that there was every possible motive to presume the most friendly relations between the two countries, and that Mr. Monroe, by bringing with him the pledge of that union on the part of his government and country, would contribute eminently to cement it.

Mr. Monroe was then received and acknowledged by the Convention as the Minister Plenipotentiary of the United States to the French Republic. The ground which he occupied was the most interesting and difficult that was perhaps ever held by any other minister. He was aware that his reception and the circumstances attending it would attract the attention and excite some feeling with the allied powers, and particularly Great Britain, with whom a negotiation was depending, and he was fearful, in the perilous state of affairs and the bearing which the cause at issue had on the United States, that the measure might not be approved by his government. He was, however, satisfied that the policy which governed him was sound, that with the allied powers the measure could do no injury and might have a good effect, and he trusted, when the considerations on which he acted were known to his government, that his conduct would be approved. With France it gave him a standing which it was impossible for him otherwise to have gained. It was a standing with the nation which would be felt and respected by every department of the government under it; and which would be disregarded by the Committee itself, however great the suspicion of some of its members might be, by causes only which would shake it with the people. To sustain this ground and to turn it to the best account for his government and country, it was incumbent on him to watch every occurrence in every quarter and to make a faithful representation of it to both governments, to that of France as well as his own. It was equally his duty to pursue such a course on his own part, consistent with his duty to his own government, as should preserve to him the confidence of the French people, to obtain which he had personally risked so much, and on which the good effect which he had contemplated by it was dependent.

A strong proof was soon afforded of the favorable impression which Mr. Monroe's appeal to the Convention had produced. A few days afterwards the Secretary of Foreign Affairs offered him, by order of the Committee of Public Safety, a house for his accommodation, as the minister of their ally, in any part of Paris which he should designate, and sent to him a carriage with horses without consulting him. To the offer of the house he gave an immediate answer, in which he declined it on the principle that it was forbidden by an Article of the Constitution of the United States, of which he sent to the Minister a copy. The carriage he retained a few weeks until he had procured one of his own, and then returned it, with the horses, asking permission to pay for them in like manner as he had procured those of an individual, which was granted.

Occupying, as he did, very delicate ground by the measure which he had adopted to dispel the suspicions of the French government and the proof thus given of the solicitude of his own for the success of the French Revolution, he deemed it very important, from public as well as private consideration regarding the divisions which existed at home, to accept no favor, however slight, from that government which might furnish any pretext to impeach the integrity of his motives. He deemed it equally important to give to that government no claim on himself personally, lest it might be counted on by it for improper purposes. Another proof was presented at this period of the good effect produced by the measure attended to on the government of France, which was equally strong with those which have been mentioned. The Convention passed a resolution expressive of its desire that the flags of the two republics should be suspended together in its Hall as a testimony of the friendship which existed between them, and called Mr. Monroe to furnish that of the United States. As this act had no personal relation to the individual, he promptly complied with it.

As soon as our citizens who were dispersed through the seaports of France saw the account of Mr. Monroe's reception by the National Convention, as published in all the gazettes, they hurried to Paris in the hope of obtaining through him a redress of their wrongs. The unfavorable ground on which Mr. Morris had stood had rendered it impossible for him to obtain justice for them and, in consequence, his aid was seldom sought. The manner of Mr. Monroe's reception inspired them with great confidence. They thought that it would form a new era in the relation between the two countries from which they should derive great and immediate advantage. His house was crowded every day with them, from the morning till the evening, each rendering a statement of his claims which was received with kindness and an assurance that his best efforts should be exerted to obtain justice for them and without delay. The citizens who had thus suffered and were still suffering were respectable men, industrious, enterprising, and intelligent. Among them there were many who had embarked and gone abroad for information as well as profit, and who had observed the course of events in France and other countries with attention and acquired a knowledge of the state of affairs generally which made an acquaintance and intercourse with them useful and desirable.

The duties which thus devolved on him were never diminished during his mission. To meet the pressure he was forced to employ several assistant secretaries, generally three, and to rent a separate house for them and afford them other accommodations and aid connected with the establishment and necessary to their comfort. There being then no consul at Paris, and the service of such an official being indispensable, he appointed to the office provisionally Mr. Skipwith, subject to the approbation of the President, who had accompanied him as Secretary of Legation, a citizen of excellent understanding, perfect integrity, and great worth, whose appointment was confirmed by the President and who retained the office during Mr. Monroe's mission and long after its termination.

To prevent any improper inference being drawn from his refusal to accept the accommodation which had been offered to him by the Committee, and to reciprocate the sentiment expressed by the offer, he was induced to purchase at his own expense a house, intimating to those in power that he made the purchase for himself, as the Minister of the United States, as a substitute for that which he had declined, and with intention to offer it to his government, on his retirement, at the price he had given for it. To this measure he was particularly and earnestly urged by many of his fellow citizens, who were fearful that his refusal to accept that which had been offered might confirm the Committee in the suspicion which had been so strongly manifested on his arrival. Of this measure he gave no intimation to his government, at the time, from a desire not to compromit it either by the acceptance or refusal at that interesting period. The refusal, he knew, would produce a bad effect. He expected when he should retire that all difficulty on the subject would be removed and that his government might act in it as it thought fit, and without any injury to the country. Of his motive in making the purchase and his intention as expressed, ample proof has been furnished. It is well known that he purchased no other property of the kind then, and that the money which enabled him to make this was borrowed of a banking house in Paris friendly to the United States, and at the insistence of his fellow citizens who had urged the measure.

Other less important incidents may be noticed here which tend to show the state in which affairs then were in France and the policy it was deemed necessary to pursue. Immediately after his recognition, a deputation was sent to him by the Poissarden, the Fishermen of Paris, of about 50 of the Corps, to compliment him on the event. The Corps, it was understood, consisted of at least 1000. It was organized, and many of them were often sent at that period in the galleries of the Hall of the Convention, uniting in applause or consent as prompted by their leaders, who were supported by the Jacobin society. The object of the visit was to obtain a gratuity, which was accordingly granted in suitable amount. Shortly afterwards an application was made to him by the poor of the section in which he resided, and to which like attention was shown. As these bodies had influence on public measures, it was deemed proper to cultivate their good opinion.

Mr. Monroe occupied ground, as has been observed, which was difficult and delicate as to himself regarding the part he had acted on it. It was eminently so to all the surrounding powers, to his own country, and to the civilized world. The people of France were engaged in a Revolution founded on principles repugnant to those of the great powers and of Europe generally, and in which they had made considerable progress. They had overthrown the monarchy, dethroned and beheaded their king and queen, abolished the aristocracy and the hierarchy, and taken the government altogether into their own hands. In the interior there was no opposition, or so inconsiderable as not to

merit the name. The revolutionary government was completely established everywhere and the people were enthusiastic in the cause.
Their armies were numerous, strong and successful in every quarter.
A complete victory had just before been obtained by Jourdan over
[the Prince of] Coburg near Charleroy, on the plains of Fleurus,
which had not only relieved France from all invasion but opened to
her the whole of Belgium and the Low Countries, a great part of which
was immediately taken possession of. On the side of Spain her success
was equally great. Her army had entered the Spanish territory and
wrested from her almost the whole of the province of Guypuscoa.
From the allied powers, therefore, no serious danger seemed to be
menaced, although no aid should be derived from the people of other
countries to whom the cause was equally applicable and a fair appeal
was made by the effort and example of France. From the overthrow
of the Roman Empire and the commencement of the governments
that were founded on its ruins by the various communities by which
that great event was accomplished, so fair an opportunity had never
been presented to their descendants or to any of them to emancipate
themselves from the slavish condition into which they had fallen, as
was now afforded by this effort of France. Many of those communities
had given proofs of their attachment to liberty and of their improvement in all those qualifications on which the institution and preservation
of free government depended, but whether they or any of them would
profit of this opportunity was altogether uncertain. Habitual rivalries,
jealousy and wars between the principal powers, which had produced
a corresponding effect with the body of the people in each, and the
violence and cruelty with which the French Revolution had been
conducted in its early stages towards those opposed to it, formed
serious obstacles to such a concert. Further discouragement had been
given it by the divisions which had occurred between those who took
the lead in support of the Revolution and the excess to which their
animosities had been carried. It followed that no reasonable calculation could be made on any aid in support of the French Revolution
to be derived from extraneous sources. The success of France, it might
fairly be concluded, would depend altogether on herself, on the
purity, the union, and wisdom of her councils in wielding her vast
resources and directing the patriotic zeal and devotion of her people
to the proper result. Two great parties had divided the Convention
from an early period, one of which was called the party of the
Mountain, and the other of the Plain; at the head of the former stood
Robespierre, and of the latter, Brissot. One was distinguished for its
violence and cruelty; the other for its moderation and humanity. The

Mountain party, impelled by the constrained fury of the Jacobin societies and the populace of Paris, yielding to every suspicion, however unfounded, which had a tendency to check its career, would stop at nothing. In this party Marat, a furious monster, had enjoyed great influence and contributed much to its enormities. Not long before Mr. Monroe's arrival, he had been stabbed in the bath and killed by Charlotte Corday, a woman of high mind and bold spirit, whose resentment he had incurred by some outrage to her family. For this she was beheaded. This party, led by Robespierre, whose power had become irresistible, overwhelmed the other, and cut off Brissot and many other distinguished men who were at its head. Danton, who next excited his jealousy by opposing the wildness and cruelty of his measures, soon experienced the same fate. By those excesses the sensibility of the nation became excited. Its humanity was shocked and its judgment as to the policy of the preceding suspended. Zealous as the people of France were in support of the great cause in which they were engaged, and prone as all people are who have just shaken off the yoke of despotism and who are menaced with its restoration to believe every charge of treachery which is made by those most vehement against those who are more moderate, yet there was a point in those excesses beyond which the people of France could not be carried. They had paused on the execution of Brissot and his associates. On that of Danton it was obvious that their judgment was made up against it. Robespierre saw his danger, but had not the judgment to avoid it. On the contrary, he was precipitated by his fears and his views into ruin. After another effort of a like kind, which was firmly resisted by Tallien, the party assailed and overset him. This event occurred on the 27th of July (9th of Thermidor), and on the 2d of August following, Mr. Monroe reached Paris; and it was in this state and under these circumstances that he had to act.

Mr. Monroe gives a full view, in his first letter to the Secretary of State of the 10th of August,[19] of the situation in which he found affairs in France on his arrival there, of their government and interior concerns generally, of the state of the war, of the temper of the people, and of every other circumstance on which the success of the Revolution would depend. In that letter, which was written on great consideration, it is obvious that he traced the foundation of the policy which he deemed best calculated to promote all the great objects of his mission. In his next letter, which was of the 25th of the same month, he announced his reception, with the measure he had adopted to obtain it, abstaining, from motives of delicacy, to state all the difficulties to which he had been exposed.[20]

Two very interesting incidents occurred at this period relating to individuals, which excited in high degree his feeling and claimed his attention, but, as he did not know precisely the ground on which he stood with the Committee, he considered it his duty to act in them with the utmost circumspection and caution. He was unwilling, after what had passed, to take any step which might rest in any degree on its confidence in his government or himself. On his arrival in Paris he was informed that Madame LaFayette, the wife of the illustrious individual who was so well known to and had such strong claims on us, was confined in prison and menaced with execution. A few days after his recognition, the Marquis de Tascher, her uncle, called and requested his interposition in her behalf. Mr. Monroe assured him that he might count on his good offices to the utmost extent that he might be able to render them, intimating, however, the delicate ground on which he stood and the propriety of moving in the affair with great caution to produce the desired effect and even to avoid doing her injury. With this the Marquis was aware, and of the caution suggested he highly approved. Mr. Monroe desired him to assure his niece that if any serious danger should be menaced, he would step forward and risk everything for her safety. The first step that was taken for her relief it seems proper to mention here. General LaFayette, her husband, was then imprisoned in Olmutz by the Emperor of Austria, a fact which in itself proved his devotion to the liberties of his country and of mankind in general. The French government, however, had acted in the turmoil of their affairs on a different sentiment. Their suspicion of his principles was then such that no aid in her favor could be hoped for by a reference to him, nor could any be expected at our instance by an application directly to the Committee itself. It was thought advisable to make an appeal to the people in such manner as to draw their aid in support of any application which might be made to the Committee. With this view the following expedient was adopted. There were then no private carriages in Paris and the hacks were generally in the worst state. Mr. Monroe procured a carriage of his own as soon as he could, had it put in the best order, and his servants dressed in like manner. In this carriage Mrs. Monroe drove directly to the prison in which Madame LaFayette was confined. As soon as it entered the street, the public attention was drawn to it, and at the prison gate the crowd gathered round it. Inquiry was made, whose carriage is it? The answer given was, that of the American Minister. Who is in it? His wife. What brought her here? To see Madame LaFayette. The concierge, or prison keeper, brought her to the iron railing in which the gate was fixed. A short time before, her mother and grandmother had been taken from the same prison and beheaded, and she expected from the first summons to her to experience the same fate. On hearing that the wife of the American Minister had called with the most friendly motives to see her, she became frantic, and in that state they met. The scene was most affecting. The sensibility of all the beholders was deeply excited. The report of the interview immediately spread through Paris and had the happiest effect. Informal communications took place in consequence between Mr. Monroe and the members of the Committee, and the liberation of Madame LaFayette soon followed, on which event she hastened directly to his house, where she was received with the warmest affection. He soon afterwards procured for her a passport from the French government and furnished her with every facility, with the aid of which she left France and joined her husband at Olmutz, where she partook with him for several years the hardship of his confinement and of the prison fare.

The other incident related to Thomas Paine, who had been imprisoned with Brissot and his party, and would have been beheaded with them, as was understood and believed by him, had it not been prevented by an accident—a mistake as to the room, or the door of the room, in which he was confined. As soon as Mr. Monroe was recognized, Mr. Paine informed him of his imprisonment and requested his good offices to obtain his relief. A like assurance was given to him and that his discharge should be demanded as soon as it might be presumed, regarding all the circumstances of the case, that it would be complied with. Mr. Paine, having incorporated himself into the society of France and become a member of the French Convention, might be supposed to have subjected himself to the fate of others in a like state. He nevertheless still retained his right of citizenship in the United States and his claim on the government and people for his services in our Revolution. In every view, however, it was proper that an application for his discharge should be made with caution. Mr. Monroe had by degrees become acquainted with many of the members of the two great Committees of Public Safety and Society General, and other members of the Convention, which afforded him opportunities to communicate with them informally on all the subjects on which he had to act. Of these he had profited in regard to Mr. Paine, as he had others of a general nature. On the first of November he made an application for his discharge, which produced a meeting of those two Committees, who deliberated on the subject the whole night, and at the dawn of day the next morning sent him an order for his release, by their secretary, which Mr. Monroe forwarded by his secretary to the prison in which Mr. Paine was confined, which was promptly obeyed and he brought immediately to his house. Being destitute of every necessity, without resource and in bad health, Mr. Monroe retained him there for a year and a half, supplied his wants, and furnished him afterwards with additional aid to some amount. The acquaintance between them personally had been slight. His claims were on the United States and from which, as their Minister he thought that he ought not to shrink.[21]

It has already been observed that the French government had injured the United States in many important circumstances. They had, in violation of our treaty of commerce of 1778, seized and condemned many of our vessels with their cargoes, embargoed others, imprisoned our citizens, and in other respects done us serious injury. They had, in fact, acted more like an enemy than a friend. The same violent proceedings which they had practiced among themselves they had extended to us, and with no other pretext to justify their conduct than that Great Britain had given the example and that we were bound to tolerate from France whatever we did from Britain. Such was the state in which Mr. Monroe found affairs on his arrival in France, with a disposition strongly manifested by those with whom he had to treat to add to the injuries rather than repair those already received. His instructions were drawn on correct knowledge of the state of affairs there, to the time of his departure, and on great consideration and with ability. They looked to every object, in a manner becoming the character of the nation. The injuries which we had received from the French government, with our claims on it in that and in other respects, were stated in detail, and for which he was instructed to demand reparation. The suspicions which were entertained by it of the policy and views of our government were known, and he was instructed to remove them. Those applicable to the mission to England were anticipated and his attention drawn particularly to that mission, with an explanation of its objects. His attention was likewise drawn to the divisions among themselves, the overthrow and destruction of one party by another, with their tendency to subvert the Revolution. It was made his duty to mark the progress of the Revolution in the establishment of a regular government, and particularly the organization of the Executive branch, with the principle on which it would be founded, and likewise to ascertain whether the people continued to be attached to the Revolution from principle, or were held together by the dread of the Revolutionary tribunal or foreign invasion. For their success in that great cause the strongest solicitude was expressed, and it was enjoined on him to inspire that government with perfect confidence in the sincerity of the declarations to that effect of which he was made the organ.

With any regular well-established government of whatever class it might have been, the path before him would have been plain, but with the existing one of France it was otherwise, and for many reasons. Mr. Monroe was instructed to demand nothing of that government but what was just in itself. For the injuries that it had rendered to the United States it was bound to make certain reparation as soon as possible, and the sooner the more to its own credit. A breach of treaty, which is a breach of faith, can never be justified without adequate cause furnished by the opposite party, nor ought motives of policy, founded on other considerations, especially the conduct of a third power, ever to be plead in justification. All the most serious claims rested on unquestionable injuries, and the greater part on a breach of the treaty of commerce; the others on acts of kindness, on voluntary aids rendered to French citizens in distress. The mere exposition of them, if justice was admitted to be the standard, would allow no other reply than the acknowledgment of them, with a prompt reparation so far as it could be rendered. But in making the demand, the nature of the government, the state of those in power, their previous compromitment and existing disposition, were to be regarded. All the injuries complained of had originated with the Committee of Public Safety and with the Mountain party, which party still ruled in the Committee. Of the hostility shown by the Committee to the United States on Mr. Monroe's arrival, and of the measure to which he resorted to avert the mischief threatened by it, notice has already been taken, as it likewise has been of the sudden change produced by that measure in the conduct of the Committee toward Mr. Monroe after his recognition by the Convention. Was that change to be counted on as dictated by a conviction of its error, a pure sense of right, or as the effort of policy from the fear of encountering the public opinion which had taken the opposite direction? Mr. Monroe was unwilling to ascribe it altogether to the latter motive, making a liberal allowance for the state in which they had been and the sudden and violent impulses under which their parties had acted, but still he deemed it improper and unsafe to calculate and act on the presumption of a real change in the sentiments and disposition of that body. Incidents occasionally occurred to confirm him in this opinion. As soon as he had rented a house, which he did in the first instance by taking that held by Mr. Morris, he invited all the members of the Committee to dine with him, which invitation was not accepted by a single member nor answered by more than two or three. This, though a trivial incident, satisfied him that the feeling of the Committee had not changed towards himself, and, in consequence, that it was impossible that it should have changed towards his government. Others much stronger frequently occurred. Inquiries were incessantly made by the members of the Committee in his intercourse with them, of the progress of our negotiation with England and of its probable effect on France, and in a manner to show that the suspicions which were entertained on his arrival had not been removed.

On full consideration of all these circumstances, Mr. Monroe concluded that in demanding of the Committee a reparation for injuries, it would be advisable for him to do it in a manner which should correspond in all respects with the friendly feeling which had been manifested in his address to the Convention and the documents which he had presented with it. He was satisfied if he should demand simply a redress of grievances, with a restoration of the treaty to its full force, without mingling with it a sentiment which should form an appeal to the magnanimity of the nation, that his note, in case it should be laid before the Convention, might be used in a manner to counteract the impression which had already been made and to defeat the object sought. If it should be drawn in such a manner as to admit such an effort or even not to prevent it, he was fearful that it would be turned to that account. The object, therefore, which he had earnestly in view was to present such a note as should exhibit in full extent the just claims of his country and demand a redress for them, but to do it in such a manner as to excite the most grateful feeling of the nation and to compel it, from a regard to its own interest and character, as well as what it owed to us, to an immediate compliance. A demand in this form, from the impression he had taken, would, he thought, be more likely to succeed than in any other that he could adopt. To make it in that form was not dictated by policy alone. Nothing would be expressed in it which would not correspond with his feelings and, as he thought, with the spirit of his instructions.

Upon this principle, Mr. Monroe's note to the Committee of Public Safety, demanding a reparation for injuries, was founded and in that spirit it was drawn.[22] He gives a full exposition in that note of the injuries which had been rendered by France to the United States and particularly of those arising from the breach of the treaty of commerce of 1778. He shows that that breach was not only injurious to the good faith of France, but to her interest in a commercial point of view and in every other view that could be taken of it: that it justified and invited in the strongest manner possible the aggressions of England on the commerce of the United States and which, as all Europe was at war against France, operated exclusively to the injury of their ally and friend, and which was the more to be regretted as it injured in equal degree the interest of France herself. He took a view also in that note of the restraints otherwise imposed by her government on her commerce, by which it appears that the whole trade of the nation had been taken into the hands of the government and that of her citizens suppressed. He showed the abuses to which such a regulation was exposed by the agents of the government and its tendency to banish foreigners from her ports and to cut off all intercourse between the nation and other powers. He observed that it formed a great object with him to show the pernicious effect which this policy produced on the interest of France herself, and concluded with a declaration that, although it had rendered to the United States, and especially by the breach of the 23d and 24th articles of the treaty of commerce relating to neutral trade, all the injury of which he complained, he was not instructed by his government to demand a restoration of those articles, and that if her government should be of opinion, on full consideration, that breach ought to be preserved in, his government and fellow citizens generally would not only bear it with patience, but with pleasure.

Mr. Monroe had now assumed an attitude with the government of France by which he risked everything in regard to himself. By his address to the Convention and the note now presented, he risked his standing with his own government. By the purchase of a house as a substitute for that which had been offered to him, and by the contingent expenses to which he was exposed by the employment of several assistant secretaries and the rent of a separate house for their accommodation, with other charges which have been suggested and which were considerable, he risked his own fortune and welfare. His situation was the more painful because he was aware that no person not on the ground and an immediate spectator of all that occurred, and in confidence, too, with many who were friends of the Revolution and had witnessed the whole movement from its commencement, and with whom he conferred, could from a correct estimate of the real state and of the considerations by which he was governed. He well knew that those least apt to form such an estimate would be those who had been parties to our own Revolution and who saw the different manner in which it had been conducted. He was satisfied that this was the only course by which any of the great objects of his mission could be accomplished, and he considered it a duty which he owed to his government and country to encounter those dangers, and the consequences be what they might, rather than shrink from them. He was the more impelled to it by what he saw of the un-merited suffering and distress of many of his estimable fellow citizens who were present and in whose favor his feeling was deeply excited.

Mr. Monroe presented this note to the Committee on the 3d of September, as soon after his recognition as he could collect the requisite information and prepare it. In making his collection, and in the remarks on the several classes of claims, Mr. Skipwith rendered an important service, which it is just and proper to mention here. It was soon perceived that it subjected the Committee to great embarrass-ment, for in the conflict of parties and the violence of proceeding, they were not aware of the excesses into which they had run and the follies they had committed. He was assured that it exhibited a picture which shocked them. More than a month elapsed and no answer had been given to it. He solicited an interview with the Committee, which was promptly granted and in which he urged with all the force he could the arguments which he had pressed in his note, with such others as had occurred, to obtain a compliance with his demands. The Committee requested him to communicate in writing what he had then stated, that they might have it more fully before them and give it all the consideration which it merited. He accordingly sent, on the 18th of October, another note entitled "Supplemental Observations to That of September 3d," and in which he reviewed the subjects treated in it, and particularly that part relating to the monopoly of the trade by the government, to which he added some general remarks respecting the breach of the treaty and the advantage thereby given to England, leaving it, however, as to the repeal of the decree authorizing such breach, on the ground on which he had before placed it.[23]

A few days after the receipt of this note the Committee invited him to a conference, with which he complied, and in which he was received by the diplomatic section, consisting of three members only, Merlin de Douay, Thuniot and Treilhard. He soon found that the ob-ject sought by the interview was to obtain from him an explicit answer to the question which they propounded, "Whether he insisted on, or demanded, the execution of the 23d and 24th articles of the treaty of commerce." As a preliminary to this question, some remarks were made as to the advantage which the United States would derive from the compliance and the injury France would sustain from it, and likewise the distress with which her citizens would see British goods protected by our flag while it gave none to them. Mr. Monroe was under the impression, while engaged in this conference, that the object was to obtain from him a demand to execute the articles and to report the same to the Convention, as the basis of a call on his government to fulfill the guarantee with respect to the West Indies Islands. He therefore replied that he had nothing to add to what had been stated in his first note, that that paper contained the answer which he now gave. The conference was prolonged by the Committee, in the course of which the interrogatory was twice repeated, and with an earnestness which increased his doubt of the motive and confirmed him in the ground he had already taken. The conference thus terminated. On a review after his retirement of all that had passed, and especially as favorable changes had been made in the Committee, he was inclined to believe that the opinion he had formed so far as related to the guarantee was erroneous, and that their object was to restore the articles of the treaty to their full force, but to make his demand the ground for it rather than take the responsibility on themselves; and from the dread of incurring the imputation of favoring England to the apparent injury of France. Mr. Monroe was, however, still unwilling to take that responsibility on his government in any other form than that in which he had presented it before the Committee, from a belief that if he rested it on the ground of a direct demand only to restore the violated articles, while Great Britain was allowed to seize our vessels on a principle different and more favorable to her than that which was pressed on France, it would defeat the object, do serious injury in many other instances. Mr. Monroe was desirous that his note should be laid before the Convention, but this he could not ask nor suggest. As those notes would have promoted the object of the Committee, supposing it to be what is here suggested, of restoring to force the violated articles of the treaty and have freed it from the responsibility, he could not otherwise account for the omission to do it than the aversion they might entertain to exhibit the proof which they afforded of the follies they had previously committed, and of which they would make an acknowledgment by proposing and supporting the change called for.

On the 21st of October, Mr. Monroe received an answer from the Committee to his note of the 18th, in which they assured him that the subject of his complaints engaged their profound attention and that they hoped that the result of their deliberations would be satisfactory to his government and country.

The first *arrêt* of the Committee was passed on the 18th of November and was communicated to Mr. Monroe, by its order, on the 24th, by the Secretary of Foreign Affairs. By this *arrêt* the restraints imposed on American vessels entering the ports of France were removed. They were permitted to enter and depart at pleasure and to sell their cargoes

or not, and either to the agents of the government or to citizens, as
their captains thought fit. If purchased by the government, they were
to be paid for according to the contract. The commanders of their
squadrons and ships of war were ordered to respect the rights of
neutral nations and the stipulation of treaties in conformity with the
decree of the Convention of the 27th of July, 1793. It was particularly
enjoined on them not to turn neutral vessels from their course; nor
to take from them their captains, sailors, or passengers, other than
soldiers or sailors in the service of the enemy; nor to seize the effects
or merchandise found on board with the exception of enemies'
property and contraband of war. A precise mode of proceeding was
prescribed, when neutral vessels should be brought in, on the presumption that they had enemies' property on board, the object of which
was to prevent abuse. Every other complaint which had been presented
was noticed and provided for, except that relating to the violated
articles of the treaty of commerce which were still maintained in
force.

On the 4th of January following, another *arrêt* was passed by the
Committee, which was communicated to Mr. Monroe on the 8th by
the Committee itself in a note which assured him of its great solicitude
to preserve the relations of a sincere friendship between the United
States and the French republic. Of this solicitude they urged the *arrêt*,
which they then communicated as a proof by which the 23d and 24th
articles of our treaty of commerce, which secured the right to transport enemies' property on board our ships and which had been violated, were restored to full force. By this act the most important and
last remaining complaint of Mr. Monroe was removed.

On the compliance of the Committee with Mr. Monroe's demands,
and the mode of proceeding on his and their part, some comments
occur which it is due to candor to make. The injuries which the
United States had received from France and of which they had a right
to complain were of great extent; but by a view of the notes which
he presented to the Committee it will be seen that he did not confine
himself within that limit: on the contrary, that they extended to
internal regulations, which although they affected injuriously the
commerce of the United States with France, they were of a nature,
as they operated on her own citizens likewise and in equal degree,
which her government had a right to impose, and of which we had
no right to complain. Every nation has a right to govern its own
people in regard to commerce as it thinks fit, and, if it places foreigners in the interior on the same footing with them, no injury
is done to them. The only rights which one nation is entitled to in its

commercial intercourse with another, or which neutral nations have with belligerents, not secured by the general law of nations, are those which are stipulated by treaty. For any violation of such stipulations by either of the contracting parties, whereby injury is done to the other, the latter has a right to demand redress. Complaints for injury arising from regulations of the kind to which Mr. Monroe's notes extended, as above adverted to, are, it is believed, seldom, if ever, made officially, since, being unfounded, they would be apt generally to excite disgust and even to prevent a redress of those for which, on principle, it could not be denied. We find, however, that a very different reception was given to those of that kind which Mr. Monroe presented: that they not only obtained a redress of all the injuries of which he had a right to complain, but produced a change of their internal system in regard to their own people, as well as the citizens of the United States. How account for this result? It can be attributed to no other cause than the very favorable impression which was made on the nation by his address to the Convention and the documents which he presented with it at the time of his recognition. It is obvious that the proofs thereby afforded of the interest which the government and people of the United States took in the welfare of those of France and in the success of their Revolution, supported as they were by his well-known devotion to that cause and his conduct then, gave him a hold on the community which favored every object which related to his country, and in which he took an interest.

The facts which have been stated, and which are supported by unquestionable testimony, justify this conclusion. Had Mr. Monroe not appealed from the Committee to the Convention, it may fairly be presumed that he would not have been received, or if received, kept at a distance and disregarded. The documents, therefore, which he presented before that body and the nation laid the foundation for the change which was made in the measures of France in favor of the United States, and in her own concerns connected with them. It was the deep-rooted hostility which had long existed between those two rival nations, England and France, and which was much increased by the conduct of England in the existing war, which induced the Convention to set aside the two articles of our treaty of commerce in favor of neutral rights, and to adopt other unfriendly measures towards our country under the pretext of following the example of England and the claim, founded on services rendered in our Revolutionary war, that we should bear from her whatever was submitted to from England. The attachment of the people of France to those of the United States, from whom they had caught the spirit of liberty, was the only hold which could be used with any effect to obtain an indemnity for past injuries or prevent still greater in future, and there was no other mode by which that hold could be used with effect than that which was adopted. The suspicions of the Committee of the object of the mission to England, after Mr. Monroe's reception, remained for some time in full force and he was fearful, if he gave them any means by which they might remove or weaken the impression which he had made on the nation by the documents which had been laid before it, that they would take advantage of them to the injury of his country. He was satisfied that the change which had taken place in that stage in the conduct of the Committee towards him, was dictated by policy rather than sentiment. It was too sudden and great and nearly connected with his appeal to the Convention to admit any other construction. He considered it as an atonement for the slight shown and indignity offered to his government and country on his arrival and the dread of reaction on themselves should their conduct be known to the community. It was to deprive them of the possibility of accomplishing any object unfavorable to the United States that, in demanding the restoration of the violated articles of commerce, he did it in the spirit which has been stated and under a conviction that, if his demand should be laid before the Convention and the nation, the ground already gained would be strengthened rather than weakened by the manner.

The slow progress which was made by the Committee in those measures furnishes a proof of its embarrassment. More than two months elapsed before the first *arrêt* passed, and nearly a like time before the second. The cause of the delay may, it is believed, be correctly traced. They would not state the demand made by Mr. Monroe to restore the violated articles of the treaty of commerce without stating the other feature in it; nor could they state that feature without communicating his notes to the Convention, or provoking or at least inviting a call for them, whereby the excesses into which they had run and the follies they had committed would be shown. They were anxious to correct those follies but unwilling to acknowledge and expose them in their full extent to the world. And there was danger in taking on themselves the responsibility of restoring the violated articles of the treaty, of incurring the odium and the censure of favoring England at the expense of France. It was owing to these causes, as may be presumed, that the Committee sought at this period interviews with Mr. Monroe, in the expectation and desire that he would alter his demand in such manner as to enable them to shift the responsibility of the proposed changes from themselves on him, without presenting his notes, and to his refusal to do it, for the reasons stated, that the delay in bringing the subject forward before the Convention was to be imputed. Thus affairs remained for some time, as it were, at a stand. In the interim the feeling of the people of France for those of the United States daily gained ground. Favorable changes of the members in the Committee were occasionally made, with whom, and other members of the Convention, Mr. Monroe gradually became acquainted, had free and friendly intercourse and communication, and of which he availed himself for all the objects of his mission. They all saw the great number of our citizens whose vessels had been unjustly seized and brought in, whose property had been taken from them, and who were there in distress. The flags of the two republics were suspended together in the Hall of the Convention, which daily called to mind the very interesting occurrence which had placed them there. All these circumstances had weight and promoted the object sought.

A general reformation was indispensable, and of which the Committee of Public Safety had become convinced, but a change in that extent did not lie within its province. To accomplish so great a revolution it was necessary to unite in the effort all the great Committees within the limit of whose powers those defects lay, so far, at least, as to authorize a recommendation to the Convention to correct them. To make this arrangement in the state in which affairs then were, the contest between parties being still violent, required time, and which accounted for the delay, but it was at length brought about. On the 22d of December, 1794, (the second of Nivose), a report was made by Johannot in the name of the Committees of Public Safety, Secretary General, Legislation, Commerce, and Finance in favor of a complete reformation, with the project of a decree corresponding therewith, which was adopted immediately without opposition. By this decree the violated articles of our treaty of commerce in favor of neutral rights were restored. How far this change, in the extent to which it was carried in other respects, was promoted by Mr. Monroe's agency will be seen by a comparison of his notes with the report and the decree referred to. If so important a change in the affairs of France at that awful epoch was promoted by the agency of Mr. Monroe, it could not fail to have measured their favorable opinion of and confidence in him, to the advantage of our country. The promptitude with which the decree of the Convention was announced to him by the Committee of Public Safety, and the manner in which it was done, are proofs that the interest which the people of France took in the welfare of those of the United States, and which the Convention and every department under it were bound to respect, was the ruling cause.[24]

Mr. Monroe had now accomplished one great object of his mission. The hostile attitude which the government of France had assumed towards the United States and pursued more than a year before his arrival was changed, and the decree by which that attitude had been assumed was revoked. The injuries which had thereby and otherwise been rendered to our citizens were acknowledged and the faith of the government pledged for their reparation as soon as possible, which in many instances was promptly made. A new duty now devolved on him which required a continuation of his unceasing attention and most laborious exertions. It was to preserve the relations then existing and prevent the resumption of the same hostile attitude with like decrees and a like practice under them. From the period of his arrival in Paris to that of the change stated more than five months had elapsed. The latter service occupied him the residue of his mission, which terminated in 1796. Of this portion of time he had to treat about nine months with the government under the Convention and the residue with that under the Directory and the two Councils. A more difficult duty, it is believed, never devolved on any person in such a trust. Their parties still existed and their proceedings were often marked with violence, especially under the Convention. For some months after the fall of Robespierre the movement was comparatively tranquil. But that party, though much depressed, was not entirely crushed by the loss of its leader. It had been so long connected with, and at the head of the popular movements in Paris and through the republic, that its power was still too great for it to abandon all hope of recovering its ascendency, and its passions too violent not to attempt it.

A more interesting and awful spectacle had not been exhibited to the view of mankind since the overthrow of the Roman republic, nor did that equal it in many important circumstances. The struggles were equally great, but they owed their origins to different causes. The first was marked by the overthrow of a republic which was badly organized and very defective in every stage, under the operation of which defects the system had become so decrepit and exhausted that it could no longer sustain itself. The struggle was between virtuous and enlightened men who labored to save the republic, who risked everything in that cause, and who perished in support of it, and those who sought their own advancement by its overthrow. The latter effort was made by a people who had been long ruled by a despotic government and held in a state of slavery, ignorance, and poverty from which the great mass had gradually emerged, and a large portion improved in property, intelligence, and in every other acquirement and qualification necessary to the establishment and support of free government. The effort in the one instance was to prevent the overthrow of free government; in the other, to establish it. The success in both instances depended altogether on the people themselves, who by their number and power had the control in their own hands. There were other marked differences between them. The one was an internal conflict only. Rome, having conquered almost the whole of the then known world, had no foreign enemies to contend with. No other power took an interest in the result. If other people acted on either side, it was as auxiliaries and instruments only. But to France, almost all Europe was opposed and from the commencement of the Republic. The governments of all the great powers were monarchist who dreaded, if the monarchy of France should be overthrown, that a like fate would befall them. They, therefore, united against her. Of this effort, Mr. Monroe was an attentive and dispassionate observer from the moment of his arrival in France until his departure from it, and of every occurrence in the conflict of parties in the operation of the government and the changes in it; and likewise in the movement of the armies, their battles and their victories, on either side, he made a faithful and interesting report to his government.

The campaign of 1794 could not be considered as terminated until the month of February, 1795, at which period Pichegru, who commanded the army of the North, had overrun and reduced under the dominion of the Republic the whole of Austrian Flanders and of the united Netherlands. In every quarter their success was brilliant. The invading powers were repelled, many of whom were seeking peace. In this line, therefore, nothing was to be apprehended. It was by the ruling power, the government itself, which was badly organized, composed of discordant materials, and acted on by disorderly popular movements, that the most serious danger was menaced to the Republic.

A few days before the last *arrêt* passed, a report reached Paris that Mr. Jay had concluded a treaty of alliance and commerce with Great Britain, containing stipulations very injurious to France. This report excited great sensation in Paris and was seriously felt by the government itself. On the 27th of the preceding month (December) the Committee addressed a note to Mr. Monroe, stating the purpose of that report, with a request that he would communicate to it as soon as possible the treaty itself, since in that mode only could all inquietude on the subject be removed. The letter was couched in strong and harsh terms. The Committee observed that no dissimulation should exist between two free peoples, and made a very unfavorable imputation against a minister who should conclude a treaty with the enemy of France, whereby the treaties between France and the United States should be violated and the claims which she had on us for the sacrifices she had made and the services she had rendered to us in our Revolution be forgotten. It stated, however, that the report was vague and declared that they considered Mr. Monroe to be as much opposed to that kind of policy as they were themselves.[25] Mr. Monroe had on the preceding day received a letter from Mr. Jay informing him that he had concluded a treaty with the British government which contained a stipulation that it should not be construed to operate contrary to the existing treaties between the United States and other powers. In reply to the letter of the Committee Mr. Monroe stated the purport of that which he had received from Mr. Jay, with an assurance that as soon as he should be informed of the contents of the treaty, he would communicate them to the Committee with a declaration also that he believed the report, as stated, to be altogether destitute of foundation. This incident gave a shock, but the causes which operated were too strong and the progress to a complete change had been too far advanced to be suspended by it. A week after this communication between the Committee and Mr. Monroe, the second *arrêt* passed and was announced to him by the Committee in the manner stated.

It occurred to Mr. Monroe, as soon as he understood that a treaty had been concluded by Mr. Jay with the British government, that it would be impossible for our government, if the treaty should be ratified, to afford any aid to that of France in obtaining a loan of money in the United States, or to interfere in any manner whatever in promoting it, and of which he immediately apprised the Committee. They had anticipated the idea and assured him that it was far from their desire to subject us to any embarrassment whatever. The countenance which had been given to the project was founded on the probable failure of that negotiation and the danger of a war with both England and Spain. As soon, therefore, as that danger seemed to be removed with the principal power, the motive for such countenance on his part ceased, and he hastened to withdraw it. Much confidential communication, however, having taken place between him and the members of the Committee respecting our interfering claim with Spain in regard to the navigation of the Mississippi, and to which the occurrence with Mr. Gardoqui gave birth, and a negotiation with the Spanish government having commenced and being still depending, and France having it much in her power, by the success of her armies, to dictate the terms to Spain, he availed himself of the friendly relation which thus existed between him and the members of the Committee to draw anew their attention to the object, with a desire to induce them to extend their good offices to procure for the United States in the treaty with Spain the right for which we contended. With this view, he presented a note to the Committee on the 25th of January, 1795,[26] in which he gave a full illustration of the subject, showing the interest which France herself had by pursuing an enlarged scheme of policy and thereby counteracting the ambitious designs of England to accomplish the object. The communication was received and acknowledged by the Committee in the most friendly manner, and had, as there is good cause to believe, a very favorable effect on the relations then existing between the two governments. They considered it a proof of a strong desire to promote the interest of France, and bond and harmony of union between the two republics, as well as the particular interest of the United States. They thanked him for the ideas he had communicated, promised to examine them with profound attention, and to inform him without delay of the result.

This was the first instance in which the attention of the French government had been drawn to that object. The incidents which afterwards occurred respecting it, in the progress of Mr. Monroe's mission, as affected by the relation between the two republics, are of a very interesting character. It may fairly be inferred that the French government contemplated from that period the acquisition of Louisiana and Florida to counteract the policy of England, to accommodate us, and to promote in other respects their own interest. It will be shown that the acquisition became an object of negotiation between France and Spain at that time, and, as there is good cause to believe, was either pressed or disregarded as the relations between the two republics were either very friendly or otherwise. As the part which the French government took in this affair gratified in some stages and gave great uneasiness in others to Mr. Monroe, we will notice them in the prosecution of this work. They tend to develop the policy of that government towards us at different stages, and in that view alone, if in none others, they would merit attention.

The party of the Plain, which might be considered the ruling power in France after the overthrow of Robespierre, gave many proofs of its moderation, humanity and wisdom during the existence of the Convention. It showed that its great object was the success of the Revolution and the establishment of a free representative government upon such pure and sound principles as should secure to the people the blessing of liberty for which they contended. At the period when Brissot and many members of that party were carried to the guillotine,

71 other members were imprisoned and held in confinement while the Mountain party remained in power. As soon after the overthrow of Robespierre as the party of the Plain found that it might liberate those members without exciting a popular movement in Paris, it passed a decree to that effect, whereby they were restored to their seats in the Convention. A few days later Mr. T. Paine was likewise called to his seat and received by the body with kindness and attention. Other instances of a like humane and liberal policy were exhibited at that period. A decree which had excluded the nobles and foreigners from Paris, our countrymen excepted, was repealed. A general amnesty was also proclaimed in the Vendée. These measures indicated a spirit which was approved by the nation, and the latter produced in the section to which it applied the happiest effect, as it essentially terminated the bloody and destructive war which had so long raged there.

The state of parties and of the public feeling is often shown by incidents of little importance in themselves. To every occurrence, however unimportant, which afforded proofs of that state, Mr. Monroe's attention was drawn with great earnestness. Having experienced the unfriendly disposition of the Mountain party towards his country on his arrival, and formed the most unfavorable opinion of its capacity to conduct the Revolution to its desired end, he saw with regret every indication of any remaining influence in that party. Of the standing which Marat had held in it, notice has already been taken. With the overthrow of Robespierre, it was hoped that his enormities would be viewed in the same light by the whole community. The fact, however, was otherwise, for a few months after that event a motion was made in the Convention, and carried, to remove the remains of Marat, which had been deposited in the Carousal, in view of the Hall of that Assembly, to the Pantheon, to do honor to his memory. Mr. Monroe was invited to attend the procession with the members, with which he complied. Walking with Merlin de Thionville, with whom he had become well acquainted, he asked him with frankness whether the sentiment was general that the deceased had merited that distinction. He replied with equal frankness that the sentiment was rapidly gaining ground that he merited the execration of all good men, and that he was confident that in three months his body would be removed from the Pantheon. He added that had opposition been made to the motion in that stage, it would have strengthened the Mountain party in the House. The event occurred as it had been predicted. At the expiration of about that term, the remains of Voltaire and Rousseau were carried in a like procession and deposited with every mark of consideration and respect in the Pantheon, and those of Marat and Mirabeau removed from it, with such as were intended to stain their memory with reproach and disgrace. Mr. Monroe and Merlin de Thionville marched together again in the procession, when the former communication between them and the presage occurred to both, and was mentioned in a like friendly conversation.

Although the party of the Plain ruled the nation after the overthrow of Robespierre, so far as it might be said to be ruled by a government, yet it was so often shaken by internal contests and popular movement that it could not be viewed strictly in that light. After the shock which that event produced had ceased, the remaining members of the Mountain party who had ranked among its leaders made an incessant struggle for power, whereby the proceedings of the Convention were much disturbed during the residue of its term. The government was therefore still that of a party, and although its views were patriotic and just, it was one which struggled for existence. A convention or single assembly cannot form a regular government. The object in calling such a body is rather to institute a government by compact among the people, than to exercise its ordinary powers. If the Convention retains the power in its own hands and exercises it in its various branches, the most extraordinary and serious dangers may be apprehended from it. No government can be sound and free in its principles, or safe in its operation, although derived directly from the people, unless it be divided into three distinct branches, legislative, executive and judicial, and each is endowed with appropriate power and enabled to support its rights and form a check on the others. A government of the people themselves in a collected body is one of the worst that can be formed, and in its operation is sure to be oppressive. A representative body, a Convention, for example, is more secure because it must be composed comparatively of a few members, and because likewise the people may form a check on them. But if the people are unsettled, tumultuous and disorderly, if they have been long ruled under despotic government and have just escaped from it, all wholesome power on their part will be lost. Parties will be formed and leaders will contend for power. Council will be given them by interested persons to gratify selfish views and, if the nation be at war and the overthrow of other governments be menaced, their agents and their money will be employed to promote seduction and disorder. One party will be apt to overwhelm the other and its leader take the rule, and will govern every department and every measure of each. Of the abuses to which such a government is subject the reign of Robespierre affords the most striking example. The party now in power was more moderate and humane. It had more the control of its own conduct; had better views; and was governed by sounder principles. It had likewise the instructive example of that which it had overthrown before it. Still it could not prevent popular and disorderly movements, nor could it pursue, in all respects, the consistent course which it sought. Though willing to forgive past enormities and injuries in regard to some of the remaining leaders of the Mountain party, with a view to higher objects, the credit and safety of the Republic, yet such was the state of affairs and the force of circumstances that they could not always resist them. A body thus organized, retaining within it a large portion of the members of the party which had been overthrown, stained with enormities and dreading punishment, and assailed also by popular movements in support of the party thus overthrown, however humane and pure its motives might be, would often act by impulses and be driven from its desired course.

The impression which Mr. Monroe had feared—that his address to the Convention and the presentation of the documents which accompanied it would make on his government—was verified, as was that respecting the other instances of a marked spirit of conciliation and accommodation which was indicated in his communications with the Committee of Public Safety. Mr. Randolph complained in a letter of December 2, 1794[27] of his address to the Convention as breathing a spirit inconsistent with the state of neutrality which existed between the United States and the powers at war with France. He thought that it expressed sentiment too warm and ardent in favor of her success in a contest in which all Europe was opposed to her, and that the presentation of the documents in that public manner, in the face of Europe, might increase the jealousy and excite the resentment of those powers towards us. He complained also of the sentiment contained in the note to the Committee of Public Safety, in which it was declared that although our government highly disapproved, and for the reasons stated, the violation of the 23d and 24th articles of our treaty of commerce, yet if the Committee should on reconsideration, after the experiment made, think proper to adhere to it, that our government and fellow citizens generally would submit to it in the manner stated—with patience and with pleasure. Mr. Randolph had received, when he wrote this letter, the third [letter] only, which was of September 15th, and could have formed in consequence a very imperfect idea of the state in which he found affairs on his arrival in Paris and of the considerations which had induced him [Monroe] to adopt the measures of which he [Randolph] complained. To this letter Mr. Monroe gave an answer on the 12th of February in which he explained fully the difficulties which he had then to encounter and the motives which had governed him in every stage which he took.[28] He referred him to that [letter] of January 13th, in which he had transmitted to him a copy of the decree by which the violated articles of the treaty of commerce had been restored and every other object contended for obtained, and, as he believed, by the manner in which they had been sought.

On the 5th of December, Mr. Randolph wrote another letter to Mr. Monroe three days after that above referred to, in which he acknowledged the receipt of his two letters of the 15th and 25th of August, 1794, and although they had given a very limited view of the motives by which he had been governed, he assured him that the President approved his conduct and desired that he should continue to cultivate the friendship of the French Republic with the greatest zeal. Had even the slightest doubt remained of the propriety of the policy he had pursued, it may be fairly concluded that on the receipt of the letter of February 12th, with a copy of the decree, it must have been removed. To this letter he gave an answer in terms which indicated the great satisfaction derived from it, with assurance that his efforts to preserve the existing state should be unceasing and equally strong.[29]

From this period all anxiety respecting his responsibility to his government for the part he had acted in the difficult state in which he was placed on his arrival in Paris, and his conduct generally as to the past, was removed. He had only to look to the incidents which had a tendency to weaken the confidence of the French government in his own and to adopt the precautions, so far as depended on him, that were necessary to preserve the friendly relation which had been restored between them. The motive for performing this duty was in every instance the same, and equally strong. It was so in regard to his government, his country, the French Revolution and himself. In regard to himself, it had indeed acquired new favor, for if he had been able under the existing circumstances to restore the friendly relations between the two countries which had been so egregiously violated by the French government before his arrival, and without any sacrifice or concession on the part of his own, it could not fail to be peculiarly distressing to him to have that ground taken from under him and to witness a change of that friendly relation and the restoration of the former hostility by France towards his country in his presence.

Mr. Monroe never doubted the purity of the President's views in the mission to England, or that they corresponded in all respects with the advice contained in his instructions. He was, therefore, satisfied that a compromitment of him was never intended. He thought it his

Reproduction of a page from James Monroe's manuscript, showing text on the opposite page. From the original in the New York Public Library.

duty also, and it comported with his feelings, to make a liberal allowance for the part he might act, should the treaty contain any stipulation which might, by the construction the British government might give it, operate to the prejudice of, and produce excitement in France. He was decidedly of opinion that should the treaty contain any stipulations of the kind suggested and be ratified, it would promote the interest of France and redound to the honor of his government to disregard it. The United States were the only people of any important nation who were friendly to her or with whom she was at peace. Hostility between those two republics would put the cause of both countries in imminent peril and render to France the most serious injury. The more, therefore, her government looked with indulgence to the difficulties we had encountered and the losses we had sustained in our revolutionary struggle, and tolerated under that policy any arrangement which, without affording direct aid to England, might lessen our losses in an effort to supply her wants, the more salutary would the effect be and magnanimous the conduct of her government. On full consideration, at an early period, he had made up his mind to pursue this course and he adhered to it with the most undeviating and persevering zeal and firmness.

On this ground Mr. Monroe stood, and such was his view as to his duties to his government and country and the obligations imposed on him by his communications with the government of France, and such, according to his judgment, was the course to be pursued to fulfill those duties and preserve the friendly relations then existing between the two countries. There was one source only from which any danger could be apprehended, which was the treaty with England. If that treaty should contain no stipulation which, by the construction it would admit of and the practice under it, would operate in her favor to the prejudice of France, there was good cause to conclude that those relations would be preserved and the good offices which had been promised likewise be rendered to us and in full extent.

It has already been observed that a few days before the adoption of the last *arrêt* of the 4th of January, 1795, by which the violated articles of our treaty of commerce were restored and the faith of the government pledged for the redress of the other wrongs which had been inflicted on us, a report had reached Paris that Mr. Jay had concluded a treaty of alliance and commerce with Great Britain, which contained stipulations very injurious to France. This report excited great sensation in Paris and was seriously felt by the government itself. It was the suspicion of such an event which had exposed Mr. Monroe to all the difficulties he had before encountered, to surmount which

he had made such strenuous and incessant exertions and risked so
much on his own part. It was natural that that report should revive
those suspicions in the Committee and place Mr. Monroe in a very
unpleasant dilemma. That such was the fact many proofs were occasionally furnished which left no doubt on the subject. On occasional
interviews with the diplomatic section on other subjects, inquiries
were frequently made of him of the contents of the treaty, with harsh
remarks on the conduct of his government towards France. Mr.
Monroe met them with becoming firmness, vindicating his government,
and particularly the President, against every illiberal or unkind imputation, but in a manner to give no offense. The friendly relation between
the two countries was thus preserved and to an extent, at a particular
period, in regard to Spain, arising from the communication which
Mr. Monroe had had with the Committee respecting the concern of
both countries of France and the United States with that power, and
the proof which he gave of the interest which he took in the welfare
of France, that he had good cause to believe that the French government would sustain our claims in the treaty which it was about to
conclude with the government of Spain. This was inferred from the
answer of the Committee to his note, which presented to its consideration the interfering claims between the United States and Spain as to
our right to the free navigation of the Mississippi. It was strengthened
by a letter from Merlin de Douay, [of the] diplomatic section, to
one from Mr. Skipwith, which was written at the instance of Mr.
Monroe and in accord with his views. It was confirmed by Mr. Pelet,
who was likewise a member of that section, in a communication with
Mr. Monroe in which he assured him that in confidence, the treaty
contained nothing injurious to France. The Committee had instructed
their Minister then negotiating with Spain to use his utmost efforts
to secure for us all the points in controversy between the United
States and that power.[30]

It may be readily conceived that Mr. Monroe had every possible
inducement, from a regard to his government, his country, and himself,
to prove that the treaty with England contained no stipulation which
could, by a fair construction, operate to the injury of France. The
loss of her good offices in the instances promised, which had been
sought on the presumption that the negotiation would fail, though
important, was an inferior consideration compared with others. He
was anxious to show that the stipulations of the treaty were confined
within the limit prescribed by the instructions given to the Minister,
according to the opinion he had inferred from his own instructions
and the representation he had given of them to the Committee. He

was fearful also, if they should transcend that limit in any instance, especially if it should be to the injury of France, that the worst consequences would result from it.

The purpose of Mr. Jay's first letter to Mr. Monroe of the 24th of November announcing his conclusion of a treaty with the British government, with the limitations contained in it, so far as they related to France, had been communicated to the Committee at an interesting period and had produced, as was inferred, a very salutary affect. It nevertheless fell short of the intimation given by the Committee, when they communicated the report of the conclusion of a treaty of a very different character, that the impression thereby made could only be removed and they be enabled by a view of the instrument itself justly to appreciate a report which was so injurious to the government of the United States. Mr. Monroe received two other letters from Mr. Jay shortly after that of November 24th on the same subject, one on the succeeding day, the other on the 28th. In the latter he stated that as our Minister in London, Mr. Pinckney, had a cypher with our other Ministers in Europe, either he or Mr. Pinckney would communicate to him in that mode at an early day the principal heads of the treaty confidentially. To this letter Mr. Monroe gave an immediate answer, which he forwarded by Mr. Purviance, an assistant Secretary in whose integrity, intelligence and prudence he had the highest confidence, and to which he was prompted by the consideration already stated and likewise by a desire to prevent a communication of the contents of the treaty unless Mr. Monroe should be left at liberty to make them known to the Committee in fulfillment of his pledge to that effect. Of the nature and extent of that pledge he informed Mr. Jay in the letter referred to, which was of the 17th of January, 1795, with an intimation of his earnest desire that he would not make to him the communication suggested on any other condition. Mr. Jay, in his reply to this letter, refused to communicate a copy of the treaty, because, as he remarked, it had not been ratified nor received its ultimate form. Ministers who negotiate treaties had, he observed, no right to publish those which were perfected, much less those which were open for alteration or rejection. He added that a respect for his government forbade his communicating, without its permission, a copy of the instrument to any person or for any purpose, especially to be submitted to the judgment of a foreign nation, however friendly. He promised to send a copy of Mr. Monroe's and his letter to the Secretary of State and to execute such orders as he might receive on the subject. Mr. Monroe was not dissatisfied with this answer, especially if the treaty should contain any stipulation which would admit a construction unfavorable to France. He had no desire to make the contents known to the French government unless this should preclude the possibility of such a construction, for although not ratified, such a stipulation would diminish the zeal which they had taken in our cause and might do other injury. It was to prevent the communication of a copy of the treaty, if any doubt should arise on that point, that he hastened to apprise Mr. Jay of his engagement to show it to the French government, his object being to remove doubts and difficulties, not to increase them. Had he received a copy and then shown it to the Committee, it would have been, as in other instances of interesting communications between them, in profound confidence not to be imparted to others. The idea of publishing it never occurred to Mr. Monroe, and he was surprised that it should have been suggested by Mr. Jay.

Mr. Monroe had concluded from Mr. Jay's last letter to him, of the 5th of February, that all further communication between them on the subject of the treaty with England was terminated, but in this he was disappointed, for about a month afterwards he received another letter, of the 19th of the same month, by Colonel Trumbull, in which he [Jay] informed him that he had authorized that gentleman, who had been his secretary in the mission to England, had copied the treaty, and was well acquainted with its contents, to communicate them to him, but to do it in perfect confidence, to be imparted to no one whatever. This letter not only surprised Mr. Monroe but subjected him to further embarrassment. The arrival of Colonel Trumbull, who was known to have been the secretary of Mr. Jay, drew attention and was calculated to inspire a belief that he had communicated to him the contents of the treaty. To withhold them from the Committee after it was believed that he had received them might lessen their confidence in him and injure his government and country. Mr. Monroe had no hesitation as to the part it became him to act, which was not to receive the proposed communication on the condition offered and of which Colonel Trumbull was apprised. The difficulty with the government still remained, and how surmount it was the question. If no communication should be made of the contents of the treaty, nor reason given why none was made, the arrival of Mr. Jay's secretary could not fail to have the ill effect suggested. On full consideration, Mr. Monroe thought it his duty to ask an interview of the Committee and to state to it what had passed between Mr. Jay and him, and the condition on which he had offered the communication by his secretary, and his reason for refusing to accept it. The interview took place; the explanation was given; and produced, as was inferred, a good effect.

Colonel Trumbull, it is presumed, was soon made acquainted by several of our very respectable citizens who were then in Paris with the ill effect which the report of the contents of the treaty with England had produced, and of the distressing dilemma in which his arrival there had placed Mr. Monroe with the French government. Under this impression, he made a communication of his view of the contents of that treaty to Mr. Hichborn, a respectable citizen from Massachusetts, with intention, as was understood, that he should impart to Mr. Monroe, with full power to make what use of him he thought proper. This act was performed by Mr. Hichborn in a letter of March 31, 1795.[31] The possession of this document subjected Mr. Monroe to a new embarrassment. The information of the proceeding put it out of his power to act on it in a regular and official form. To withhold it would be thought improper, since, regarding the source from whence it came, it might produce a good effect. On a view of all circumstances, he decided to send it to the Committee by Mr. Guavain, a respectable youth of Navre whose house was much connected in commerce with several of like character of the United States—and who had supplied, by a temporary appointment, Mr. Skipwith a place after his appointment to the Consulate as secretary to Mr. Monroe— with instruction to explain the causes which had produced it. The previous explanation which Mr. Monroe had given personally to the Committee of what had passed between Mr. Jay and him, and of his refusal to accept through Colonel Trumbull the communication which he had authorized him to make on the condition offered, would show the cause why this informal procedure had been resorted to, and satisfy the Committee, if any doubt existed on the subject, that that explanation was strictly correct.

This terminated all correspondence between Mr. Jay and Mr. Monroe respecting the treaty with England and the effect produced by the report of its contents in France. Mr. Jay had intimated his intention to transmit to the Secretary of State a copy of the correspondence, to obtain instruction as to the part he should act in the point in which they differed. Mr. Monroe had invariably communicated to his government his correspondence with the government of France, with Ministers to other powers, and with every other person, which treated on subjects interesting to the United States. He transmitted, of course, this correspondence with Mr. Jay, with such comments on it as the occurrence seemed to justify and require; to that letter which contains his full view on the subject we beg to refer.[32]

The treaty was now before the government of the United States; its contents were unknown, and the decision uncertain. Mr. Monroe's sense of his duty, under any circumstances which might occur, has already been explained, and to this he adhered. It was to reconcile the government of France to the decision of his own on that treaty, although it might contain stipulations which would admit a construction unfavorable to France, and be ratified by his government. He was satisfied that a rupture between them would prove very injurious to the cause in which France was engaged, to which both nations were devoted, and in support of which the United States had suffered so much. He likewise was [satisfied] that the more liberally any stipulation of that kind was viewed by the government of France, the more magnanimous would its conduct be, the better the effect in the United States and throughout the civilized world. Of the fidelity and judgment with which he performed this duty an impartial estimate may be formed by the documents which are presented and likewise by the course of events which followed.

The attention of the French government was now drawn to the government of the United States and whatever might be the contents of that treaty. The French government had no right to take any steps in regard to it until it should appear that they were injurious to France and that the treaty was ratified by the President with the sanction of the Senate. As the result in both respects was uncertain, it was incumbent on Mr. Monroe to move with the utmost circumspection and caution in his intercourse with the French government. The explanation which he had given in an early stage of the motives of the mission to England he could not retract, nor could he, if the limit stated had been transcended, with the information he then possessed, do justice to his government by placing its own explanation on its proper ground. How this affair stood he knew not, and was very anxious to say nothing on it which might impair the confidence of the government of France, either in his own government, or himself.

On the 16th of May, 1795, Mr. Monroe received a letter from Mr. Randolph of the 9th of March, informing him that the treaty with England had arrived the preceding night, but that his perusal of it had been cursory and his opinion was not formed whether it ought to be ratified or not. He stated that the Senate would be convened to deliberate on its ratification on the 8th of June, and that it would remain secret in the interval. He made some general remarks on its stipulations of a favorable character, in which he adverted to its contents, specifying the parts: spoliations on our commerce, and the regulation of trade. In these subjects he observed that we had a right to make treaties and that no power had a right to complain of them unless we violated its rights. From this letter it was concluded that a treaty of commerce had been formed and extended whereby an object was embraced which Mr. Monroe had understood, and represented to the French government, was not authorized by his instructions. This communication showed the propriety of Mr. Monroe's decision to observe great caution in intercourse with the French government, so as to let nothing escape him which might produce an ill effect or prevent his turning to the best account every incident which might occur.

Two very important objects claimed his attention. The first was to make a faithful representation to his government of the progress of the French Revolution, of the state of the public councils, of the divisions in them, of the probable result of the success of the contending parties in the war, and on which side the scale was likely to preponderate.

It was equally proper to report the impression which the treaty made on the government of France, in its several stages, and the course which it seemed probable that government would pursue should its stipulations be thought unfriendly and the treaty be ratified by the President. So far as policy might be justifiable, regarding the treaty with France, and be permitted by our government to have any influence on the decision, a knowledge of these circumstances was very important. The other object related to France. It was equally incumbent on him, should inquiry be made, to report the time the treaty was received, when the Senate would be convened to decide on its ratification, the uncertainty of its decision or its ratification by the President, and to avail himself of every suitable opportunity which might avail in the interim to reconcile the government of France to the decision, whatever it might be, and whatever might be its contents. A summary view in each instance is all that we deem necessary or shall attempt.

To accomplish the first object, it was necessary for him to mingle much in the society of the members of the Committee and of the Convention generally, and likewise of other leading and public characters of the community, so far as it comported with his station. It was by such intercourse that he could acquire the best information on all the points on which it was important for his government to possess it. It was by that intercourse also, well known as his friendly feeling for France and ardent desire for the success of the French Revolution were, that he would have it most in his power to reconcile the government of France to the ratification of the treaty by the President, should that be the decision. Such friendly and familiar intercourse was the more necessary because it corresponded with what had preceded. A sudden change, which might be attributed to the cause, might, and most probably would, produce an ill effect. The members were invited to his house and hospitably entertained. He cultivated also an acquaintance with the generals of their armies, particularly with Pichegru, Moreau, Hoche and Berthier, and with others of inferior grade, and likewise with some of their admirals, particularly with Truguet and Blanquet, the former of whom had served under the Count d'Estaing in our Revolutionary War, in which he had been wounded. With the most distinguished of the scientific men of Paris he likewise became acquainted, and especially with the astronomer Lelande and the chemist Foureroy, to whom he showed great attention. By this intercourse Mr. Monroe gratified his own feelings as well as promoted the important object which he had in view.

It has already been observed that the party of the Plain was the preponderating party in the Convention, but such were the divisions in that body that it could not pursue, in many instances, the policy which its judgment dictated as best calculated to preserve order in the government and accomplish all the other great objects contemplated by the struggle in which they were engaged. There were several members in the Convention, of the Mountain party, who had been intimately connected with Robespierre, who partook in the violence and cruelties which he practiced and, as was believed, had justice been rendered then, ought to have shared his fate. The most distinguished among these were Collet d'Herbois, Barrère, and Billaud de Varennes. It was obviously the policy of the party of the Plain to view with indulgence the conduct of these men and to take no step which had for its object their crimination, and to criminate and inflict punishment on them. It did not accord, however, with the view of those members, nor with that of their party, to remain, as they thought, in a state of degradation. Many proofs had been furnished from an early period of their disposition to risk everything in an effort to recover the power which that party had held and to place themselves again at the head of the nation. The trial of Carrier, a member of that party, furnished an incident which proved the boldness of their policy as well as the depravity of their principles. He had been during the reign of terror a representative in mission to Nantes, where he had committed the greatest enormities. A number of respectable citizens of that town, whom he had arrested and sent to Paris, were now brought before the tribunal of that city. Their trial disclosed a scene of horror which excited the public indignation to such a degree that his trial, which was generally demanded, could not be resisted. Condemnation was the inevitable consequence. It was expected, so great and well established was his guilt, that the leading members of the Mountain party would have separated themselves from him and left him to his fate. They pursued, however, a different course by giving to him all the support in their power and identifying themselves with him. Proofs were furnished, while the subject was before the Convention, that those members held communication with the Jacobins in Paris and calculated on their support. In this mode the resentment of many of the members of the party of the Plain was so much excited that it could not be restrained. A motion was made against Barrère, Collet d'Herbois, and Billaud de Varennes, which was sent to the Commission of Twenty-one, who reported that there was cause of accusation. The subject was then brought before the Convention who decided, by what was called the appeal nominal, in favor of the report. The trial of these members, which was in vain, was supposed to involve the last remaining men of the Mountain party and, in consequence, its whole force then in Paris was exerted for their relief and the restoration of the party. Thus commenced a new series of events which inspired with many a fear that the Revolution would fail in its great object and furnish a motive to the coalesced powers to continue their exertions to subvert it.

On the 12th of Germinal, 1st of April, 1795, an attack was made on the Convention by a large body of citizens of the laboring class, principally from the Faubourg of St. Antoine, who forced their way into the Hall and suspended its proceedings. The crowd in the Hall, it was supposed, amounted to three or four thousand and in front of it, to a greater number. The cry was loud and incessant for bread and for liberty to the patriots, meaning the accused members. They remained in possession of the Hall three or four hours, suspending all proceedings and continuing the same tumultuous uproar. The members of the Convention retained their seats and acted with becoming firmness. Some indications were seen, on the intrusion of this body and of its retreat, of an understanding between its leaders and some of the members of the Mountain party. The Committees performed their duty. By their order the tocsin was sounded and the citizens throughout Paris called to arms, whereby an appeal was fairly made to them whether they would support the existing government with those in power or overthrow it. The call was promptly obeyed by a large force, by whom the invaders were driven from the Hall and the crowd gathered near it dispersed. General Pichegru, who had happened to be in Paris, took the command of the force collected for the defense of the Convention and, by his disposition of it, rendered essential service to his country. At about six in the evening the Convention resumed its deliberations, commencing by a review of the attack on it. Among the measures adopted was a decree for the banishment of the accused members to the Isle of Oleron, and another for the arrestation and imprisonment of eight or ten others of the Mountain party to the Castle of Ham, both of which were immediately executed.

Of this movement, in all its stages, Mr. Monroe was a spectator near the Convention, in frequent communication with its members and obviously and deeply interested in their welfare and in the success of the Convention by the repulsion of the invaders. He had, before its commencement, become acquainted with General Pichegru and invited him to a dinner with the members of the Committee of Public Safety on a day which had been designated, and which happened by a singular casualty to be that which succeeded the suppression of the insurrection. On that day they met at his house, and on which occasion the occurrences which had preceded became the subject of conversation, and the part which Mr. Monroe had acted being known to all, the conversation was free and unreserved and his participation in it admitted as a right, common to him on principle, as well as to them.

Of this occurrence Mr. Monroe gave a full account to the Secretary of State in his letter of April 14th, tracing the causes to their origin, with his opinion of the effect it would have on the fortune of the party in power and on the Revolution.[33] His impression was that it would be favorable to both. In that letter he intimated that the ruling party had it in contemplation to establish a constitution essentially different from that which had been reported in 1793. He informed the Secretary also that since the late commotion a treaty had been concluded with Prussia, at Basle, and to which he thought its fortunate issue had contributed.

The impression made by the result of the late movement was that the ruling party in the Convention would acquire new strength, and that the Convention would enjoy, in its subsequent career, some degree of tranquility. That it gained strength is certain because it confirmed on its side, under its direction, the prevailing sense of the nation. It did not, however, so completely overwhelm the opposite party as entirely to suppress it. Another movement of the like kind, but of a more violent and serious character, took place in Prairial the 20th of May, composed of many thousands from the same quarter and excited by the same motives: the redress of grievances, among which the scarcity of bread was made the principal, and which they said could not be accomplished otherwise than by the establishment of the Constitution of 1793 and the recall of the patriots Barrère and the other banished members. They forced the sentinels, entered the Hall with tumultuous cries, a large body of women at their head, and suspended all proceedings. The person of the President was menaced and in a contest for his defense, Ferraud, one of the members, a person of distinguished character, was slain and his head, severed from his body, was fixed on a pike and carried in triumph through the Hall. The members for some time kept their seats and Boissy d'Anglas, who presided, behaved with the utmost composure and dignity. At length, the number of insurgents was so great and their purpose so decided, no resistance could be made to them. The President withdrew, and they became possessed of the Hall. In their state they organized themselves as a body, placed one of their members in the chair, assumed the reins of government, and passed several laws in accord with the avowed objects of the movement. They repealed all the laws which had been passed since the 9th of Thermidor [July 28], recalled Barrère and his associates, and were proceeding by other measures equally violent to revive the reign of terror. This state of disorder and confusion lasted till midnight, at which time a force which was collected from the neighboring sections by the Committees of Public Safety and *Sureté général* entered the Hall, attacked the invaders with sabre and bayonet, and expelled them from it.

Of this movement Mr. Monroe gave a full account to the Secretary of State in his letter of June 14th, with all the incidents attending it.[34] His deportment through the whole occurrence, |as| far as circumstances permitted, corresponded with that which was observed on the movement of Germinal and had, as may be presumed, a like effect.

At the commencement of this movement, Mr. Pinckney arrived in Paris on his route to Spain, with whose government he was charged with a negotiation for the settlement of our claims with that power. Mr. Monroe communicated to him what had passed between the Committee and himself on that subject, with his opinion that if he could satisfy the Committee that the late treaty with England had not injured France, they would give him all the aid in their power in support of his negotiation. He showed him also a letter from Mr. Short, our Minister at Madrid, written at the instance of the Prime Minister of Spain, to request Mr. Monroe to promote a negotiation between that power and France, with an assurance that our demands should be yielded and adjusted at the same time. Mr. Pinckney was very sensible that the aid which the French government could give to his negotiations would be important and wished it, but thought that he could not ask it unless he showed it the late treaty with England, which he did not feel at liberty to do. Mr. Monroe announced his arrival to the Committee and asked an interview which was granted, in which he presented Mr. Pinckney to the members, who received him with attention. The interview was formal but respectful. Nothing was said in it on the subject of his mission, and from that time it was inferred that the French government would instruct its Minister, then engaged in a negotiation with the Minister of Spain, not to interfere with our claims but to leave the adjustment of them to the Minister of the United States, who was charged with that subject and who had just passed through Paris on his way to Madrid.

Mr. Monroe, in his next letter of June 26th, informed the Secretary of State that it was reduced to a certainty that the British government had revived its order of the 6th of November, 1793, and that under it 30 or 40 of our vessels, laden with provisions destined for the ports of France, were seized and carried into those of England.[35] He observed that the measure had excited a ferment in their councils, and that he was fearful it would produce an ill effect towards the United States, but assured him that he would make every possible exertion to prevent it. The scarcity of bread was great and the distress of the laboring class throughout Paris excessive. He indulged a sanguine hope, however, that those considerations which had obtained the repeal of unfriendly decrees and restored the relation of friendship between the two republics in an early stage of his mission would still have full force and prevent any change of policy in the government of France towards the United States. But as he was doubtful of the result, two attacks having so recently been made on the Convention under that pretext, he added that if such change should occur, he would advise his government of it by a vessel which he would dispatch for the purpose.

The 4th of July, the anniversary of our Independence, was approaching. It comported with Mr. Monroe's principles and feelings to pay a tribute of respect to that great event by celebrating it on that day. The motive for it at that period was peculiarly interesting. The revolutions of the two countries resting on the same basis, he thought that it furnished an opportunity, under a suitable arrangement, to produce a favorable effect on the councils of France towards the United States. He resolved, therefore, to avail himself of it for that purpose. With this view he took the entertainment into his own hands, provided a dinner at his own expense, and regulated it in every circumstance according to his best judgment. All the Americans then in Paris were requested to attend, and who complied therewith. He

invited to the entertainment, specifying the object, the members of
the government Committees, many members of the Convention, and
the officers of the French government, with such as were distinguished
who were then in Paris in the military and naval service and who
attended. He invited also the foreign Ministers, then there, from
Sweden, Tuscany, Holland, Genoa, Geneva and Malta, who likewise
attended. The assemblage was, in consequence, very numerous, comprising at least 150 guests. It being impossible to entertain so great a
number in his house, he asked of the Minister of War a loan of 12
marquees, which was granted, and which he arranged on a terrace,
and under which the party dined. The toasts were adapted to the
occasion. Due respect was paid to the Revolution of his own country
and to the memory of those who had fought, bled and died in defense
of it, to the President of the United States and other officers of his
own government. A like respect was paid to the principles of the
French Revolution, to the talent and skill of the Commander, and to
the heroic bravery of their armies, and likewise to those in the public
councils who braved all difficulties with firmness and sustained their
stations with dignity. A tribute of respect was also paid to the
Ministers then present who represented powers friendly to France.
It is believed that the entertainment produced the desired effect.

About the middle of August, gazettes from the United States
arrived at Havre and were sent to Paris which contained the treaty
with England, with the proceedings of the Senate on it. The publication had been made by a member of the Senate, in opposition to the
rule of the House, on his own responsibility. The government of
France thus became acquainted with the contents of the treaty and
the proceedings on it to that stage. Mr. Monroe gave immediate
intelligence of this event to his government in a letter of 17th of
August, 1795,[36] but as the treaty had not then been published in
Paris and he had not heard from the Committee on the subject, he
could say nothing of the impression it had made on the French government. He stated to the Secretary that he did not expect to hear from
the Committee on it otherwise than in reply to such communication
as he might make to it, founded on the desire of his own government.
The President had not ratified the treaty nor was it known that he
would. Till ratified, the French government had no right to complain
of any article, and the more silent it should be in the meantime, the
more correct would its conduct be. Mr. Monroe concluded that whatever might be the decision of his government, early information on it
would be given to him, and that his course would be marked out with
great precision. He assured the Secretary, therefore, that he should take

no step on his own part, but would await his instructions and keep the affair entirely under his control. He deemed it proper, however, to communicate to him the report of a secret agent of the French government, who had been employed in England, that the British government had said, on the seizure of our vessels laden with provisions destined for France, that they knew that it would give no offense to our government, the affair being provided for by the treaty. He treated this report with contempt and was happy to hear that it was disregarded by the French government. He was the more induced to mention it from the consideration that after the arrival of the treaty the attention of many had been drawn to the second paragraph of the 18th article, and [it] was said that, as the law of the nations had not been settled by the treaty, and payment was provided for seizure in cases of contraband, and of course for those which were not contraband, the French government would have a right, if the treaty should be ratified, to complain of it. He was fearful, as the scarcity of bread which had become severely felt for some months still continued, that this stipulation would be objected to; and as it was not known at what time the President would decide, he thought it incumbent on him to direct the attention of his government to it, that it might be duly considered.

The letter of March 8th from the Secretary of State is the last which has been noticed. In that, it was stated that the treaty with England had been received and that the Senate would be convened on the 8th of June to give their advice as to the ratification, and that its contents would be kept secret in the interim. Some general remarks were added, respecting its stipulations, of a favorable character which, by repelling any of the objections which the French government might have to it, seemed to countenance, according to his view of it, its ratification. In the interval between the receipt of that letter and the arrival of gazettes from the United States with the treaty and proceeding of the Senate on it, other letters were addressed to Mr. Monroe from the Department of State and from Mr. Randolph which it is proper to notice here, with their contents. These letters date on April 7th, May 2d, June 1st, and breathe the same spirit with that of March 8th.[37] That of June 1st, written a few days only before the meeting of the Senate, and which had been promised in those which preceded, is the more marked in that respect. It reviews at great length our relations with France, from the commencement of the French Revolution, to repel every idea of unfriendliness to France in any stage or measure, and to reconcile with that sentiment, and to qualify the ratification of the treaty in accord with it, on a principle of strict right, on the precaution, as was inferred, that such would be the decision of our government. It gave many reasons to prove the impolicy of embarking in the war on the side of France, such as the contention between the parties, the destruction of one by another, and, in general, the disordered state of affairs there. He [Randolph] observes that all Europe was against her and had we formed a commercial treaty with her government, war with England would probably have ensued. He does not enter into examination of any of the stipulations of the treaty, but leaves their bearing on France to be estimated when the government shall have decided on it and the instrument be published. In the conclusion of this letter, Mr. Randolph adverts to the construction which Mr. Monroe had given of his instructions, respecting those to Mr. Jay, and contends that he had misunderstood them, since in stating that the surrender of the forts and compensation for our plundered property were the motives of that mission, the formation of a commercial treaty was not pretended.

These letters were received at periods subsequent to the arrival of the gazettes containing the treaty and proceedings of the Senate on it. They furnished no light of which advantage could have been taken in that stage with the French government, had they been received in time; nor did they, so far as they manifested a disposition in our government to ratify the treaty, furnish any that could be useful with that government in any stage. They were useful, and when received, by putting Mr. Monroe on his guard to make no suggestions to the French government of a presumption that the treaty would not be ratified. The letter of June 1st embraced other objects, but as it did not enter into the treaty by an examination of its stipulations, it was equally inapplicable to that stage. The French government, as heretofore observed, had no right to complain of the treaty until it should be ratified, be its contents what they might, and this general view of our conduct could be useful only admitting it to be correct in every instance, so far as any part of the view might be applicable to the objection which might be made. It is just to remark, as to the charge of unfriendliness, that every impression of that kind, though great, had been completely overwhelmed on Mr. Monroe's arrival by his address and the documents which he presented to the Convention, on his recognition, so that no question could arise on that point unless adequate cause should be furnished for it by the treaty with England.

The subsequent letters which were written to Mr. Monroe from the Department of State, while Mr. Randolph remained in office and which claim attention, bear dates on the 2d, 14th and 21st of July.[38] That of the 2d, which was after the proceeding of the Senate on the treaty, stated that he had sent to him a copy of the treaty with the vote of the Senate, but that the President had not decided on the ratification: that he had delivered to Mr. Adet a copy, who had made some remarks on it, to which he should give a reply which he thought ought to be satisfactory to him. Mr. Adet's remarks, he observed, would be laid before the President. In that of the 14th, he stated that the treaty as published, and likewise his correspondence with Mr. Adet, were then forwarded to him. He informed him that the treaty had not been ratified by the President, nor did he believe that it would be until it should be returned from England, if then. The late British order for seizure of provisions, he observed, was a weighty obstacle to the ratification: he could not believe that such an attempt to starve France would be continued. In that of the 21st, he stated the difficult dilemma in which the President was placed by the situation in which the affair then stood: that doubts occurred whether the Senate would sit again on the article to be added; whether the President could ratify without the sanction of the Senate to that article; whether he could ratify before he inspected the new article after it had been agreed to by the British government; and what effect the suspension of the 12th article might have on all those subsequent to the 10th. His own impression was that the President would not ratify the treaty until it should be returned from England with the addition of the suspending clause, nor then, if the British government had issued the order for the seizure of our vessels laden with provisions going to France, as was understood. He adverted to the movements of the people which had already taken place in Boston and New York, and were menaced elsewhere against the treaty, with an intimation that countermovements might be expected. By those proceedings he said that the President would not be guided, but would be governed in his decision by his own estimate of his duties and a just regard for the interest of his country. He was aware, however, that a crisis had occurred, let his decision be either for the ratification or rejection, which involved the highest interests of the nation.

These letters, although the view which they presented as to the probability of the ratification were different from that which had been given in those which were written after the receipt of the treaty, before the meeting of the Senate, yet as they left the result uncertain, they furnished no ground on which—had they been received in time —to authorize a communication to that effect to the Committee. Caution in his remarks on that point in his interview with the members of the Committee, were still incumbent on him, and such was his conduct. The correspondence with Mr. Adet, to whom a copy of the treaty had been presented, in that stage, was an interesting paper which would claim attention whenever a suitable opportunity should present itself. Mr. Monroe's course was firmly fixed, as has heretofore been stated, which was, should the treaty be ratified, to use his best exertions to reconcile the French government to it. To the result the attention of that government was drawn, and on it would its own policy and conduct be founded. In the interim, it was Mr. Monroe's duty to pursue a course, in his general deportment, which should correspond with the past and preserve so far as he might be able the confidence and good feeling towards him which had been shown on many preceding occasions. It was by a preservation of that confidence only, should the treaty be ratified and the French government be dissatisfied with any of its stipulations, that he could contribute, in any degree, to moderate its councils and to render any service to his government and country.

In the course of this period of suspense and anxiety, complaints were made to Mr. Monroe by the Departments of the government on different subjects which related to the intercourse with England. The Minister of Foreign Affairs complained that our Consuls and their agents granted passports which gave to the bearers the qualification of American citizens. He remarked that the Minister only had that right and that in the ports such document from him was not necessary, since if the parties were engaged in commerce, the local authorities would give them the necessary protection either to leave the country or pass into the interior. The Minister of Marine complained of an irregular and illicit intercourse in the Channel, between the British and French ports, under the protection of American documents. The Committee afterwards interposed and to the same effect. To those complaints Mr. Monroe gave prompt answers, which led to an arrangement which, while it secured to his fellow citizens in every instance the full enjoyment of their rights, was very conciliatory and satisfactory to the French government.

It has already been remarked that the Convention, under the direction of the party of the Plain, had it in contemplation to prepare and submit to the people a Constitution very different from that which had been reported in 1793. In pursuit of this object, a Committee had been appointed who were engaged in the work and anxious to acquire every light from every source which might aid them in the execution of so important a duty. Their attention was naturally drawn to the constitutions of our several states and also to that of the United States, whose revolution rested on the same basis with their own, the sovereignty of the people, and whose Constitution had been

founded on it. Some of the members requested Mr. Monroe to prepare for them a digest of those constitutions, with which he complied, had it translated into French, and gave it to them.

At this very interesting period an incident occurred of a peculiar
character regarding the relations then existing between the two countries which is entitled to attention. By the treaty of amity and commerce between the United States and France of 1778, the French
government bound itself to exert influence with the regimes on the
Barbary Coast to protect our commerce against their piratical deprada-
tions. After the conclusion of the treaty with England and its reception
by our government, Mr. Monroe was instructed to apply to that
government for aid in a negotiation which it was about to institute
under the direction of Colonel Humphreys, our Minister at Portugal.
Colonel Humphreys attended at Paris to obtain that aid in July, 1795,
through the interposition of Mr. Monroe, who applied for it, to
whom it was promised, and in concert with whom every necessary
arrangement was made to carry it into effect, and complied with on
the part of the French government.[39] This incident is material because
it affords a strong proof that this aid would not have been asked by
the President, highly respected as he deservedly was for loftiness of
sentiment, if he had then decided to ratify the treaty or believed, in
that event, that it would violate our engagements with, or operate to
the prejudice of France. It was equally interesting because it proved
that the French government was disposed, until some event should
occur of which it might think it had a right to complain, to indulge
friendly feelings and to pursue a corresponding policy with us.

It is proper to state here that, while this arrangement was in train,
Mr. Monroe called on the Committee to obtain a passport for Mr.
Barlow, who was charged with the management of the business with
each of the regimes and who was on the point of departure. He was
received by Mr. Jean de Brie, of the Diplomatic Section, to whom
that portion of that branch which related to American affairs was
committed. As soon as that object was accomplished, Mr. Jean de
Brie adverted to another of the most interesting character, that of our
treaty with England. He informed Mr. Monroe that the Committee
were of the opinion that that treaty was injurious to France, and
that he was then preparing for the Committee, and by its order, a
letter to Mr. Monroe on the subject. An interesting discussion ensued
in which Mr. Monroe endeavored to obviate the objections that were
stated and to moderate the excitement there. Mr. Monroe at length
asked Mr. Jean de Brie if the Committee had received the correspondence which had taken place between the Secretary of State and Mr.

Adet, their Minister, on the subject, to which he replied that they had not. Mr. Monroe then requested that he might be permitted to send him a copy of that correspondence and likewise that he would decline addressing to him the letter which he had suggested until the Committee had perused and weighed it, which was promised. A copy was, in consequence, delivered to him either on the next day or immediately afterwards. The events which soon followed prevented, as was inferred, any communication from him on the subject.

As early as the month of June the Committee of Eleven, who had been appointed by the Convention to prepare a new Constitution, made a report of one essentially different and much better in many of its most important features than that which had been reported in 1793. This report was immediately taken into consideration by the Convention, examined with care in all its parts, and finally adopted the latter end of August or first of September following. It was then submitted to the decision of the people in their primary assemblies. The Convention thought it expedient to submit to the people, at the same time, two decrees the object of which was to transfer from its body as many of the members as would constitute two-thirds of the legislature under the new Constitution, should it be adopted. The object of the Convention obviously was to keep in power a majority of those who were friendly to the Revolution and who had experience in the management of public affairs. Two very important subjects were then submitted to the people under circumstances which were calculated to put to the test their attainment to free government, their zeal in the cause, and the further sacrifices they were willing to make in its support. If wearied with the war, willing to get rid of it and return to the ancient despotism, the opportunity was favorable for such an event.

The epoch was in other respects peculiarly interesting. Violent parties still existed among them and as the party of the Plain preponderated in the Convention, it might be inferred, if the decree should be approved, that a much larger number of its members than of the opposite one would be introduced into the legislature of the new government. There was good cause to apprehend, therefore, that all that [the Mountain] party, especially in Paris where the excitement had been greatest, would be opposed to the decree. It was equally presumable that the Royalist party, though hidden, as it were, for a long time from view, would seize the opportunity to promote its views so far as it might be practicable. Thus an appeal was made to the people under circumstances which put in motion all the conflicting elements of which the society was composed.

In deciding on the Constitution, the people acted in their character as the sovereign power of the state and had a right to view the subject and that of government generally in all the lights of which they were susceptible. The range, therefore, which might fairly be taken was very extensive. The existing government could adopt no measure on principle to check their deliberations or movements in any department or section until it should be manifest that the object in such quarter was, not simply to decide on the merits of the Constitution before them, but to subvert the liberties of the people. If the proceeding should take that shape in any quarter, it would then become the duty of the Convention, in support of the rights of their constituents, to suppress it. Every anticipation which might have been formed of the opposition which would be made to the Constitution to which they would respectively make it, was verified. The Royalists and terrorists moved in harmony and endeavored by a combined effort to overthrow the Convention and thus to throw everything into confusion, the one having in view the restoration of monarchy and the other that of their party. The movement, however, was in fact, so far as principle was involved, guided by the Royalists and for the restoration of monarchy, but without knowing the object. The discontent and disaffection of the other party were taken advantage of for that purpose, and they were made the instruments in an attempt to ruin their own cause.

The opposition commenced in the primary assemblies, and the decrees were made the ground of it and in the most popular form. It was contended that the right of suffrage, in the choice of representatives, could not be abridged in the principles of free government, although the abridgment proposed was made dependent on their sanction. Five days were allowed by the law to the primary assemblies for the performance of the important duty assigned to them. In many, in Paris, their session was prolonged and other measures adopted in contempt of the law and in defiance of the existing authority. They were at length dissolved. The sections of Paris then took the subject up under the same influence and in the same spirit. An invitation was given by one of the sections, in which the Royalist party had the control, to the others to form a commission of 48 members who should address France on the actual state of affairs, and in subversion, as was inferred, of the existing system. It then proposed that the Electoral corps should sit at the Theatre Francais on a day specified, and that the several sections should escort their members there by an armed force and protect them during the session. A partial meeting ensued. The whole proceeding being in defiance of the government and in opposition to the law, the Convention issued a proclamation ordering the members to disperse and instructed General Menou, who commanded the National Guard, to enforce it. He failed to execute the order and was, in consequence, degraded. The command was then given to Barras, under whom Generals Berruyer and Napoleon Bonaparte acted.

The leaders in this revolt had in this mode organized in the disaffected sections a strong force which was led, under officers elected for the purpose, directly against the Convention, with intention to destroy it. The attack was made on the 5th of October, 13th of Vendémiaire, at five in the afternoon, and continued till ten at night, at which period the assailants were completely repulsed in every quarter. The assailing force, which approached through every avenue that led to the National Palace, amounted to at least 10,000 while that of the Convention did not exceed 6,000. The arrangement of the latter was judicious and well conducted, and the gallantry of the troops distinguished. On the side of the sections, the movement partook of the haste with which the force had been collected and the indecision which often marks the conduct of those in a state of revolt. Six or eight hundred were killed in the action. The assailants withdrew tranquilly after their defeat to their respective sections and were not pursued in their retreat. The members of the Convention kept their seats during the encounter and through the whole night, and acted with the greatest firmness and decision.

Of this movement Mr. Monroe was an attentive observer in every part and in every stage. He considered it by far the most formidable that had been made against the Convention and the Revolution, the period being most favorable, the combination most extensive, and the character of those who took the lead in it most distinguished for talent and avowed for principle. The old *ci-devant* Duke of Nivernois was placed at the head of the Electoral corps at the irregular meeting which had been mentioned, a majority of which consisted of Royalists, as might be inferred from his appointment. Mr. Monroe's impression was, from the period at which this attack was made on the Convention and the Electoral corps put in motion—being before an election of new members was made and a new government could be formed— that had the attack succeeded and the Convention been destroyed, there being then no regular government whatever, the object was to place this Corps at the head of the nation in the character of a government in the hope that by the advantage thus gained, and a dextrous management of it, a counterrevolution might be accomplished. The failure, however, of the whole movement, under the favorable circumstances attending it, was a convincing proof that the nation and Paris itself were decided in favor of the Revolution and resolved to sustain it, notwithstanding the difficulties they had already borne and those which they might encounter in the prosecution of the struggle. Mr. Monroe passed occasionally on the day on which the attack was made, under the protection of his card as Minister of the United States, through the troops on both sides, and was in the Convention until a short time before the action commenced. His presence there, at a moment so critical, excited the attention of the whole body and left no doubt of his solicitude for their welfare and the success of the cause in which they were engaged. Several of the members, his friends, came to the box in which he sat, pressed his retirement, and led him from the Hall, through the carousal, by their cannon, where they parted. He then passed up the street by the cannon of the troops of the sections, which were not distant, to the quarters of a friend, and immediately afterwards the action commenced.[40]

The Convention had no further difficulty in carrying into effect the new Constitution. It had been approved, as had likewise the decrees, by a great majority of the people, in accord with which the two Councils were formed and the members of the Directory immediately afterwards elected. On the 27th of October the Convention terminated its career and on the 31st the new government was completely installed. Réveillère Lépeaux, Reubell, Sieyès, Le Tourneur and Barras were placed in the Directory. Sieyès declined the office and, in consequence, Carnot was elected to the vacant trust.[41]

The last letter which Mr. Monroe received from Mr. Randolph, which has been noted, was of the 21st of July, shortly after which he resigned and Mr. [T.] Pickering was called provisionally into the Department of State by the President. The first from Mr. Pickering bears date on the 12th of September, which was received about the last of November or first of December. By this letter Mr. Monroe was officially informed for the first time that the treaty had been ratified by the President. The fact, however, had been established at least a month before, and particularly by Mr. Fauchet, the later French Minister in the United States, who had arrived at that period. In this letter Mr. Pickering does not enter into an examination of any but the 18th article of the treaty, to which he says that his attention was drawn by the late seizure of our vessels laden with provisions destined for the ports of France and the inquietude it was calculated to produce. He contends that the first clause admits no article to be contraband which was not so considered by the ablest writers on the law of nations, and that the insertion of all the articles in the treaty was necessary to admonish our citizens of the danger to which they would be exposed in attempting to enter the ports of France with any of those articles. The second clause he considers a compromise between contending parties, in a doubtful case, and to which we had a right to accede to protect our commerce against a much greater injury. Great Britain, he says, maintains the doctrine that provisions may become contraband when destined for ports not blockaded; which doctrine we consider repugnant to the law of nations, especially in the extent claimed by her. Neither party would yield its claim and, in consequence, a stipulation was agreed to which provided payment for provisions and other articles not generally contraband, but which when they should become such, should for that reason be seized. He considered the stipulation beneficial to France as well as to the United States, for as our merchants would make a profitable voyage, in either event, of their safe arrival in the ports for which destined, or capture, the invitation to their enterprise would be proportionably increased and France in like degree be better supplied with our provisions. He disclaimed the idea that the seizure was adopted in consequence of the stipulation because it applied alike to other nations and was practiced by the British government before the mission was decided on. He adverted to the objection which had been made to the formation of a treaty with Great Britain, whereby our situation would be improved, while she was engaged in a war with France, with whom we had a treaty of amity and commerce. This objection he considered absurd, since having treaties with many other powers, if we waited for a time of peace, we might make none or amend those existing. No nation would have a right to complain unless treaties with them should thereby be violated or advantage be given in other respects to the powers with whom the treaty was formed, to the injury of the other, which he affirmed had not been done in that instance. He observed that we had many causes of variance with Great Britain the adjustment of which could be no longer delayed, that war and negotiation were the alternatives, and that we preferred the latter. He concluded with a declaration of the sincere friendship of the United States for France and of the earnest desire of our government to preserve the most friendly relations between the two countries. A copy of the correspondence between Mr. Randolph and Mr. Adet was forwarded with this letter, as it had been before by Mr. Randolph, and of the early application of it to the purpose for which it was intended notice has already been taken.

On full consideration of the contents of this letter, Mr. Monroe was of opinion that there was no part in it of which advantage could be taken in a communication with the French government. The exposition of the 18th article of the treaty, and especially of the second clause could not fail, as he thought, if the doctrine advocated in it should be urged, to produce the opposite effect. The variance in sentiment between the United States and Great Britain respecting the instances in which provisions would be free or become contraband, so far as payment for the seizure was involved, had been settled, but in what manner? Not by fixing the boundary between them and defining under what circumstances they might be viewed in the one or the other light, but by prohibiting the seizure in no case and securing the payment in all. It could not be doubted, if the British government should be bound to pay us for the seizure of vessels about to enter a blockaded port (when we should admit the provisions to be contraband), that it would not refuse to do it when entering a port not blockaded, respecting which the difference arose between the two governments, and we contended that they were free. He was fearful, therefore, that this stipulation, if viewed in the light stated by Mr. Pickering, would be considered as the abandonment of the principle that provisions were free in any case, and the admission of the British claim, or at least of the right to seize them in all, for the indemnity provided. And as to the encouragement which the indemnity thus secured would give to our merchants to seek the ports of France, as the British Navy preponderated at sea and might seize every vessel about to enter them, and actually had seized them, he knew that that argument would have no weight. He was anxious, therefore, to keep this article out of view as much as possible, and never to glance at it unless he should be forced to do it in reply to such objections as might be made to it, and then in the best manner that he could.

The other passages in the letter did not promise to afford him greater aid. The idea that the order was not issued in consequence of the stipulation in the treaty was a delicate one for him to touch. A principal object of the mission had been to obtain compensation for our plundered property and, of course, to provide against like spoliations in [the] future. This provision had not been made and the treaty was ratified after the order for like spoliations was renewed and in operation. Mr. Monroe was fearful, if he touched that subject, that it would be urged that a sanction was thereby given to the order with the knowledge of its injurious operation on France. With much less force could it be contended that the spoliations which were committed by the British government before the treaty furnished a proof that those committed afterwards, especially as payment was secured for every seizure, were not sanctioned by the treaty. As to its application to other powers as well as to the United States, it being known that neither Denmark or Sweden supplied provisions, or if any to a very small amount, and that we alone were looked to as the great resource, it would follow that we were the object of the order with Great Britain. It would follow, for the same reason, that the extension of it to them would tend but little to moderate the excitement of the French government towards us, should it suppose that the measure was countenanced by the treaty. He was resolved, however, to avail himself of every aid which could be derived from this letter, so far as any might, in any discussion which might arise between the French government and him respecting the treaty.

Under the new government, the organization being different, its powers were distributed between its several branches in accord therewith. The Executive powers were vested in the Directory, including all foreign concerns, the control of the Armies and Navy, and an agency in the internal affairs to the extent authorized by the Constitution. With that department, through the Minister under it, the representatives of foreign powers had to treat on all affairs in which their respective governments and countries were interested. The proceeding became, in consequence, under the new government, more subject to form and rule than had existed under the Convention. With the members of the Directory Mr. Monroe was acquainted, particularly, with Réveillère Lépeaux, Reubell and Barras, with whom he had had a friendly intercourse. With Le Tourneur and Carnot his acquaintance was less familiar, but they had been in society together and were known to each other. His deportment towards the members of this branch and to those of the two Councils corresponded in all respects, so far as circumstances permitted, with that which had been observed to those in power under the preceding government. It was in all instances respectful and conciliatory, so far as comported with a just sense of the respect due to the station which he held.

The Diplomatic corps was received in a body by the Directory immediately after its organization. The members were introduced by the Minister of Foreign Affairs. The interview was short, the object being simply to give a formal commencement to the new government and to establish the relation which should exist between the Directory and that corps.

With the Minister of Foreign Affairs Mr. Monroe held communication on ordinary topics, from the commencement of the government, in occasional interviews, but nothing materially interesting was touched on for some months, during which Mr. Monroe was attentive to every incident and very anxious to ascertain the view which the

Directory might take of our treaty with England. On the 15th of February, 1796, he called on the Minister to represent to him the distress of some of our citizens arising from the protest of bills given them by the government for supplies furnished, and to request his aid for their relief. The Minister immediately drew his attention to another much more important subject, that of our treaty with England, by informing him that the Directory had at length decided how to act in regard to that treaty, that it considered the alliance between France and the United States as dissolved by it and had, or should, appoint an Envoy Extraordinary to repair to the United States and declare that sentiment to our government. Mr. Monroe expressed his astonishment and deep concern at the information given him and endeavored to obtain from the Minister a full communication of the objections to the treaty that he might answer them, but this could not be done. The Minister made some general remarks on the treaty, tending to show that it was considered as throwing us into the scale of the coalesced power, but would enter into no detail. He observed that he should address a note to Mr. Monroe on the subject, being instructed so to do by the Directory. To such remarks as were made Mr. Monroe gave the proper answer, and on the subject generally expressed his earnest desire that the utmost candor and moderation might be shown in the discussion and in all transactions with us, since we were their best friends. To this the Minister made no reply, and it appearing that he was about to withdraw, Mr. Monroe left him. On the day following this interview (the 16th), Mr. Monroe communicated at length to the Secretary of State the information given him in it with an assurance that he should see the Minister on that day, and if he permitted him to consider the communication official, that he would demand an audience of the Directory and endeavor to divert it from the measure contemplated.[42]

On the 16th the interview suggested with the Minister took effect, and in which Mr. Monroe remonstrated with all the force and in the strongest terms that he could use against the measure which had been suggested. He stated that such a mission, to declare to our government the dissatisfaction of his government with our treaty with England, would make an impression in both countries and throughout the world that war or peace would depend on the result: that the enemies of both republics would rejoice at it, while the friends of liberty would behold it with horror: that the mission would place both governments in a new and embarrassing dilemma from which both could not extricate themselves with honor: that something was due to the character of the mission; its success must be brilliant or disappointment would ensue, which might induce his government to augment its demands and make an accommodation more difficult: that as soon as the mission should be known to foreign powers, they would commence their intrigue to separate us; that all were interested in our separation, and although the success of the French Armies might force many nations to withdraw from the contest, yet there did not exist on the earth a power in which either could confide, except the other.

Mr. Monroe remarked that France had gained credit by her conduct towards us, for while England had seized our vessels, she had pursued a more magnanimous policy, which had produced a corresponding effect in the United States toward both countries: that if France should change her policy and assume a hostile attitude towards us, that impression would cease. He added that he did not wish that well-founded complaints should be withheld; on the contrary, if such were supposed to exist, it was his desire that they should be brought forward and discussed in a frank and friendly manner, to obtain redress where due, and to make known in every instance the sentiments which each entertained of the conduct of the other. He assured him that he would enter into a discussion of the subject before him with pleasure, that his government, being possessed of our views of the subject, would be better enabled to decide whether its complaints were well founded or not, and how far any measure of the kind suggested would be expedient or proper.[43]

The Minister, in his reply, urged in terms equally strong with those he had used before the dissatisfaction of the Directory with the conduct of the United States toward France. He observed that they had other causes of complaint against us, but that our treaty with England had annulled theirs with us. He admitted, however, that the objections which Mr. Monroe urged to the measures contemplated had weight and promised to report them immediately to the Directory, by whom he was satisfied due attention would be paid to them.

Mr. Monroe obtained an interview with the Minister immediately after that which has been noticed, in which he had the satisfaction to hear that the Directory had agreed to relinquish the idea of sending an Envoy Extraordinary to the United States to remonstrate against our treaty with England, and would make its representation on the subject through the ordinary channel. He stated, however, that the Directory had not changed its opinion of the injury done to France by that treaty. Mr. Monroe asked him again what were the objections to the treaty, to which he replied in general terms that we had thereby violated our treaties with France and greatly to her injury in the present war. Mr. Monroe assured him that it was not admitted by our government that the slightest violation had been committed, and urged with great earnestness that the presumption of such violation ought not to be acted on, nor any measure of an unfriendly character be taken, until it should be shown by a fair examination of its stipulations in the discussion which he had invited. The Minister replied that he should certainly enter into the discussion and that the measure would |not| be taken by his government until it should be concluded, but that the subject being then before the Directory, he could not engage in it until he should receive its orders so to do.[44]

It appearing by the communication of the Minister in the last conference that the subject was still before the Directory and nothing decided, and fearing that some measure might be taken—that of the extraordinary mission—before the discussion, Mr. Monroe deemed it incumbent on him to go to the source of power and to ask an audience of the Directory in the hope of preventing that measure and of procuring by its order the discussion which he had invited. The audience was granted in which the Directory were attended by the Minister of Foreign Affairs and the Minister of Marine. Mr. Monroe stated the information which he had received from the Minister of Foreign Affairs, of their dissatisfaction with our treaty with England and some other measures of our government since the war, and that it was contemplated to express to it that sentiment by a minister who should be dispatched for the purpose to the United States. He expressed his regret to hear that the Directory should view in that light any act of our government, since nothing could be more remote from its intention than to violate our engagements with France, or to injure her in any other respect. He had asked the audience to request that he might be made acquainted with the complaints suggested and thereby furnished with the opportunity to answer them. He did not seek such an exposition from the Directory. He wished that the Minister of Foreign Affairs might be instructed to give it at length, to receive his answer, and to enter into a full discussion of each complaint, and that the Directory would suspend its decision until the subject should be thus brought fully before it. The request was promptly granted. Objections were then urged to the conduct of our government in certain instances, to which explanations were given that were satisfactory in some, and particularly as to the countenance which it was understood was shown to the emigrants. This objection had been urged and repelled under the Convention. Mr. Monroe assured the Directory that the complaint was altogether destitute of foundation; that the President received none who were obnoxious to the French Revolution and to the existing government of France; that all such persons were excluded by a positive order from his Hall.[45]

On March the 8th, the Minister of Foreign Affairs addressed a note to Mr. Monroe in which he stated the objections entertained by the Directory to the conduct of our government towards France during the war. As the discussion [which] had been invited and was thus commenced involved the propriety of the conduct of the two governments toward each other and likewise that of Mr. Monroe in the discharge of his duty to his own government and country, it is thought proper to present in a summary manner a distinct view of the complaints which were urged on the one side, with the arguments in support of them, and of the answers which were given to them on the other.

The Minister classed his complaints under three heads: first, the inexecution of our treaty with France; second, the failure to present with becoming energy the outrage to the Republic in the person of its Minister, Mr. Fauchet, by the British ship, *Africa*, in concert with the Vice Consul of that nation; and third, the late treaty with England by which the United States had evidently and knowingly sacrificed their connection with the Republic and the rights of nations, the most essential and least controverted.

In support of the first charge he stated: first, that our courts of justice took cognizance of prizes taken by French privateers, which was expressly prohibited by our treaty; second, that British vessels of war were admitted and, on some instances, with their prizes, into our ports against the stipulation of the 17th article of our treaty; third, that the Consular Convention had not been carried into effect in two of its most important stipulations. By that Convention the Consuls had a right to decide all controversies between French citizens, but of which they had been deprived by a failure in the law to enable them to execute their judgments. By the Convention the Consuls had also a right to arrest marine deserters, a right of the highest importance to their naval service in the United States. Of this right they had likewise been deprived by the demand of the judges, whose warrants were required to give effect to the stipulations of the original register of the equipage, although by the 5th article, copies [were] admitted as sufficient evidence in the tribunals of the two countries; and fourth, the arrestation in the Port of Philadelphia of the Captain of the Corvette *Cassius* for an act committed on the high seas which was repugnant to the 19th article of the treaty of commerce which stipulates "that the commandants of public and private vessels, should not be detained, in any manner." It violated also the right of nations by which the officers of public vessels were protected by their flag. The Captain had been imprisoned, and with difficulty had obtained his discharge.

In support of his second complaint he stated that the packet boat in which their Minister had sailed was arrested by the British ship, *Africa*, in the waters of the United States, and his trunks searched for his papers: that after this outrage, that vessel had blocked up the French frigate, *Medusa*, for a month at New Port and was not ordered to depart till the *Medusa* had sailed: that that order was then given for another outrage, an insult offered to our government by the British Consul by a menacing letter, and for which offense his exequatur was withdrawn.

In support of that third complaint he urged that the United States had abandoned the principles of the armed neutrality, which were maintained during the war of our independence, and had likewise extended the list of contraband to the injury of their ally to articles which were made free by the law of nations by their treaties with all other powers; and likewise by the treaties of England with most of the maritime powers. In noticing the second clause of the 18th article, he observed that we had gone still further by comprising within the list of contraband provisions which were admitted to be free in all cases except when destined to a blockaded port. He added that by this concession we have tacitly acknowledged the pretentions of England to extend the blockade to the islands, and even to France herself, by a proclamation. He considers this stipulation as the abandonment of their Colonies to Great Britain and repugnant to that by which we were bound to defend them.

To these complaints Mr. Monroe gave an answer, reciting distinctly the nature of each and extending the answer to every feature in it.[46] To the first article in the first complaint, which stated that our courts took cognizance of prizes taken by French privateers in breach of our treaty with France, he asked whether it was asserted as a general principle without exception? As a general principle he contended that it could not be maintained. If, for example, the prize should be taken within our jurisdiction, we should be forced in support of the rights of sovereignty, as well as the obligation of neutrality, to interpose and compel the restitution of it. Or if the privateer which took the prize and brought it into port was fitted out within our jurisdiction, the obligation to do it would be equally binding on us. Our treaties with France did not extend to such cases, and if the instances complained of were of that character, France had no right to complain of the conduct of our government in them. It was our duty as an independent nation to support the rights of sovereignty and equally so to fulfill the obligation of neutrality. He admitted the principle that if the prize was taken on the high seas, by a privateer fitted out by the Republic or its dominions, we would have no right to interfere, but declared it as his opinion that no such case had occurred.

The second article of this complaint stated that we have admitted into our ports British ships of war, even those which have taken prizes and in some instances with their prizes, in violation of the 17th article of our treaty of commerce. To this Mr. Monroe replied that the article referred to did not prohibit the entry of British ships of war without prizes, and that under particular circumstances—the stress of weather and the danger of the seas—they might enter with their prizes. The only ground of well-founded complaint, therefore, would be the failure to remove them, when they entered with their prizes, as soon as possible. It did not appear that the ships of war of that nation had entered under other circumstances, and well satisfied he was, when they entered under any circumstances, that his government had used every means in its power to compel them to retire. He observed that our coast was extensive; our harbors were numerous; that we had no Navy; and how difficult it was without one to enforce a compliance with the orders of the government by the ships of war of a nation whose maritime force was so great.

The third article of this had stated that we have failed to execute the Consular Convention in two of its most important stipulations, the first of which secures to the Consular the exclusive jurisdiction over controversies between French citizens and the second, the right to recover marines who desert from their vessels. To the first, Mr. Monroe replied that as no specific defect in the law alluded to had been shown, no precise answer could be given to the objection. To the second, he observed that by the 5th article of the Convention, the instances in which copies were admitted to be sufficient applied to other objects and not to this, and by the 9th, which obviously related to it, the originals seemed to be required. To vindicate his government more completely against this charge, he enclosed to the Minister an extract from the act of Congress of the 9th of April, 1792, which was enacted expressly to carry both stipulations into effect and which it had done, as he presumed, in a manner that would be satisfactory to the Directory.

The fourth and last complaint under this head states that the Captain of the Corvette *Cassius* was arrested in Philadelphia for an act committed on the high seas, contrary to the 19th article of our treaty of commerce, which stipulates that the commandants of vessels, public and private, shall not be detained in any manner whatever, and likewise is the law of nations, which puts the officers of public vessels under the protection of their flags. It states also that this vessel had been seized, though armed at the Cape, on the pretext that she had been armed in Philadelphia. To this Mr. Monroe replied that as the act with the commission of which the Captain had been charged was not stated, he could give no explanation respecting it; that the article specified was of a general nature intended to regulate the intercourse between the two nations in the instances to which it applied: to secure to the ships of war of each the right to enter and retire from the ports of the other with the kindness and favor which they should enjoy in those ports; that it was not intended to protect the officers who commanded them from the punishment due to crimes, nor were they protected by the law of nations. He presumed that the act for which the Captain had been arrested was such that the court was bound to investigate it. He was happy, however, to hear that he had been released, as it proved that the procedure was altogether judicial and mingled with it in that branch of our government no unfriendly policy to France. As to the seizure of the Corvette, if she was armed in the United States it was the duty of the government to seize her, such right not being secured by treaty, and when brought before the court on that charge, it was the duty of the government to prevent her sailing until it should be disproved and her right to sail be established by the decision of the court.

To the second complaint, which states that our government had not reacted in a proper manner [to] the outrage committed on the French Minister by the British ship of war, the *Africa*, within the waters of the United States, in concert with the British Consul. Mr. Monroe replied that the measures which were adopted by our government in resentment for that indignity ought, and he was persuaded when thoroughly understood, would be, satisfactory to the Directory. The exequatur of the Consul was revoked for the part he acted in it, and an order was given to the Commander of the ship forthwith to depart; that all supplies should be withheld from her pending the blockade. The Minister of the United States at London was also instructed to represent the outrage in all its circumstances to the British government and to demand an adequate reparation for it. A copy of the instruction to our Minister in London and likewise of that to the government of Rhode Island to withhold supplies from the ship was communicated to the Minister of Foreign Affairs with this reply. Mr.

Monroe observed that the outrage in all its parts formed only one transaction and for which the measures adopted were intended as the punishment. He added that as we had no fleet, it was impossible for his government to have acted with more decision or vigor.

The third and last complaint applies to the 18th article of our treaty with England, by which the Minister charges us with the abandonment of the principle of the armed neutrality and the extension of the list of contraband, without limitation, to articles made free by the law of nations, by our treaties with other powers, and likewise by England in her treaties with several of the maritime powers. By the second clause of that article, he observes that we have made provisions contraband not when destined to a blockaded port only, but when about to enter ports not blockaded and in every case in which vessels thus laden and destined for that country might be seized. To this charge Mr. Monroe replied that the principles of the armed neutrality, which were supported by the Empress of Russia and other neutral powers, and by all the powers at war with England in our revolutionary contest, were very dear to us because they were sound in themselves and important to our welfare. He admitted that on this principle we had inserted them in our treaties with every power who would adopt them, and that he hoped they would become universal. He reminded the Minister that in that war when the combination against England was so powerful, she did not accede to those principles. In the then state, when the combination was broken and many of the powers who were at war with her in the former instance were now engaged on her side, it would be impossible to force her into it. He lamented that we had not been able to obtain more strict limitation of the articles of contraband, for no nation on the earth was more interested in it than we were, all our exports being articles of the first necessity in demand in France and in every other country. He contended, however, that we had intended in that list no article which was not considered by the law of nations. In reply to the objection to the second clause of the 18th article, he observed that we had not authorized the seizure of provisions in any instance in which they were made free by the law of nations; that we left them on the ground, in that respect, which they held by that law, having authorized the seizure only when about to enter a blockaded port, and in which case we had provided payment for them. He urged that by this stipulation, which exempted our provisions from confiscation when made contraband by the law of nations, it was presumed that encouragement would be given our citizens to increase their enterprises for the supply of France, since if they succeeded in entering her ports, their profits would be considerable, and if seized they would sustain no loss.

Mr. Monroe concluded his reply to the objections which had been urged by the Minister of Foreign Affairs to the conduct of his government in the existing war with the expression of an earnest hope that the explanations which he had given would be satisfactory to the Directory. He assured him that should there have occurred any incident in the relation between the two republics to excite a suspicion on the part of his government that we were not sincerely and affectionately attached to the welfare of France, [it] would give great pain to the government and people of the United States. It was his earnest object to promote the harmony and affection which had so long existed between them, and if by his feeble efforts he could in any degree accomplish that end, it would form one of the most gratifying occurrences of his life.

Of this communication with the Minister of Foreign Affairs Mr. Monroe informed the Secretary of State in a letter of May the 2d, to whom he transmitted with it a copy of the notes which had passed between them.[47] An important result had been obtained by the communication, since it seemed to preclude any unfriendly step towards the United States without affording to Mr. Monroe an opportunity to remonstrate against it. He trusted by such remonstrance and the explanations he should give, should such be contemplated, that he should be able to prevent it, as he enjoyed great facility of communication by his acquaintance with the members of the Directory, with the Minister and members of the two Councils, who were connected with and most respected by the Executive. He stood at his post, therefore, with the same steadiness and zeal which had animated him with the government under the Convention, resolved to watch every incident that might occur and to use his utmost efforts to prevent any such measure, and to preserve the friendly relations which still existed.

Immediately after this correspondence with the Minister of Foreign Affairs, Mr. Monroe received from the Secretary of State a letter of January 7th, enclosing one from the President of the United States to the President of the Directory, announcing the presentation to him of the French flag by the Minister of France, and the transmission of it by him to Congress, with the resolutions of the two Houses which were passed on the receipt of it.[48] As those resolutions were couched in the most friendly terms for the welfare of France, with an earnest desire for the success of the Revolution, and the letter of the President breathed in all respects the same sentiment, Mr. Monroe hastened to deliver them in person to the Minister for his government, in the hope that they would produce a favorable effect in the then state of affairs. A few days afterwards, Mr. Monroe received a note from the Minister in which he assured him that his government received with satisfaction everything which tended to confirm the bonds which united the two nations.

On May 25th, Mr. Monroe addressed a letter to the Secretary of State in which he informed him that he had heard nothing from the French government since the late communication between the Minister of Foreign Affairs and himself, of which he had sent him a copy, nor had he heard through any other channel that any decision had been formed on the interesting topic treated of in it. He informed him also that no successor had been appointed to Mr. Adet, who had solicited his recall before the discussion commenced, whence he inferred that no satisfactory conclusion could be drawn respecting the decision until such appointment should be made.[49] On the 12th of June he informed the Secretary that in a late informal conference with a member of the Directory, he was advised by him that the Directory had done nothing in regard to us on the subject of its complaints, and that he presumed that they would do nothing.[50] Mr. Monroe observed, however, that no successor had yet been appointed to Mr. Adet, a circumstance which still involved the result in obscurity.

In a letter of June the 28th, Mr. Monroe informed the Secretary of State that the favorable prospect of which he had given him an account in his letter of the 12th had changed, as appeared from a letter of the 25th which he had received from the Minister of Foreign Affairs, stating that his government was informed by the latest intelligence from the United States that the House of Representatives had expected to carry the treaty with Great Britain into effect, and demanding of him whether that vote had been officially communicated to him. The Minister observed that if that branch had given its sanction to the treaty, his government ought to consider it in full force, in which event the effect which it would have on the interest of France would merit their profound attention. To this letter Mr. Monroe replied that he had received no official communication on the subject, nor had he any information respecting it other than what the gazettes referred to by the Minister contained. He added that, having already answered in a detailed and, as he hoped, satisfactory manner, his objections to the treaty, and to which he had received no reply, he could not then enter further into the subject; but if there were any points on which doubts still existed and he would state them, further explanations should be immediately given and he hoped to the satisfaction of his government.[51]

On the 7th of July the Minister addressed a note to Mr. Monroe in which he gave a more explicit character of the sentiments entertained by his government, of our treaty with England, and of the attitude it intended to assume towards the United States in consequence thereof, than had been done since the commencement of their discussion. He informed Mr. Monroe that the opinion of the Directory had never varied on that point and that their complaints had acquired new force by time. He should not enter into details, but would content himself by announcing to him that the Directory considered that act, concluded in the midst of hostilities, a breach of the friendship which united the two countries, and that the stipulations respecting the neutrality of the flag were an abandonment of the tacit agreement which had subsisted between them since their treaty of commerce of 1778. He repeated what he had urged before, that the abandonment of those principles was the more objectionable because we had secured them in all our treaties with other powers and were so generally acknowledged that they had become the law of nations. He concluded with remarking that the Directory thought that the stipulations of this treaty in regard to the neutrality of the flag had altered and suspended those of our treaty with France of 1778 relating to that object, and that it was incumbent on it to modify its own regulations in accord therewith: that the treaty of 1778 would never have been consented to otherwise than on the conditions of reciprocity, which had been departed from and violated by our treaty with England.[52]

Mr. Monroe considered this last note from the Minister of Foreign Affairs as intended to terminate, on his part, the discussion respecting the objections of his government to our treaty with England and to our conduct in other respects during the war. From the declaration which it contained, that the opinion of the Directory on those points had not varied and that it had decided on the measures it ought and should adopt in consequence thereof, no other conclusion could be drawn. He did not, however, consider himself prevented from making such remarks in reply to that letter as were applicable to it, or which he might presume or hope would produce a change in the policy suggested. A reply to the objections stated in the letter was indispensable because silence would have admitted their force, and on other accounts he deemed it equally necessary. A favorable effect had been produced by the discussion which had already taken place, several months having elapsed since its commencement, which showed that the mind of the Directory was undecided. This inference was confirmed by the information given him by the members in informal conferences with them. He indulged a strong hope, therefore, that he might be able, by his reply to that note, to give a further and more decided check to any unfriendly acts towards our government and country, especially as he still enjoyed the advantage of personal interviews and conferences with those members.

The Minister made one objection only in this letter to the conduct of our government in the existing war, although he reported that the mind of the Directory had not changed on any of the points brought forward in his first note. This objection applied to our treaty with England, which he considered a violation of a tacit agreement which had been entered into by our treaty with France of 1778, respecting the neutrality of the flag and likewise of the law of nations, the principles consummated by that treaty having become a part of that law. To those objections Mr. Monroe confined his reply, commencing with a declaration of his opinion that no violation had been committed in either instance. He asked what were the nature and ˜extent of the stipulations in the treaty between the United States and France, a violation of which had been charged? They undoubtedly had their object, which applied in equal extent to both parties, the fulfillment of which by each, when placed in the relation contemplated, would discharge the obligation imposed on it. The articles in the treaty referred to stipulate that if either of the parties shall be engaged in a war with another nation, the vessels of the other party shall be respected in its trade with that nation and be allowed to transport the goods of that nation in its vessels. It adopts the principle that free ships shall make free goods. And the reciprocity is to be found in a change of circumstances when the party lately at war shall be in peace, and the party at peace be in war, and the advantage which was enjoyed by the latter be enjoyed by the former in equal extent. Mr. Monroe affirmed that this was the sole object of the stipulations referred to in that treaty and this the utmost extent to which they could be carried. The parties to the treaty were not bound to impose that rule on other nations, nor were they bound not to make a treaty on the other principle with another nation. He considered the idea of a tacit agreement as destitute of foundation, since it was precluded by the notice of the stipulations which had a dear and distinct object and limit, which showed in what the reciprocity consisted.

Mr. Monroe contended that the failure to obtain in our treaty with England like stipulations in favor of neutral rights with those which were adopted in our treaty with France. was no breach of the law of nations. He observed that no principle was better established by that law than that when two nations were at war, either might seize the goods of the other in neutral bottoms if it was not prohibited by treaty. For proof of this doctrine he referred to the most eminent writers on that law. If such was not the law of nations, why were treaties formed by different nations in favor of the opposite principle? If secured against seizure by that law, what further protection would be necessary? Was it supposed, when our treaty of 1778 was entered into, that it made no change, that no advance was made on liberal principles in favor of neutral rights? That the law had undergone no change was certain. How could such a change be made? When a law is established, no nation can be deprived of its right under it without its consent. A portion of the civilized nations have no right to dictate the law to the others. A contrary doctrine would substitute force to right and might be productive of the most fatal consequences. Among nations who have adopted the free rule a change has taken place, but it applies to them only. That Great Britain opposed the principle that free ships should make free goods in the last war, and likewise has done it in the present, is well known, as it is that all your enemies in the present war have done the same, including some who are now your friends, and to the great injury of the United States. If the majority of civilized nations had a right to bind the minority, how could it now be done when many of the powers who formed that majority had shifted sides and were now arranged in support of the opposite principle?

Mr. Monroe concluded this note by reminding the Minister that in his preceding communication he had declined stating the injuries which France had rendered to the United States in the present war. He might, however, have stated that by a decree of the Convention of 1793 the articles of their treaty of commerce of 1778 in favor of neutral rights had been set aside, and in violation thereof, about 50 of our vessels had been brought into port and their cargoes taken from the proprietors, who were yet unpaid: that about the same time upwards of 80 of our vessels were embargoed at Bordeaux and detained there more than a year, to the great injury of the proprietors, who had never been indemnified: that for supplies furnished to their Indie Island and enumerable spoliations committed on our commerce in those islands, and for supplies furnished to France, immense sums were due to our citizens, as authenticated by the highest authorities there and here, for the want of which many of them were ruined. He had abstained from presenting this view because it would have borne the aspect of recrimination, which he wished no part of his conduct to bear in any transaction with the French Republic; and because he was disposed to yield every accommodation to their exigencies which his duty would permit. Nor did he then mention these injuries in that spirit. He did it under a conviction that such a review should be taken by the government of France before any decision should be formed on the subject under consideration, as he deemed it equally important to both Republics to preserve for ever the good understanding which still existed between them. For what had passed the United States had always found an excuse in that unhappy state of affairs attendant on the Revolution, and had looked to the establishment of a free and happy Constitution as the period when the two Republics should harmonize, not in peaceful review of any unpleasant incidents which had occurred and were attributable to the difficulties which pressed on them, but in devising the means, founded on their mutual interest and secured by a permanent arrangement, to cement their union; and greatly mortified they would be if this should not be the case. He trusted, however, that it would be the case, under which impression, and on the observations already made, he submitted the subject in discussion to the wisdom and candor of the Directory.

It remained for Mr. Monroe to watch occurrences, as he had done before, and to use his best exertions in informal conferences with the members of the Directory, when he could obtain them, to prevent any unfriendly measures toward his government and country, should such be contemplated. On the last of July or first of August he heard that the Directory had appointed Mr. Mangourit, who had been Consul of France at Charlestown, South Carolina, and who was then Secretary of Embassy in Spain, chargé d'affaires to the United States.[53] As Mr. Mangourit had given offense to our government in his office of Consul, Mr. Monroe concluded that his mission would produce an unfavorable effect. He was also concerned at the grade given to the person about to be employed, as it indicated an unfriendly feeling to his government and country. In consequence he called on the Minister of Foreign Affairs and remonstrated against the appointment, but who gave him no encouragement to hope for a change. He then sought and obtained an interview with a member of the Directory, to whom he stated frankly the objections which applied to the person, and with the desired effect. The *arrêt* for his appointment was rescinded.[54] Mr. Monroe then indulged a strong hope that the crisis had passed and that the friendly relation which then existed would be presumed. But this prospect soon vanished. He was informed a few days afterwards, through a channel entitled to confidence, that

the Directory decided to recall Mr. Adet and to instruct him to declare to our government that the customary relations between the
two countries should cease on account of our treaty with England.
The same advice added that no successor would be appointed to
him. Mr. Monroe assured the Secretary of State, in the letter which
announced this event, that he should see the Minister on the next
day and endeavor to draw him into a communication on the subject,
and in any event renew his exertions to prevent the measure, though he
began to despair of success, so often did they return to the same
subject and with the same disposition.[55]

Mr. Monroe had become satisfied that his further efforts to prevent
the government of France from expressing in its own form, with
the light before it, its sentiments respecting our treaty with England,
would not only prove abortive but produce irritation. He thought that
he saw distinctly an aversion to a further communication with him in
the then stage on that subject. Under these circumstances he instructed
Major Mountflorence, who was Chancellor under Mr. Skipwith in
the Consulate at Paris, and who passed daily through the several departments of the government and was well acquainted with the chiefs
employed in them, to collect what information he could of the views
of the Directory towards the United States and to report it to him.
The Major called occasionally and communicated what he had heard.
He also made three reports in writing to the following effect. The
first bears date on the 26th of August, 1796, in which he states that
he should have called on that day to give such information as he had
been able to acquire respecting the forwarding of orders to America,
but was prevented by indisposition. He was at the office early that
morning and was advised that the packet was made up but had not
been dispatched. Positive orders for its departure had not been given,
but the former were not rescinded. They proposed to inform Mr.
Monroe of it officially only eight days after they should have departed. The second was of the 30th of August, in which he states
that he had seen a person the preceding evening who assured him
that he believed the dispatches were gone and sent by an aviso which
had been prepared for sea some time before. The government pretended that they had been prevented for nearly eight months taking the
measures which were consistent with the dignity of the nation and
their general plan. They did not censure his government. Their determination was, in his opinion, fixed, and we had only to wait for
events. His third letter, of 29th of September, states that the person
whom he had mentioned to Mr. Monroe the day before intimated
an apprehension that they had it in contemplation to notify to him;

their having recalled their Minister to the United States, they could not communicate with him officially. He hoped and believed that this was groundless, for if such an event should take place, it would indicate a disposition to push matters to an extremity which it was [in] the interest of both countries to avoid.

At this period and under these circumstances, Mr. Monroe received a letter from the Secretary of State of June 13, which gave him great surprise and inexpressible concern. The Secretary charged him with having remained an idle spectator of the discontent of the French government on account of our treaty with England, from its origin at a distant period back and in its progress until it had risen to its greatest height and assumed its most menacing form, without making the slightest effort to remove it, although he had been possessed, both before and after the ratification of the treaty, of the views of his government respecting it, and furnished with ample means for the purpose. The letter, by a fair construction, goes still further. A charge of inactivity and silence under such circumstances plainly indicated a suspicion, and were the belief, that he had seen those discontents not only with indifference but pleasure, if he had not fomented them. A person capable of the charge alleged would be equally capable of the latter act. Other parts of this letter confirmed this construction. The information which had been communicated to Mr. Monroe on the 15th of February, 1796, by the Minister of Foreign Affairs, was at an interview which he had obtained on other business. This circumstance was urged as a cause of reproach; and the delay in commencing the discussion as late as the 25th of March, the date of the last letter he had received, during which time the subject was under the consideration of the Directory, before whom it had been brought by Mr. Monroe, was regarded as an additional proof of his unwillingness to engage in the discussion and of his desire to withhold from the French government the lights which had been furnished him, by his own, for that purpose. The Secretary instructed him |that| if by any possibility they should not have been imparted, to withhold them no longer and to communicate them in writing, of which he should make a copy and transmit it to the Department. By requiring the evidence of his communication with the French government in writing, considered with the charges in the letter, the Secretary showed that he required better proof of the fidelity of his conduct than his own declaration, and, in consequence, had no confidence in him. This letter, therefore, impeached in the most distinct form the integrity of Mr. Monroe. To one who had always stood at his post and encountered so many difficulties from the commencement of his mission; who had labored with incessant zeal in support of the character and conduct of his government in every situation in which it had been placed, and was animated with an ardent desire to avoid any calamity from his country, such a charge, and especially under the high sanction which it bore, could not fail to be very afflicting to him.

It was obvious that this letter formed a crisis in Mr. Monroe's own life which menaced the most serious consequences to his future fame as well as to his private fortune and the welfare of his family. He weighed its contents, therefore, with profound attention, and in which he cherished great liberality and the kindest feelings for the President. He knew the danger which had arisen after the conclusion of the treaty, and especially after the sanction it had received from the Senate, that its rejection might terminate in a war with England, which would be very calamitous to the country. He knew likewise the violence of the party divisions which existed at home and the hostility which some of those, who had essentially contributed to the establishment of the Constitution, bore to himself, with which, and more especially with the causes which produced it, the President was probably unacquainted. These persons were nearly connected with the President and would most probably be consulted by him in the existing emergency. By the course which the affair had taken and the state in which it then was his sentiment of independence and pride of character might have been roused, and although he had great self-command in his general conduct, yet those were feelings, if excited, which would have great influence over him. Mr. Monroe resolved, therefore, to take no step by resignation or otherwise in connection with his mission, in consequence of this letter. His mind had been made up long before as to the course he ought to pursue in any state in which the public affairs might be placed, and he was incapable of making any change in it by considerations relating to himself. He was satisfied that the President had acted with perfect integrity and with the best views in the interest of his country, under the impression which he had taken from the light communicated to him from various sources, some of whom might be in Paris, of the opposite party and unfriendly to him, though of this he had no proof nor any cause for suspicion, as both parties there had uniformly approved his conduct and been kindly received and treated by him without distinction. Still an answer to this letter was indispensable, and in a manner to do justice to his conduct and character to show that he feared nothing and asked no favor.

In reply to these charges, Mr. Monroe declared to the Secretary, in a letter of September 10th, that they were altogether destitute of foundation and that the facts which he had urged in their support, if they proved anything, proved directly the reverse of what he deduced from them. The discontent existed on account of our treaty with England, as it certainly did, and from a much more distant period back than that suggested by the Secretary. How happened it that it was suppressed through so long and interesting an interval? He reminded the Secretary that such discontent was shown, and in a marked manner, in December, 1794, shortly after the conclusion of the treaty, when the first accounts of its contents reached Paris, and in a variety of instances afterwards of which he had apprised his government, and of his dread of the consequences if the cause continued to exist. Why did it not break out under the Convention and especially in August, 1795, when Paris was starving and our vessels laden with provision destined for the ports of France were seized and carried into England? That was a crisis difficult for him to sustain, the eyes of France being fixed on him as the representative of a nation on whose friendship they had calculated and who had just before been the organ of declarations the most friendly. Why leave us afterwards, until the last stage, to our unbiased deliberations, without an effort to disturb them? Did difficulties like those, with the result which followed, prove that he had been a calm or indifferent spectator of a storm that was rising and threatened injury to his country, or that he withheld any light that came to his aid that might tend to dissipate it? He did not claim to himself the merit of this delay because he knew, under the unfavorable impression which the French government had imbibed, that it was due to the sincere and strong affection which the people of France entertained for those of the United States. He declared, however, that he had exerted his best faculties with unwearied zeal through the whole of his mission to prevent the French government from adopting any measure, let the merit of the points in discussion be where it might, which might disturb the friendly relation existing between the two republics, and which he had done from a conviction that such a policy would redound more to the interest and honor of France, as well as of the United States, than any other that her government could pursue. He added that it was from a knowledge which the French government possessed of the sincerity of his motives that he had been heard in friendly communication, and often in remonstration, against its projected measures, with an attention which he could not otherwise have expected.[56]

Until the 16th of February, 1796, no complaint was regularly made by the government against the treaty, nor was it certain that any would be. The object of Mr. Monroe had been to prevent such complaint, and in which he had succeeded with the government under the Convention. So well acquainted had he become with the members that opportunities often occurred in private conversation to ascertain their views, and |those| of the government itself, and to reconcile them to a mild and friendly course. One incident, however, occurred under the Convention, on which he founded the communication which he made to the Secretary in his letter of October 20, 1795, and on which the Secretary relied as a proof of his inactivity and neglect to apply the lights which had been furnished him to the object intended by them. Calling at that period on Jean de Brie, a member of the Committee of Public Safety, and who had the American branch under his care, on the subject of our Algerian affairs in which the French government had afforded its aid, he found him engaged on the treaty, and to which he promptly called Mr. Monroe's attention by informing him that he was preparing for him a letter to be submitted to the Committee on the subject. Jean de Brie made many charges against the treaty and spoke with great asperity of it, and to which Mr. Monroe gave the answer and explanations which appeared to be proper. He at length asked Jean de Brie if he had received the correspondence which had taken place between Mr. Randolph and Mr. Adet on it, to which he replied that he had not. Mr. Monroe then informed him that he had that correspondence, and of which he asked permission to send him a copy, and likewise that he would suspend his report to the Committee until he had perused and weighed it, which he promised. A copy was, in consequence, immediately sent to him. This incident occurred just before the movement of Vendémiaire, at the termination of which the government was transferred to the Directory and the two Councils, and by which the measure contemplated was probably prevented. The ground was sufficiently strong to justify the intimation which he gave to his government of the consequences which might be apprehended from the ratification of the treaty. From motives of delicacy he did not communicate the details, in the hope that the project would not be reviewed and from a desire to give no pain which could be avoided, especially as it was soon afterwards known that the treaty had been ratified.

From the organization of the Directory until the 15th of February, 1796, nothing was said to Mr. Monroe by any of its members or by the Minister of Foreign Affairs on the subject of our treaty with England. His relation with the members continued on the same friendly footing that it had done before. He frequently called on them at their separate apartments at the Luxemburg and was received with kindness and attention. Their reserve and silence on that subject gave him concern, but he still indulged a sanguine hope that they would abstain from any unfriendly act towards his government. On that day the communication was made to him by the Minister of Foreign Affairs, which has been noticed, as have been the consequences which ensued. From the moment that that opportunity was presented, he seized it and never quitted the subject, regarding the state in which it stood, during the residue of his mission. The letter from the Secretary of State of the 13th of June was received at the period after the discussion with the Minister was finished and the government had evidently made up its mind as to the course it intended to pursue, and likewise that a further pressure from him would not only produce no change but probably have a bad effect. It was at the period when Major Mountflorence had been instructed, the intercourse between the members and Mr. Monroe being essentially suspended, to ascertain the decision which the Directory had formed and to report it to him, and after he had made the report contained in his two first letters. Copies of every communication which had passed between the Minister and himself in the discussion had been previously transmitted to the Secretary. A correct account had also been given to him of what had passed in the audience he had obtained of the Directory, in his interviews with the members separately, and with the Minister. His conduct, therefore, in a very important occurrence to his country and also vital to himself, was placed on a ground peculiarly his own, and which furnished the best possible means to form a correct judgment of his integrity, of his zeal and devotion to his government and country, of his assiduity, and of the judgment with which he discharged all his public duties through that great emergency. It might be asked on due consideration of facts which cannot be controverted, whether there is any proof of connivance between him and the members of the French government, either directly or indirectly, under the Convention or Directory, whereby it was encouraged to take any measure against his own? Whether the whole proceeding does not prove that he exerted his best faculties and effort in every stage to prevent such measure, and that those in power under both governments believed that he meant what he said? Could he have prevented such measure under the Convention when the excitement had risen to such a height, by the distress to which Paris was ordered, if the popular feeling had not been on his side, founded on the documents which he presented on his recognition declaratory of the interest which his government and country took in the welfare of France and the success of the French Revolution, supported as they were by his own uniform conduct afterwards? To attack his government and country was to attack him, and to which there was obviously a great repugnance.

Such was the state of affairs between the two republics and such had been the conduct of Mr. Monroe in those affairs at the period when the letter from the Secretary of State of the 13th of June, above referred to, was received.

As soon as it was known that the Directory had decided to express its dissatisfaction to our government with our treaty with England, and to adopt some measure in that spirit, various reports were circulated respecting those which it had or probably would adopt. Different representations were made of the instructions given to Mr. Adet as to the extent to which he should go in declaring to our government the dissatisfaction and the part he should act afterwards, whether he should remain there to receive the explanation of our government and to accommodate the difference between them, provided they should be so disposed, or to withdraw and leave our government to pursue its own course. It was likewise stated that an order had been issued for the seizure of our vessels laden with enemy's property, whereby the articles in our treaty of 1778 in favor of neutral trade were violated. It was further said that a still more hostile attitude would be assumed towards us: that a treaty with Spain had been or would be soon concluded whereby Louisiana and the Floridas would be ceded to France, and that an attempt would be made to sever Canada from England, unite it with those provinces, and invite the western parts of our union to separate from it and join this new power which was thus to be reared in that quarter.

These reports gave to Mr. Monroe extreme inquietude, especially as he could obtain nothing explicit on either from the Minister of Foreign Affairs. In this state he sought and obtained an interview with some members of the Directory in which he endeavored to draw from them a full and frank communication of the measures they had adopted or decided on in every instance. He began by expressing his concern to hear that they were still dissatisfied with us and intended to take some measure in consequence thereof, which he sincerely regretted, because he had concluded that the explanations which he had given in reply to their several complaints had been satisfactory and because also, he was concerned that any unfriendly measure towards us would be equally injurious to both countries. They replied that they were dissatisfied with us on account of our treaty with England, and thought that the honor of their country would be sullied in their hands if they did not declare it. Mr. Monroe endeavored to head them into free communication on the points to which they had objected, but found that it was impossible, as they distinctly showed they thought that too much time had already been bestowed on it. One of the members observed that the abandonment of the principle adopted in their treaty with us in favor of neutral rights was a serious injury to France. Mr. Monroe replied that nothing was abandoned, since such was the law of nations, as he had fully proved in his note to the Minister of Foreign Affairs. The member observed that if we could not carry that principle with England, nor protect our flag against her seizures in breach of it, that that was a sufficient reason why France should not complain: that they did not wish us to engage in the war with England, but that the abandonment of the principle, formally by treaty, while they were engaged in a war with that power, stood on different ground. Mr. Monroe saw that it would be useless to press this point further, and proceeded in consequence to hint what he had heard, of the intention respecting Canada, Louisiana and the Floridas, to which he [the member] replied that with respect to Canada, they had no object for France; and in regard to Louisiana, none which should disquiet us; that they wished us well and hoped that matters might be amicably adjusted, since they would meet suitable propositions to that effect with pleasure; that the Minister of Foreign Affairs was instructed to communicate to him the *arrêt* they had passed, but in a manner to satisfy him; that to that communication he must look for a knowledge of its contents and not to them. These details were added in his letter to the Secretary of State of September 10th, to the reply to the charges which had been alleged against him.

Being extremely distressed at the report which circulated of their intention to acquire Louisiana, the Floridas, and Canada, and to invite our western people to join them, he obtained shortly afterwards another interview with a member of the Directory, in which he led directly to this point and obtained from him an explicit and satisfactory answer. The member assured Mr. Monroe that their sole object in regard to Canada was to dismember it from England and weaken her; that they were not anxious about Louisiana, and if they took it, it would be in the event of a war between Spain and England, and to keep the British from it, who would avail themselves of the opportunity to seize the mouth of the Mississippi; that with respect to our interior we had no cause for inquietude, for there did not exist in the breast of a single incumbent of the government an intention to disturb it; that they would adopt no measure which they did not avow to our government, and that we need harbor no suspicion of any design on their part which they did not avow. In the information derived from this source Mr. Monroe had entire confidence, and in which he was soon afterwards confirmed by that from others, whose opportunities were favorable, and of the correctness of whose reports ample proof had before been afforded. He was satisfied, therefore, that no such project existed either on the part of the government of France or of our western people, and that the report was either the suggestion of slander to do mischief or of some few disaffected who wished it.[57]

It may clearly be inferred from a view of what had passed that the French government never thought of making the acquisition of Louisiana and the Floridas until it was suggested by Mr. Monroe's note of January, 1795, respecting the Mississippi. It is obvious from the reply to that note, of the 8th of February, that the view presented of it made a very sensible impression on the French government, as well from a desire to promote the interest of the United States, under a feeling which was then strong, as to weaken England. It would have been strange if such should have been the change of sentiment and feeling in that government that a suggestion which was made and adopted with intention to promote our welfare, should have become instrumental to the opposite purpose.

Mr. Monroe, being very anxious to obtain from the Minister the note which the members of the Directory had informed him he was instructed to write, he addressed one to him [the Minister] on the 21st of September, requesting information whether an order had been issued by his government to seize enemy's property in neutral bottoms, as was reported. He expected, in giving an answer to this inquiry, that information would likewise be given of the nature and extent of the instructions to Mr. Adet, on which, however, he deemed it improper to touch. To this note Mr. Monroe did not obtain an answer until the 7th of October, and which embraced, as he had anticipated, all the objects alluded to in his conference with the members of the Directory. The Minister stated that he was instructed by his government to inform him that the functions of the Minister of France to the United States were suspended, and that an *arrêt* had passed by which their ships of war were ordered to treat our vessels as the United States permitted the English to treat them. On the first point he observed that it was painful for him to dwell; that their Minister, Mr. Adet, would give further explanations to our government, which he presumed would justify to it the measure which had been adopted; that the ordinary relations between the two people, by virtue of treaties, would not be suspended; that the courts would superintend their execution; that the modifications which would be produced by the *arrêt* were not attributable to them, but to the violation of the general laws of neutrality which was committed by the English; to the fulfillment of the treaty between the two republics; and the consequence of the treaty between the United States and England. He assured Mr. Monroe that it would not be the fault of the Directory if the relations between the two nations were not speedily reestablished on the footing they ought to hold, and if the clouds which cast a gloom on their alliance were not speedily dispelled by frank and loyal communications to which his government would be particularly anxious to listen if they should be made through him.

To this note, Mr. Monroe gave a reply on the 12th, in which he expressed his great concern at the information he had received, because he had presumed that the explanations which he had given in reply to the complaints of his government in the discussion which had passed between them had been satisfactory. He deeply regretted, also, that any incident should have occurred, and especially during his mission, which indicated a diminution of that friendship which ought always subsist between the two governments. He trusted, however, that the discontent would be transitory, and that he should soon see the restoration of that cordial amity which had before united them. He declined entering again into the merit of their complaints; the subject being then before his government, he deemed it his duty to await orders. In concluding his note, he acknowledged in terms of respect the attention with which they had heard his communications, official and informal, with an assurance that he should always remember it with great sensibility.

At this period Mr. Monroe received a letter from the Secretary of State of the 22d of August, announcing his recall, with the appointment of General Charles C. Pinckney of South Carolina as his successor, who was daily expected in Philadelphia and would soon embark for France in discharge of the duties of the trust. For the considerations which produced his recall, he referred him to his letter of the 13th of June, and in support of the charges alleged against him in that letter, repeated that the information communicated in his letters of February 16th and 20th, of March 10th and 25th, had been decisive. These letters, it will be recollected, gave the first intimation to the Secretary of the discontent of the Directory on account of our treaty with England, and that it was contemplated by it to adopt any measure in that spirit towards our government. The Secretary observed that, as Mr. Monroe had anticipated that discontent and had not removed it by a timely application of the lights which had been furnished him, and which he affirmed might have been easily done had they been

thus applied, the proof of his negligence and inactivity at a very
important crisis was conclusive, that the President had deemed it his
indispensable duty to recall and appoint a successor to him. To this
letter Mr. Monroe gave no reply, having already answered the charges
alleged against him in his reply to that of the 13th of June. He was
satisfied that the more tranquil and silent he was while he remained
in office, the better the effect would be as to his government and
country, and less the compromitment as to himself with both governments. Conscious that he had discharged his duty according to his
best judgment with integrity and zeal, his object was to retire home
as soon and as quietly as possible. When he should reach that ground
he would have a right, as a private citizen, to explain his conduct
and vindicate his character, which was most dear to him. General
Pinckney arrived in Paris on the 6th of December and carried with
him Mr. Monroe's letter of recall, bearing date on the 9th of September.
Of his arrival at the port in the south of France intelligence had been
received before he reached Paris. The Minister of Foreign Affairs,
being apprised of it, addressed a letter to Mr. Monroe of the 2nd of
December, prescribing the formalities which should be observed on
the occasion by the transmission of the letter of recall of the one and
the credence of the other, and which he requested him immediately to
do if he had arrived. Mr. Monroe informed the Minister on the next
day that General Pinckney had not arrived, according to his information, but that as soon as he did, he would pursue the course which
he had designated. From motives of delicacy Mr. Monroe remained
at home, avoiding interviews with those in the French government
and all others with whom he could avoid it, not in his confidence and
immediately connected with him. On the 6th, Mr. Monroe advised
the Minister that General Pinckney had arrived, and requested that
he would appoint a time when they might attend and present him the
documents incident to the occurrence. On the 9th, the Minister
acknowledged the receipt of Mr. Monroe's of the 6th and invited
him to attend his office on that day, accompanied by his successor.
They waited on him accordingly and delivered to him the documents
referred to. On the 11th, the Minister addressed a note to Mr. Monroe
in which he informed him that the Directory had charged him to
declare that it would not recognize or receive any Minister from the
United States until reparation had been made for their grievances,
which it had demanded of our government and which the French
government had a right to expect. He assured Mr. Monroe that this
determination did not oppose the continuance of the affection between
the French Republic and the American people, which was founded

on mutual good offices and reciprocal interest, and which Mr. Monroe had cultivated by all the means in his power.

In the interview which Mr. Monroe had obtained with the Minister for General Pinckney and himself, and in which a copy of the letter of recall of the one and of credence of the other were delivered, Mr. Monroe requested the Minister to obtain for him an audience of the Directory as soon as possible, that he might take his leave of the government, which he promised. No notice having been taken of the time when such audience would be given to him in the letter of the 11th in which he [the Minister] communicated the decision of the Directory not to recognize General Pinckney, he immediately addressed a note to the Minister in which he repeated his request. On the 27th, he received an answer from the Minister, informing him that the Directory would give him a private audience on the 30th for the delivery of his letter of recall, and if he would attend his office at eleven o'clock, they would proceed thence together to the Directory, to whom he would present him on the occasion. He attended at the hour appointed and the Minister conducted and presented him to the Directory, to whom he delivered his letter of recall and of whom he took leave in an address in which he communicated the instruction of the President to renew the assurance of the solicitude which the United States felt for the happiness of the French Republic. Mr. Monroe availed himself of the opportunity to declare the delight with which he had beheld their success in Council and the field, his earnest solicitude for the continuance of perfect harmony between the two republics, and to acknowledge, with great sensibility, the attention and confidence with which he had been honored in his mission. The President of the Directory replied in terms full of reproach to our government, charging it with condescension to Great Britain, claiming to France the credit of our success in the War of Independence, discriminating between the people of the United States and their government, ascribing to them correct and honorable motives, and declaring that they possessed the esteem of the people of France. Of Mr. Monroe they took an affectionate farewell, assuring him that he departed with their regret, and carried with him their best wishes for his future welfare.

As soon as it was known to the citizens of the United States that Mr. Monroe was recalled, they assembled, without distinction of party, and agreed to an address expressive of their high sense of his faithful and unabated application to the duties of the arduous office he had held, and of the important service he had rendered in it to his country. They acknowledged, also, the promptitude and zeal with which he had advocated their interests individually in the difficult circumstances in which they had been often placed in the unsettled and critical situation of that country during his mission, and of which they assured him they should always retain the most grateful sense. They expressed their deep regret of his recall, both on public and personal considerations. Five of these citizens, who were appointed for the purpose, offered to present the address on the 8th of November, but he then declined to receive it, as it might become known to the French government and do harm. On the arrival of General Pinckney they presented it, but the contents were not then published and the incident itself was kept as secret as possible.

Mr. Monroe having received his recall in the winter, and there being no American vessel in France which could afford suitable accommodations for his family had he been willing to encounter a passage at that season, her ports being generally blockaded, he was compelled to delay his departure till the spring. Perceiving, however, that his recall by his own government had removed from the most jealous and prejudiced in that of France all doubt of the good faith with which he had promoted a good understanding between the two republics, and labored to prevent the French government from adopting any unfriendly measure towards the United States in consequence of their treaty with England, but had excited a generous feeling towards him under the sense of the injury they had done him by that suspicion, he was very anxious to show, so far as he might be able, every expression on its part of that sentiment in his favor. He saw distinctly that every indication of kindness towards him by the government of France, especially after the rejection of General Pinckney, would be considered by his own as a proof of connivance between him and that government, and of the charges alleged against him by the Secretary of State; and that the stronger the expression, the more complete would be the proof of his guilt. He resolved, therefore, to leave France and to proceed to Holland, to remain there during the winter, which he accordingly did. In the spring he returned and passed hastily through Paris to Bordeaux, from where he sailed on the 20th of April, 1797, and arrived in the Delaware and in Philadelphia the latter end of June.[58]

Some questions are involved in the recall and censure of Mr. Monroe on which the public may now form an impartial and correct opinion. The first is: whether there was a connivance between him and the French government, whereby he had indicated a disapprobation of the conduct of his own, excited the discontent of that of France, and stimulated it to unfriendly acts towards his own; or in other words, whether he had performed his duty to his country with integrity and zeal in every stage of his mission. The second is: whether he had, by the standing which he had acquired with the French government, checked its resentment after the conclusion of the treaty with England and thereby produced a delay, and moderated in the measure it finally adopted the tone which it would otherwise have assumed. The third is: whether his recall did not remove such restraint and leave them at liberty to pursue the course most agreeable to themselves: to reject General Pinckney and assume the violent tone which was then displayed; or whether, had he not been recalled, he might not have been able to heal the difference which had been produced by the treaty with England and to restore the friendly relations between the two governments without a rupture. The decision on either of these points seems to involve that of the others, and so fully have the facts on which they respectively rest been stated, and so well supported are they by unquestionable documents, that it is deemed unnecessary to dwell on them.

We will simply ask: in what state did he find affairs on his arrival and how did he retrieve them? How preserve them in the state thus retrieved while the Convention remained in power, although the causes which had produced the former state, by the breach of the treaty of 1778 and other injuries, not only continued to exist, but after the conclusion of the treaty with England and the report of its contents had acquired much greater force? To what cause was the delay of the Directory in forming any decision or taking any measure in reference to the treaty for more than three months to be imputed and by what means were many of its decrees moderated, for nearly eight months afterwards? Why was he left in power after the decision to suspend Mr. Adet, their Minister to the United States, in the discharge of his ordinary functions, the motive being equally applicable on principle to the Minister of the United States to France? Did the explosion which took place on the arrival of General Pinckney indicate any underhanded communication between him and the French government, or was it imputable to the removal of the only obstacle to such a step, whereby they were left at liberty to pursue the course most agreeable to themselves, to reject General Pinckney and assume the violent tone which was then displayed? Can any reason be assigned for these results other than the weight he had acquired by his conduct in France and the respect entertained for him personally by the French government, and could he have had any weight or produced any effect on the policy it preferred if he had not acted with perfect integrity and been so understood by that government?

Page three of the account book kept by James Monroe, in which he lists expenses which he incurred during his first Mission to France, 1794 to 1796, and which he tried to collect from Congress in later years. (See Introduction, page 2) The heading is from page one of the account book.

It is certain that this mission, by the expenses attending it, sub-jected him to debts which have embarrassed him through life. Its duties were of vast extent and of a nature the most complicated, arising from the peculiar character of the French government and disordered state of the interior; from the distress of our citizens, of whom a great number were collected there, and to which they were reduced by the previous measures of the French government, and likewise from other causes. To meet the demands made on him by the performance of his various duties, the labor which was indispensable required three or four times the aid necessary in ordinary missions. A distinct establishment with three or four assistant secretaries was necessary through the whole mission. The purchase of a house, at the instance of his fellow citizens, as a substitute for that offered to him by the French government, and the heavy loss incident thereto by his recall; the charge incident to the relief and aid afforded to Mr. T. Paine and to others of his fellow citizens; occasional contribu-tions to the poor and others of the city who demanded it; his detention nearly four months after his recall, by the season, for which no allowance was made, and the expense attending which was much increased by the obligation imposed on them, for the reasons stated, to leave France and pass that time in Holland. These items will give an idea of the debts which were incurred in that mission and of the effect which they must have had on his private fortune.

On his return home, two objects claimed a primary attention, both of which were connected with his character. The first related to his recall and the charges alleged against him, as the motive to it. The second to his account with the government incurred in his mission. On the first he opened a correspondence with the Secretary of State, in which he asked what were the additional circumstances alluded to in his letter of recall of the 22d of August, 1796, which induced that measure. By this inquiry an opportunity was afforded to him to state whether, on a view of the documents which he had afterwards re-ceived, any change of opinion had occurred respecting his conduct in the discharge of his duties. No such change was acknowledged, and remarks were made in reply to show that the circumstances alluded to had increased the motive to his recall, without, however, specify-ing what they were. Mr. Monroe considered it his duty, in vindication of his character against those charges, to make an appeal to his fellow citizens throughout the union by the publication of his instructions and correspondence with both governments, with other documents connected with the mission. He added, in illustration of the whole subject, an introductory view with such explanations, in each instance,

as the case required.[59] This view was written under a deep sense
of the injury he had received, in a spirit of independence and a defiance of all scrutiny. In regard to the President, we are happy to state
that the opinion which Mr. Monroe had formed in early life and
entertained at the time of his appointment of his transcendent services,
exalted merit, and great purity of principle, had undergone no change,
even at the period when the burden of his censure lay heaviest on him.
He well knew that his situation had become peculiarly delicate, by the
treaty itself, in its bearing on all the parties and interests connected
with it, especially after the decision of the Senate. Had he rejected
it, he would have taken on himself the responsibility of all the consequences which would have followed, of a war with England, for
example, had that ensued. He was aware also that the popular movements in the United States against the treaty might have formed an
additional obstacle to its rejection, as it might have been inferred
that it had been produced by those movements, and by intimidation,
to which he was the last of men to yield.

Such had been the division of parties, and so great were the excitement and animosity between them at this moment, and so far had
the measure advanced, that to have rejected the treaty would have
thrown him essentially on that party which was in direct opposition
to the whole proceeding. He was instilled to the confidence of the
nation, and actually enjoyed it, but in the state in which the affair
then stood, he could expect support in the course which he might
adopt from one party only. By ratifying the treaty and relying on
the party which had supported the policy pursued, he was sure of its
uniform and continued support, and might calculate on the acquiescence of the other after the excitement of the moment had passed
away. By rejecting it, especially if war with Great Britain should
ensue, there was danger that the Federal party would have been
offended and the other have afforded only a moderate support. His
situation was therefore peculiarly delicate and difficult, not in regard
to himself only but the nation, as to the consequences attending his
decision. It was known that he hesitated after the British had commenced the seizure of our vessels laden with provisions destined for
the ports of France, and it cannot be doubted, had he foreseen the
state in which we then were, at a period while the proceeding was
under his control, that he would have prevented it. In the decision
which he did form, which was to ratify the treaty, he was compelled
to view the actual state, and in which we are satisfied that he was
governed by the present principles. The recall of Mr. Monroe seemed
to be incidental to that decision. Those near him, whose council he

had respected and with whom Mr. Monroe had had collision—we allude particularly to Mr. Jay and Mr. Hamilton—would press his recall, and the President might suppose after the ratification of the treaty that his recall and the appointment of another Minister would indicate more tone and have a better effect with the French government.[60]

The other object, the settlement of his account with the government, he committed to the care of Mr. Dawson, a friend in whom he had great confidence, but under an injunction to make no difficulty as to the manner: to let the Department settle it as it thought fit. By the settlement, no provision was made for any of the extra charges which have been specified, and in those which were usual, the utmost rigor was observed. General Pinckney arrived in Paris on the 6th of December, 1796, with an instruction to Mr. Monroe to take a friendly leave of the French government, and for which he requested an audience of the Directory as soon as it could be granted, in his interview with the Minister in which he presented General Pinckney, but could not obtain it until the 1st of January following. His compensation was suspended on the day that General Pinckney arrived, and for all the contingent expenses of the mission, one hundred and ten dollars only were allowed, which must have fallen far short of the sum disbursed for stationery and the flag which he presented to the Convention, without noticing others which are incidental and allowed to every mission. All the extra charges specified fell on him, and for which he was forced to make provision by the sale of property, by loans of banks and individuals, to meet the measures made on him in the best manner that he could. Those extra disbursements were, it is presumed, not even mentioned to the Department. A Minister who had been recalled and censured on the charge of failing to perform his duty, with imputations much stronger, could not expect that a claim for those extra charges would be listened to, nor would he, from a respect to his own character, bring them forward.

Thus terminated Mr. Monroe's first mission to France, and such is the view which we present of it, founded on consequential documents in every detail. We will now proceed to other instances of his public service and his discharge of the duties incident to each trust.

Items which belonged to James Monroe—collection of books,
Bible, eyeglasses, sander, inkstand,
quills and snuffbox.

4

"Vindication"

Mr. Monroe, having made an appeal to his fellow citizens in vindication of his conduct and character in the discharge of his duties in the late mission to France by the publication of his instructions and correspondence with both governments, and other documents connected therewith, he deemed it improper to seek, by any movement of his own, the public favor. He remained tranquilly at home about two years, devoting his time and labor to the care of his private concerns, and particularly to an effort to make such an arrangement as would enable him to meet the debts which pressed on him from France by the sale of a part of his property and the disposition by mortgage of other parts as a security for loans with the least sacrifice. He was resolved, if any attention should be shown him, that it should be voluntary and the result of the opinion formed, on a view of the documents which had been published.[61] While thus engaged on his farm, his attention was drawn, in the commencement of December, 1799, to a citizen of Richmond who was well known to and respected by him, Colonel Alexander Quarrier, who approached him in the field and delivered a dispatch which had been committed to him by the Speaker of the two Houses of the General Assembly, and of which he added that he was happy to be the bearer. On perusing the dispatch, Mr. Monroe found that it announced to him his election to the office of Chief Magistrate of the state, with a request that he would repair to Richmond to take on himself the duties of the office as soon as it might be convenient to him. He resolved to depart without delay. He required one day only to make such arrangement of his private affairs as would admit of his absence. Early on the ensuing morning, Mr. Jefferson, his venerable neighbor and friend, called on him, and immediately afterwards, Colonel Thomas M. Randolph arrived with a troop of horse to manifest their respect for him personally and for the decision of the General Assembly in electing him to the office of Chief Magistrate. He departed immediately for Richmond, accompanied by the venerable Mr. Jefferson to Milton, and by Colonel Randolph and the troop to the boundary line of the county. Many friends saluted him on the road, and as he approached Richmond, he was met by Dr. Foushee and other friends, with whom he entered the city. As they advanced, he was informed by Dr. Foushee that an authentic account had been received of the death of General Washington, an event which shocked and deeply affected him, for it was his intention, now that he was placed on independent ground by the generous confidence of his fellow citizens, to make advances and indicate a desire to restore their former friendly relation. The report made to him by his friend Dr. Edwards of the favorable sentiment expressed of him by the General after his recall, he thought would justify such advance from the station he then held, and it accorded highly with his feelings and principles to make it.[62]

Court suit worn by Monroe when he was presented to
Napoleon during his second mission to France.
It is made of cut velvet with cut steel
buttons. The vest is hand-embroidered.

5

Minister to Napoleon:
Louisiana Purchase

As soon as Mr. Monroe had terminated his service in the office of Chief Magistrate of the State, he resumed his station at the bar with intention to devote himself to the profession until he should place his affairs in an independent state.[63] In that office he had done little to retrieve himself from the debts contracted in his mission to France. He took a house in Richmond, gave notice in the gazette of his intention, and had business to some amount immediately committed to him. At this moment an incident occurred which deeply affected the interest of the western states and roused the indignation of the union. By the treaty of San Ildephonso, between France and Spain, which was concluded on October 1st, 1800, the latter had ceded to the former the province of Louisiana and had suppressed, at the instance of the former, as was inferred, our right of deposit at New Orleans, which was secured by our treaty with Spain of 1795. The act justified war, to which ever government it might be imputed, and many were prepared to risk it by removing the obstruction by force. The President preferred a different policy. He resolved to make the experiment of a special mission, and with that view nominated and appointed him in that character to both France and Spain, without consulting him. Mr. Monroe had, in repeated instances before, given strong proofs of the interest which he took in favor of the free navigation of that river. He had evinced this disposition by his opposition to a projected treaty between our Secretary of Foreign Affairs and Mr. Gardoqui, the representative of Spain, in 1786, by which it was proposed to suspend our right to the free use of that river for a certain time, that of twenty-five years. It was known that he drew the paper which was presented by the delegates of the state against that project, and which had since been published from the Secret Journals of Congress. He had evinced a like disposition in his mission to France, by a note which represented to the Committee of Public Safety, in 1795, the details of which have already been noticed. Full confidence was, therefore, entertained throughout the union in the zeal which he would carry with him in the negotiation. It was equally presumable that he would be well received in France, regarding the incidents of his former mission, the revolutionary party still being in power, and among them, many of those with whom he had been closely connected and in great confidence during that mission.

Other considerations operated with peculiar force. The intimate and cordial friendship and great harmony in political life which he had so long enjoyed with the President and Secretary of State,[64] with his high respect for their talents and merit, rendered it impossible for him to decline a cooperation with them in support of this great cause in which they were engaged. Under these circumstances Mr. Monroe did not hesitate to accept the appointment, although he knew that his relinquishment of the bar and absence from the country would increase the debts then existing and feared that the new mission, however short it might be, would subject him to still further difficulties, especially as he was informed that no outfit would be allowed to him. He repaired immediately to the city and sailed as soon afterwards as his instructions were prepared. His departure from the state being sudden, he gave to Colonel James Lewis, a neighbor in whom he had confidence, a power to sell his tract of land above Charlottesville of 950 acres, and a large tract in Kentucky, should any exigency require it. As his new mission would commence with France, where the debts which had not been paid of his former mission were due, he hoped that by the decision of the suit respecting the balance due for the house, which he was confident would be in his favor, he should derive considerable aid; and that by his presence with those to whom he was indebted, with whom he held a friendly relation, be the decision as it might, he should be able to prevent any pressure from that quarter. The debt of the neighborhood, therefore, in the concerns of an estate which had been neglected, the precise amount of which he did not know, were those only for which he thought a provision would be absolutely necessary. He deemed it proper, however, in that which he did make, to anticipate the possibility of other demands and to provide for them.

He sailed from New York with his family on the 8th of March, 1803, and arrived at Havre de Grace, in France, on the 8th of April following. Colonel John Mercer of Fredericksburg, the son of General

Hugh Mercer, who fell at Provincetown in our Revolutionary war, accompanied him as a friend, and with intention to afford him all the aid in his power. Mr. Monroe was not allowed a secretary. Colonel Mercer was a young man of talents and great worth. From Baltimore, his family took under their protection Mrs. Benthalou, the wife of Colonel Benthalou who had been an officer in Count Pulaski's Corps, distinguished for his gallantry and wounded in the attack on Savannah. He was then in France in pursuit of claims, and she went to join him.

On landing at Havre de Grace, he was saluted from the battery, and as soon as he reached the hotel to which he was conducted, a guard with an officer and 50 men were sent to his quarters as a further tribute of respect. To have sent back the whole guard might have wounded the feelings of the commanding general. Two sentinels only were retained, and by the officer who commanded and led back the others an acknowledgment was made to the General for his kind attention, with an assurance that by permitting two only to remain the sensibility would be increased. In the morning the General with his *état-major* attended to pay their respects in person to Mr. Monroe, and on the ensuing day the commanding officer of the Navy, with all the officers of the corps at that port, called to pay their respects in like manner. This attention, if it proceeded from the parties themselves, was a strong proof of the favorable impression which Mr. Monroe had made on the nation in his first mission, and if it was shown in obedience to the orders of the government, it was equally a proof of that effect on the nation, as of a corresponding feeling of those at its head. It is believed that no examples of a like attention had been shown to a minister from any other power. On entering the territory, they are usually furnished with passports which specify their grade and the sovereign whom they represent, under which protection they pass from the frontier to the city. Mr. Monroe advised Mr. [Robert R.] Livingston of his arrival on the 8th, the day on which he reached Havre, and the government was advised of it, as he understood, on the same day by the telegraph.

What attention might be shown Mr. Monroe by the acquaintances he had formed in his first mission could only be ascertained by their conduct after his arrival. He thought it incumbent on him, however, to have that circumstance in view, and so to regulate his conduct as to derive from it such advantage to his government and country as it might afford, if any, and in any event, to prevent its doing any injury.

Between his first and second missions six years had elapsed. During his absence from France an important change had been made in the government: that the Directory and her Councils had been overthrown and the Consular government established in its stead. The latter was founded likewise on the sovereignty of the people, but their agency in it and their power in that character was essentially impaired. Those in the latter government had supported the Revolution and were all revolutionary characters, but with different views, as was inferred from those who had been put down. Mr. Monroe had held a friendly relation in his first mission with almost all who were in office, and with many of those who had been removed by the change. Between the parties he was aware that serious hostility must exist, and that any intercourse on his part with those opposed to the government would be noticed by and diminish its confidence in him, which might operate to the injury of his mission and of his country. He considered it his duty, therefore, to adopt a rule as to his intercourse with society, before he reached Paris, which would prevent that effect. The government of the country, acquiesced in by the people, is the legitimate government for foreign powers to treat with and is entitled to the respect of their ministers. In internal changes they should take no part, the society alone having the right to make them. In his first mission he treated the government while in the hands of the Convention, and those of the Directory and two Councils, with equal respect. A like respect was now due to the Consular government, which he was resolved to show it. In the former instances the sovereignty was in the people unimpaired, to which principle it was known that he was devoted. Should any radical change be now contemplated, his conduct would be more attended to and his intercourse with those opposed to it more injurious. He therefore considered himself bound, however painful[ly], to designate those at variance with the existing government whom it would be improper for him to see. He did so, and of whom he made a list which he gave to his principal servant with instruction should any of them call, not to admit them, always giving some excuse which should not be offensive.

On Mr. Monroe's first mission to France his attention was drawn by his instructions to the progress of the Revolution, to the state of the interior, the division of parties, the prospect of the establishment of a good republican government, and the competency of the people to sustain such government, and likewise of their probable success in the war with the allied powers who were combined against them. To all those objects a faithful attention was paid by his letters to the Secretary of State, which gave a full development of every interesting occurrence, in all the views suggested, through the whole of his mission.

At that epoch there was cause to apprehend, from the motive which led the allied powers to assail France—a desire to crush the people in their effort in favor of liberty—that if they succeeded they would strike at the source from whence the spirit originated, which was known to be the United States. While there was a probability, or even a possibility, of their success, the fortune of France seemed to be connected, if not to involve the welfare of the United States; but as soon as it became certain that the subjugation of France was impossible, and that so great was her force that she not only repelled invasion on every side but menaced the overthrow and subjugation of the surrounding powers, the danger ceased, and the object as to the form of government in which the revolution would terminate, or the principle on which founded, became afterwards rather an affair of speculation and anxiety as to the competency of such a people to institute and support free government, than of a danger from those who had assailed it.

In whatever form of government the revolution might terminate, it might fairly be presumed, as those who would be placed at its head would be revolutionary characters, men who had contended either in council or the field against the allied powers, who had acquired that fame and derived their direction from the revolution itself, that a separation would still exist between them and the old dynasty of Europe, which would form a barrier and bulwark in favor of the United States. As early as the end of the campaign of 1795, Mr. Monroe considered the question as to the success of the war decided. France was triumphant and had nothing to fear from the surrounding powers. The demonstration of that result was still more complete at the end of the campaign of 1796. During his first mission the government of the Convention and of the Directory and the two Councils was in both instances the government of the people. It was not only founded on their sovereignty but had such an immediate dependence on their will and agency as to be ruled by them. It was, therefore, Mr. Monroe's duty to treat it with respect, and in so doing, and evincing his solicitude for its welfare in certain movements against it, he gratified his own feelings as well as the feelings of those in power and thereby promoted the interest of his country. In his absence a change had taken place in the government, which placed the people in a different position. The sovereignty was still in them, but their power in that respect had become nominal rather than real and was still more so in the exercise of it. The actual government, however, being the legitimate government for foreign powers, the principle was the same as to the respect due to it by their ministers; although with those devoted to free government, the satisfaction in treating with it would be diminished. His mission was likewise special and temporary, produced by a recent and serious aggression which required prompt adjustment with the existing government, to which his instructions were adapted. With this sense of his duties, in their relation to the government with which he had to treat, Mr. Monroe entered on the execution of them in his mission to France, and he adhered to it strictly afterwards in his mission to other powers.

Mr. Monroe left Havre on the 10th of April and reached Paris on the 12th and took the quarters which had been provided for him by his friend Mr. Skipwith, who had accompanied him as Secretary in his first mission [and who] was appointed soon after his arrival as Consul for Paris, which office he still held, having discharged its duties with integrity, ability and diligence. Mr. Monroe received in reply to his letter to Mr. Livingston of the 8th, one of the 10th by Colonel Benthalou, who had advanced by the route to Havre to meet his wife. In this letter Mr. Livingston gave a very discouraging prospect of the success of the mission. He congratulated Mr. Monroe on his safe arrival and expressed an anxious hope that his mission might answer his and the public expectation. War, he said, might do something for us; nothing else would. He had paved the way for him by his memoirs and if he could add an assurance that we were in possession of New Orleans, we should do well. On the evening of his arrival, he waited on Mr. Livingston accompanied by Colonel Mercer and Mr. Skipwith, on which occasion a conversation occurred on the state of affairs in the United States at the period of Mr. Monroe's departure, and in which Mr. Livingston asked what had been the fate of Mr. Ross's resolutions. On being informed that they had been rejected, he expressed his regret, with a remark that force only could give us New Orleans and that nothing but the actual possession of the country could give success to the mission in which they were associated. In this interview Mr. Livingston observed to Mr. Monroe that as he had seen that part of his correspondence with the French government which had reached the Department of State before he sailed, he presumed it would be agreeable to him to peruse that which had followed to the present period. To this Mr. Monroe promptly assented and, in consequence, it was agreed that he should attend there at an early hour the next day, when it should be submitted to him. He attended accordingly, accompanied by Colonel Mercer, and perused the whole. Among the letters of Mr. Talleyrand, that of the 24th of March drew their particular attention because it afforded strong ground on which to presume that the mission would succeed in all its great objects. The sentiment which it expressed was conciliatory, and in regard to

Louisiana, it stated that the First Consul considered the possession of it, whereby new means were afforded him to convince the government and people of the United States of his friendly disposition for them, in the number of the advantages which he ought to derive from that acquisition. In regard to any negotiation on that subject, the Minister observed that as Mr. Livingston had announced to him the approaching departure of Mr. Monroe, whom the President had appointed Envoy Extraordinary to treat on it, he had concluded that his government expected that that Minister should be waited for and heard, that every matter susceptible of contradiction should be completely and definitely discussed. He requested him to assure his government that the First Consul, far from thinking that their new position in Louisiana should operate to the injury of the United States, he would receive the new Minister whom the President had appointed with the greatest pleasure, and that he hoped, to the satisfaction of both countries. (See Mr. Talleyrand's letter of March 24, 1803). As nothing had been done respecting the Mississippi, the great object of the mission, before Mr. Monroe's arrival, and the Minister had pointed to it as an event which he deemed important to that object, Mr. Monroe concluded, notwithstanding the unfavorable impressions of Mr. Livingston arising from what had passed between him and the government, that the First Consul looked to it as one which would form a new relation between the United States and France. Mr. Monroe inferred, therefore, from that letter, that a negotiation would be immediately opened, and in a spirit corresponding with the sentiment expressed in it.[65]

Some incidents of a very interesting nature occurred at the moment of Mr. Monroe's arrival in Paris, which it is proper to notice here. So far as any circumstance in either was connected with the mission, in that degree should the order of time be respected. The first to which we shall advert we should be sorry to postpone, because it relates to an individual in whose welfare and fame the whole nation take a deep interest.

On Mr. Monroe's arrival at his quarters in Paris, a message was delivered to him from his estimable friend, General Lafayette, requesting that he would call on him as soon as convenient at his aunt's, Madame de Tascher, where he lodged, and with whose address he was apprised. He was informed by Mr. Skipwith that he [Lafayette] was confined to his bed in consequence of a fall on the ice in the winter, by which his hip joint had been dislocated, and that he could not rise or change his position. Mr. Monroe called on him the next day and found him in the state described. Their interview was affecting, by a recollection of the incidents which had occurred between them and those relating to Madame Lafayette on Mr. Monroe's first mission, when the General was confined at Olmutz. The President, Mr. Jefferson, had committed to Mr. Monroe the act of Congress which allowed to the General the land and commutation which officers of his rank were entitled to for service in our Revolutionary war, and to which he had set up no claim, preferring to bear his own expenses and to render his service gratuitously. Mr. Jefferson had likewise committed to Mr. Monroe a letter for the General, explanatory of the motive which led to the act, with a renewed assurance of his own undiminished attachment. Mr. Monroe delivered to the General the letter and act, and was most sensibly affected by the impression which they made on him. He was evidently overwhelmed. You are the only people on the earth, said he, from whom I would accept it. Mr. Monroe assured him that this grant allowed him nothing more than what was due to him and what all our officers of the same rank who had served the same time had received. Mr. Monroe heard from other sources that at that time he possessed the estate of La Grange only, a chateau with about 300 acres, the sale of which his condition then pressed, and that Madame Lafayette, who had signed deeds for the conveyance of his other property for the payment of debts, was then hesitating whether she ought to sanction the sale of the last remaining resource and home for her husband, herself, and children. The grant, by the act of Congress, relieved him and the family from the pressure and preserved to them that domicile. It is proper to mention that this relief was promptly obtained by an advance which was generously made to him by the House of Baring on the credit of the land thus granted. The claim of General Lafayette on the citizens of the United States and the friends of liberty everywhere was the stronger from the consideration that the First Consul had offered to him a seat in the Senate, which was entitled to a liberal compensation, and which, as Mr. Monroe understood, he had declined from a fear that the government was taking a direction which he disapproved.

In this interview General Lafayette communicated to Mr. Monroe an incident which excited his surprise. He informed him that General Bernadotte, who had been appointed some short time before Minister to the United States, had left town for Rochfort, the port from which he expected to sail, on the 10th in obedience to the order of his government. General Lafayette and General Bernadotte had served together in the commencement of the Revolution and were intimately acquainted with each other. Knowing that it was the wish of General Bernadotte to see Mr. Monroe before his departure, and that he was on the route from Havre and expected to arrive in Paris on that day, he sent a messenger to apprise him of it that he might remain and have the interview he desired. His orders, however, were so positive as to compel his immediate departure, depriving him of the opportunity. From this communication it appeared that the movement of General Bernadotte was connected by the French government with the arrival of Mr. Monroe, the motive for which he could not comprehend.

In the morning of the day which ensued Mr. Monroe's arrival, he was called on by a confidential friend, who informed him that on the Sunday preceding (the 10th of April), the First Consul had held a cabinet council at St. Cloud in which he apprised his Ministers of his decision to cede to the United States the province of Louisiana, and that he should commit the arrangement of the negotiation to Mr. Marbois. This friend enjoyed likewise the confidence of the two great Houses of Hope and Baring. He stated that the object of Mr. Monroe's mission was known to those Houses, as it was, that he might and probably would require the loan of a considerable sum of money to accomplish it. He assured Mr. Monroe that he was authorized by those Houses to inform him that they would make the loan for any sum he might require. Mr. Monroe asked to what amount and on what conditions would they make it? For ten millions, should you desire that sum, and on the terms your government will approve, at six per cent per annum. Mr. Monroe replied that he did not expect to have occasion for anything like that sum but that it was important and gratifying to him to know that he might obtain it if necessary. As this communication was confidential and differed so entirely from the opinion entertained by Mr. Livingston, as expressed in his letter to Mr. Monroe of the 8th, and in the interview which took place at his own house on the evening of Mr. Monroe's arrival, no notice was taken of it when he called in the morning to peruse his correspondence with the French government, according to appointment.

Mr. Monroe was gratified by a communication which he received at this period from the Consul Cambacères, through his secretary, Mr. Monvil, a young man of merit, that he should be glad to receive him whenever it might be convenient for him to call on him. He observed that by rule a Foreign Minister might be presented to the First Consul before he was received by the other two, but that that rule would be dispensed with in his case. He assured him, on meeting, that he recollected, with due sensibility, the kind attention and hospitality which had been shown to him by Mr. Monroe in his former mission, and was happy to have it then in his power to evince it. A like attention was shown to him by the Consul Lebrun, on both of whom Mr. Monroe called at an early day, and by whom he was treated with the greatest kindness during his mission.

An interview took place at this period with Joseph Bonaparte, which it is likewise proper to notice. Mr. Monroe took a letter to him from Mr. Pichon, the chargé d' affaires of France in the United States, which he left at his house in Paris immediately after his arrival. Mr. Bonaparte was then in the country. As soon as he received the letter, he sent a message to Mr. Monroe with a request that he would call at his house in the city at an appointed hour, which he did, and was received in a very friendly manner. The object of the mission was adverted to in the interview, and to which Mr. Bonaparte expressed a desire that it might succeed, as he thought we had a just claim to our demands, and that an amicable arrangement would be advantageous to both countries. Mr. Monroe believed that he held the same language to his brother and on very disinterested motives.

The family of Mme. Beauharnais, the wife of the First Consul, had been in a great measure domesticated with that of Mr. Monroe in his first mission. Her daughter, Hortense, had been educated under the celebrated Mme. Campon with Mr. Monroe's older daughter, Mrs. Hay, and her son, Eugene, with young Jones, the son of his estimable relative, the judge, whom he took with him. The nieces of Mme. Campon, the Misses Auguie, were likewise under her care. Mme. Beauharnais had been married to General Bonaparte during that mission and in Mr. Monroe's absence from France, Hortense, her daughter, had been married to Louis, the brother of Napoleon; and one of the Misses Auguies to Marshall Ney, and the others to distinguished officers in the French Army. Mr. Monroe's situation, in the turmoil of that period, enabled him to show kindness to Mme. Campon, to Mme. Beauharnais, and their families, which produced a grateful feeling in their bosoms towards him. From the moment of his arrival an intercourse with him and his family was sought and cherished on their part, and so far as they had any influence on the mind of the First Consul, it cannot be doubted that it was exerted to produce a favorable feeling with him towards Mr. Monroe and his family and, in consequence, his country.

Mr. Monroe dined with Mr. Livingston the day after his arrival, the 13th, accompanied by his friends Mr. Skipwith and Colonel Mercer, and while at dinner they were informed that Mr. Marbois had arrived and wished to see Mr. Livingston, but being apprised that they had not left the table, he amused himself by a walk in the garden. On retiring from the table, Mr. Marbois had a private interview with

Mr. Livingston, in which he informed him that the First Consul had decided on the 10th to make to the United States the cession above stated and had intrusted to him the negotiation. An interview between Mr. Livingston and Mr. Marbois, at the house of the latter at eleven o'clock that night, was agreed on between them, and which took place accordingly. From this period no doubt was entertained of the decision of the First Consul to cede the province. The points to be adjusted respected the extent to which the cession should be carried and the conditions on which it might be obtained.

Mr. Monroe was presented to Mr. Talleyrand, the Minister of Foreign Affairs, by Mr. Livingston, immediately after his arrival, who received him with kindness and attention.[66] He assured them that the First Consul was much gratified by the disposition which had been manifested by our government in adopting the mission and had expressed himself in very favorable terms of the Minister employed in it. He promised to see him that evening and would endeavor to fix the time when Mr. Monroe should be presented to him. He observed that no Minister had been presented except at public audiences, but that a person would be appointed to treat with them and with whom they might proceed in the same manner as if he had been already presented. On the next audience day he was presented to the First Consul, and his reception corresponded with the communication which had been made to Mr. Livingston and himself by the Minister of Foreign Affairs when he was presented to him. "You have been here before," said he to Mr. Monroe, who replied that he had been, and at a very interesting epoch. The diplomatic corps, which was very numerous, being present, the remarks which the First Consul made were of general nature, but of a character very friendly to our government and country. The diplomatic corps dined with the First Consul on that day. On retiring to the drawing room after dining, he advanced to Mr. Monroe and communicated more freely with him. He made inquiries respecting our President, Mr. Jefferson, of whom he spoke in very favorable terms. He asked where he resided in the recess of Congress, whether in the city or on his own estate. He adverted to our relations with other powers and to the state of our interior with apparent interest. The conference being in some measure private, it attracted the attention of other ministers, and particularly of Lord Whitworth, from England, and in consequence, it was not long continued.

In compliance with the assurance which had been given to our Minister by Mr. Talleyrand when Mr. Monroe was presented to him, that a minister would be appointed to treat with them, a notification was immediately afterwards sent to them that the appointment had been conferred on Mr. Marbois, and from whom an intimation was received that he would commence the negotiation as soon as it might be convenient to them. They were unwilling to lose a day. The negotiation immediately commenced, and terminated in a treaty and two conventions, bearing date on the 30th of April, by which the whole province of Louisiana was ceded to the United States and provision made for the payment of the sum stipulated to be given for it.

Our government contemplated only the acquisition of the Island of New Orleans and the territory eastward of the river, for which our Ministers were authorized to give ten millions of dollars. It was ascertained in the first conference that the First Consul would cede no part of the province if he did not cede the whole, and on a comparison of the value and the condition on which they were able to obtain it with that of the part sought and the sum they were authorized to give for it, our Ministers did not hesitate between the alternatives thus presented to them. The province extended, under any view which could be taken of its limits, far to the south and west on the right of the river, and on the left it was understood to extend to the river Perdido. Should France retain the right bank or should it fall into the hands of another power, of Great Britain for example, disputes might arise which might involve us in war, the charge of which would exceed in a single instance more than the sum for which the whole might be acquired. The mere adjustment of the presiding controversy with France, by the removal of the obstruction to the free navigation of the river, with the content which it would spread over the union and particularly the part dependent on it, would afford an ample indemnity for the price given for the whole.

Eighty millions of livres were stipulated to be given for it, of which sixty were to be paid to France and twenty to our citizens in discharge of the debts due to them by France. The sum to be paid to France, equal to eleven million, two hundred and fifty thousand dollars, was to be paid in stock, with a credit of fifteen years, on the payment of six per cent annually. At the expiration of that term, the principal was to be discharged by installments, by the payment of three millions each year. Cash instead of stock was asked for the sum to be paid to France, and a perpetual exemption of French vessels from foreign duties, instead of one for twelve years, which was agreed on. The negotiation was conducted by the Ministers on each side in a spirit of great candor and liberality. They had been long and intimately acquainted and had great confidence in each other.

This very important transaction being thus concluded, the agent of the two Houses of Hope and Baring, who had communicated with Mr. Monroe on his arrival, requested our Ministers to place them on the same ground with the French government which they had held with them, which they readily undertook and for which an opportunity was immediately afforded. It being the object of the French government to convert the stock into cash, Mr. Marbois asked our Ministers to whom it might be disposed of with most advantage to both nations. They designated to him those two great Houses, with an assurance that they thought them competent in Europe, and that they would act with great candor and liberality. They had had occasion to mention them in the course of the negotiation, to show the estimation in which our stock was held. In the present instance they were more full and explicit. A contract was formed by the French government with these Houses, by this the stock was sold to them at a fair price, and who fulfilled their engagement with great punctuality and credit.

Whether the employment of Mr. Monroe contributed in any degree to the success of the mission, a correct opinion may be formed by the facts just stated and others which preceded. Mr. Marbois has composed a work entitled, *The History of the Province of Louisiana, and of Its Cession to the United States*, which furnishes useful light on the subject. This history is a well-digested and able work. It commences with the discovery of the province and gives a detailed account of all the incidents attending it from that period to the cession, and of the causes which led to it, and of many of the most interesting circumstances attending the negotiation. We shall confine ourselves to those which bear immediately on the special objects of inquiry. It appears by this work that until the 10th of April, 1803, the First Consul had given no intimation to his Cabinet of his intention to cede the province to any power. Till then, the idea of the cession had not occurred to any of them, nor had they any suspicion that he contemplated it. On that day he opened the subject in a conference with two of his Ministers, one of whom advised, and the other opposed it. The prospect of a war with England, and the loss of it by her preponderance at sea, which he suggested, was the argument used by the one, and the uncertainty of that war and his preponderance on the Continent, which would enable him to take Hanover, by which, by exchange, he might recover Louisiana, was that which was urged by the other. It appears through the whole discussion that he had made up his mind to cede the province, although he did not declare it in that conference. On the next morning, the 11th, at the dawn of day, he sent for the Minister who had advised the cession, declared to him his decision to make it on conditions which he then stated, and committed to him the management of the negotiation. On the 10th it was known to the First Consul, as may fairly be concluded, that Mr. Monroe had arrived at Havre and might be expected in a day or two at Paris. It was known to Mr. Livingston on that day that he had arrived, as his letter to Mr. Monroe in reply to one from him announcing it from Havre, bears that date. If the report that his arrival had been announced by the telegraph to the French government was correct, and which the manner of his reception at Havre seems to sanction, it must have been known to the First Consul on the 8th. That the movement should have been delayed to that moment and acted on then with such promptitude and decision can admit of no other conclusion.

Other facts are stated by Mr. Marbois which confirm it. In the conference with the Minister to whom the negotiation was committed [Mr. Marbois], the First Consul observed that Mr. Monroe was on the point of arriving, and as his government was distant 2,000 leagues, the President must have given him explicit instructions, more extensive as to the sum to be paid for the territory which might be ceded than could be inferred from the proceedings of Congress. That fact alone proves that he thought that nothing could be done until he did arrive; that he delayed the movement until he knew that he had arrived, and hastened afterwards to make the necessary arrangement for the commencement of the negotiation as soon as he should reach the city.

The war with England was anticipated from the debates in the British Parliament and particularly from the speeches of Lord Grenville and Mr. Canning, as early as the 23d of November, 1802, and it is obvious from the communication of the First Consul to the Corps Legislative of the 20th of February following, in which he proposed that 500,000 men should be raised to defend and revenge the Republic in that war, that he then deemed it inevitable. Had the war with England been the sole or even the ruling motive to the cession, it being known that it would occur at the period referred to, and particularly on the 20th of February, before any account of the mission which had been adopted by the President had reached France, advances would have been made to Mr. Livingston in reference to it or his communications met in a very different spirit; but such was the impression made on him, as is shown by the statement which he expressed in his conference with Mr. Marbois after Mr. Monroe's arrival, notwithstanding the assurance given him that the cession would be made, that it is obvious he had no confidence in it. The impression which he made on Mr. Marbois was that he thought the overture to cede the province illusory, to avoid the payment of the sum due for the prizes they had taken. So sudden had been the change in the temper of the French government as previously manifested to him, that he could view it in no other light.

The first and only communication of the French government which authorized a presumption that any accommodation would be afforded to us respecting the Mississippi, which was much before Mr. Monroe's arrival, is to be found in Mr. Talleyrand's letter to Mr. Livingston of March 24th, at which time he was at sea on his voyage to France. In that letter Mr. Talleyrand speaks in friendly terms of the United States, acknowledges in like manner the effort made by the President to remove the ferment which had been excited among our citizens by the suppression of the deposit at New Orleans, and intimates the desire of the First Consul to meet us in such an arrangement as would be advantageous and satisfactory to both countries. He refers also, in a marked manner, to the mission of Mr. Monroe, and states that his arrival would be waited for and that the First Consul would receive him with the greatest pleasure.

That the approaching war with England contributed to the cession there can be no doubt, but that it was his sole motive is not believed. We were satisfied, on the contrary, that the excitement produced in the United States by the suppression of our right of deposit at New Orleans and the menace of restoring it by force, which he knew that we could accomplish, and the measure adopted by the President to prevent a rupture and settle the affair by a friendly mission and amicable arrangements, gave the first and a decided impulse to his mind to make the cession. Had the deposit not been suppressed and the affair turned on the relation between France and England only, we do not think that any proposition of cession to our government, or even the idea of it, [would] have occurred. A contempt of danger was a marked feature in the character of the First Consul, and this applied as well to France, whose power he wielded and whose fame was connected with his own, as to himself personally. He estimated her strength and resources, of which he had seen so many, and the decisive proofs too highly to adopt any measure, and especially the cession of territory, under a different impression. That the statement made by Mr. Marbois of what passed in the conference is correct is readily admitted, but still that statement leaves the subject open to other views as to the policy of the individual in whom the government was vested.[67]

An incident occurred after the treaties were concluded and had been ratified by the First Consul which excited equally the surprise and concern of our Ministers. Symptoms of discontent appeared which excited a suspicion that he was dissatisfied with the compact and regretted that he had formed it.[68] After some days a letter was received from Mr. Marbois which stated that by the 2d article of the Convention, which stipulated the sum which should be paid directly to France for the territory ceded, it was agreed that that stipulation should be executed within three months, at the latest, after the treaties should be ratified and possession be obtained of the territory by our government. If not executed in that time, he observed that the parties would be restored to their original rights in the same extent as if the treaties had not been formed.

Our Ministers scarcely knew in what light they were to view this communication or what answer they should give to it. Their difficulty was increased by one from Mr. Talleyrand, in an intercourse they obtained of him on the subject, who observed that the First Consul considered the ratification under his control until the exchange should take place, and that he might annex to it such conditions as he thought proper; that he wished every act stipulated on the part of the United States to be performed strictly within the periods specified, or on failure that the parties should be restored to the state in which they were before the treaties were formed.

Our Ministers asked what had excited a doubt on that point or raised the difficulty which then existed? He observed that by the article in the Convention which stipulated the payment of sixty millions of francs to France, the payment was made dependent on the delivery of possession of the territory to the United States, which some incident might prevent: the Spaniards might not surrender it in time, the British might seize it. They replied that those contingencies were contemplated when the treaties were made; that they could not add a new article nor explain any other of them; that our government would be responsible for such delays only as proceeded from bad faith on a fair construction of the treaties. He observed that after what our government had given in the last treaty, the First Consul might annex a condition to the ratification, explanatory of the sense of this treaty, which he would do if they did not satisfy him either that the treaty would be promptly executed, or expunge the provision in the Convention relating to the taking possession of the territory. Our Ministers observed that they could not alter the treaty: that it must be ratified, rejected, or modified by the parties who had a right to do it, not by them.

The affair remained in this state several days, and our Ministers were much embarrassed what course to pursue. They saw distinctly that an answer to Mr. Marbois's letter was expected and apprehended very unfavorable consequences if a satisfactory one was not given. They therefore gave one, in which they admitted that our government was bound to execute the treaty and conventions within the time specified, and that any neglect on its part which should produce a failure would put it in the power of the French government to decide how far it would be bound thereby, or be entitled to compensation for the injury sustained by such neglect. They observed that in making these concessions they confined themselves within the letter of the treaty. They were gratified to find that this letter was satisfactory and removed every difficulty to the transmission of the ratifications, under the care of our Ministers, to Mr. Pichon, their chargé d'affaires in the United States, for exchange, when our government should be prepared for it. That feeling was still further increased by the effort produced in the French government, for a few days afterwards the letter addressed to them by Mr. Marbois was taken back and theirs restored.

Shortly after this event Mr. Marbois read to Mr. Livingston, in an interview with him, the order which would be given to Mr. Pichon as a substitute for the correspondence which had been restored, and desired him to request Mr. Monroe to attend at the Minister's office that it might be communicated to him. He attended accordingly and the letter was read to him, Mr. Marbois being present. Mr. Talleyrand asked how he liked it? Mr. Monroe replied that it was not for him to decide, it being the act of the government only. But which did he prefer? The latter, most certainly. Mr. Talleyrand assured Mr. Monroe that it was on the presumption that it would be more agreeable to our Ministers that the measure was adopted, since by suppressing the letters it became, as it ought to be, the act of the government only. Adverting then to the late negotiation and the result, he observed that he hoped no difficulty would take place hereafter, as our government had sufficient time to perform the stipulations we had entered into, and that his government had it much at heart to preserve future harmony between the two nations. Mr. Monroe assured him that similar sentiments animated his government; that he was satisfied the treaty would be ratified, as he was that after the ratification, the President would promote the payment before the creation of the stock, so far as in his power, to evince his desire of a prompt execution of the treaty; that the Ministers on their part would on their own responsibility, if desired, prevail on the Houses of Baring and Hope to advance their first payment according to their contract with his government, of six millions of francs, before they heard from their government, in confidence that their conduct would be approved. Mr. Monroe stated that he thought his colleague would concur with him in that sentiment. Mr. Talleyrand expressed himself to be highly gratified by this communication, which he considered a strong proof of the friendship of the people of the United States for the government and people of France, and being made after everything was concluded, was the more honorable to the United States, and would be so considered by the First Consul, though he did not think that he would accept anything otherwise than as it became due under the treaty.[69]

Mr. Monroe made the suggestion of promoting the payment by the Houses of Hope and Baring of a sum within the limit of the two millions of dollars, over which a control had been given to our Minister by their instructions, in a firm belief that Mr. Livingston would concur with him in it. They had repeatedly offered in the course of the negotiation to apply that sum in payment in part of the amount stipulated to be given for the province, if a reasonable allowance should be made for it, but which had been declined by Mr. Marbois. They had likewise both been equally concerned at the difficulty raised by the First Consul, by his decision to annex a condition respecting the execution of the treaties by the United States after he had ratified them, and equally apprehensive of the injurious consequences into which the temper then manifested might lead. The object of the interview and of the remarks made by Mr. Talleyrand invited a corresponding reply, which being reported to the First Consul, and promptly, as was inferred, might produce good effect. Mr. Monroe regretted Mr. Livingston's absence on an occasion so interesting, but that was voluntary and intentional on his part: the attendance of Mr. Monroe having been produced by a message from Mr. Marbois, through him, for a purpose on which he had been already consulted and on which he had given his opinion. Mr. Monroe communicated to Mr. Livingston immediately after the interview what had occurred in it, and particularly the disposition which he had expressed and in which he thought that he would concur to promote the payment of the sum specified by the Houses of Hope and Baring, before the treaties should be ratified by their government. Mr. Livingston remarked that he was glad that the offer had been made, as he likewise was that it had been refused.

All difficulty thus terminated with the French government, and the treaty and Conventions, with the ratifications, were transmitted by three of our citizens, by different routes, to our government. The ratifications were enclosed, under its care, to Mr. Pichon, the charge d'affaires of France, with instructions how to act in regard to them.

The object of the mission with France being thus accomplished, and the treaty and conventions forwarded to the government, Mr. Monroe had to decide whether he would remain in Paris until he should receive the order of his government on a view of those documents, as to the course he should pursue, or proceed directly to Madrid and endeavor to settle the boundaries of Louisiana and to acquire that portion of the territory which still belonged to Spain on the eastern side of the river. His opinion was that it would be advisable to proceed immediately to Madrid, under the impression that the cession which had been made by France would be felt by the government of Spain and induce it to make like cession. He was persuaded that all the considerations which applied to one power were equally applicable to the other: a desire to accommodate the United States and the danger of a war with England. He thought also that as the remaining territory of Spain in that quarter would be included within our limits, it would be of little value to her, since her government must know that at no distant period we should acquire it, the United States being a rising and Spain a declining power. Under this impression, he addressed a letter on the 19th of May 1803, to Mr. Talleyrand, communicating his decision and requesting the good offices of his government which had been promised under Marbois in the late negotiation in support of that contemplated with Spain.

Several days elapsed and no answer was received. Mr. Monroe had an engagement at this period with the Consul Cambacères, and attended at his house at the hour appointed. The party, consisting of civil and military officers, was numerous and very respectable. The Consul was absent and did not return till a late hour. His secretary, Mr. Monvil, informed Mr. Monroe that he had gone to St. Cloud to attend the First Consul in a cabinet council, and that interesting concerns must have detained him. As soon as he entered he advanced to Mr. Monroe and said to him, in a low voice, there being many present, that he must not go to Madrid. Mr. Monroe asked the reason, observing that he had nothing to do in Paris, and thought that the present was the most favorable moment. He repeated the advice several times without explaining the motive for it, and finally referred him to Mr. Marbois, the Secretary of the Treasury, who, he said, would give the explanation desired. He immediately left the Consul and called at the house of the Secretary that evening, well knowing that he would act with the utmost candor and withhold nothing from him which he could with propriety communicate, but did not find him at home.

In this state of suspense, dispatches were received from Mr. Madison, the Secretary of State, of the 18th and 20th of April, authorizing Mr. Monroe, provided our affairs with France should have been satisfactorily adjusted, to proceed to England, Mr. King having retired, no chargé d'affaires having been appointed, and war menacing between England and France. Mr. Monroe did not hesitate to adopt that measure and of which he immediately apprised the Minister of Foreign Affairs in an interview which he obtained for the purpose. In this interview the Minister expected that a pressure would be made by Mr. Monroe for an answer to his letter calling [on] the French government for its aid in his negotiation with Spain, which had been promised in that with France by Mr. Marbois. He soon relieved him from all anxiety on that subject by informing him that he had just received a dispatch from his government to that effect, and by a full and frank explanation of the motives which led to it and of the contingency on which it was made to depend. The Minister was gratified by the communication, which he considered a new proof of the good faith of our government in its conduct with his and of its sincere desire to preserve peace and friendship between the United States and France. In adverting to what had passed in the late negotiation, he declared that nothing short of the course which had been pursued by our government would have obtained the result which had attended it. Mr. Monroe requested the Minister to communicate to the First Consul the information which he had given to him, with his intention to depart at an early day and his desire to be favored with a private audience, to take leave of him, before his departure, which he readily undertook. He expressed, however, a doubt, as the Consul intended to commence his tour of the Belgic in a few days and was pre-engaged by appointments for the whole interval, whether it would be in his power to comply with the request.

A few days after the conference with the Minister of Foreign Affairs, Mr. Monroe received a note from him requesting his attendance at St. Cloud at one o'clock the next day, when he would present him to the First Consul, which was accordingly done. The interview was interesting. Mr. Monroe made to him, in substance, the same communication which he had made to the Minister, to which he added that he was instructed by the President to assure him, before his departure, of his high respect for him personally and of his earnest desire to preserve peace and friendship with France. The First Consul reciprocated the sentiment in favor of the President and the United States in terms that were strong and explicit. He said that he considered the President an enlightened man, a friend to liberty, who understood and pursued with zeal the interest of his country. No one wished, he observed, more than he did the preservation of friendship between the two republics. He had ceded to the United States Louisiana, not so much on account of the sum obtained for it, as to preserve that relation. He had seen that we entertained a jealousy of their possession of that province which threatened to force us into measures which might prove equally injurious to both nations, and which he wished to prevent by an act which should remove all cause for anxiety on that point and leave us at liberty to pursue the course which interest and feeling might dictate.

Mr. Monroe assured him that he viewed the cession in the light in which he had placed it, as an act of enlightened policy which had for its object the great result which he had stated. The First Consul observed that there was no rivalship or conflict of interest between the United States and France, their relation being principally commercial, and each requiring what the other had to spare, but that we must be careful not to give the protection of our flag to the commerce of England. Mr. Monroe suggested that in the latter remark he touched an interest which would merit his most mature deliberation and might, in the consequences, incident to the existing war, form an appeal to his candor. If he admitted that free ships made free goods, as he understood that he did, no difficulty could arise on that head. He acknowledged that it was one not free from difficulty, and to which due attention should be paid. He then observed that the present was not the proper time to treat with Spain for Florida; that she complained much of the cession which he had made to us of Louisiana and that he must have time to reconcile her to it. Mr. Monroe remarked that as Florida would be within our limits, she had better cede it to us than retain it, since we could not fail ultimately to acquire it, and it would be more admirable for her to cede it by amicable negotiation, at a fair equivalent, at once, than risk the consequences of a rupture. He persisted in the idea that that was not the proper time to treat for it, but left Mr. Monroe under the impression that at some future time he would afford the aid which had been pledged, and thus they parted. The First Consul set out on the evening of that day on his tour along the coast bordering on the Channel, with intention to menace a descent on England.[70]

Mr. Monroe having been treated with great kindness and attention by the Consuls Cambacères and Lebrun, and likewise by Mr. Marbois during the mission, he called on them and made an acknowledgment of it, and likewise explained in a full and candid manner the motives which led to his mission to England. They parted as friends, a relation which was always afterwards preserved between them. He had deemed it proper, as has been observed, on his return to France, not only to treat with respect the existing government but to guard by a suitable precaution against the possibility of injury to the mission from an intercourse with that portion of the friends whom he had formed in his first mission, who had been put down by the change which had occurred in the government in his absence. He was gratified to find on his leaving France that not one of those whom he had particularly designated ever called. He considered it a strong proof of a liberal sentiment and generous feeling on their part towards him. In taking leave of Mr. Marbois, he mentioned the precaution which he had adopted on his arrival and the fact that not one of them had called, which he did as an act of justice to them, and the only retribution which he could then make. Mr. Marbois received the communication in the spirit in which it was made, with a remark that Mr. Monroe might have received whom he pleased without injury or exciting attention. Mr. Monroe assured him that he knew that such would have been the light in which he would have viewed it, but that he had deemed the precaution necessary as a general rule.

Mr. Monroe could neither enter nor leave France on his second mission without the excitement, in a high degree, of his sensibility. It was natural that all the incidents of his first mission should recur to his recollection and especially those relating to the progress and probable fate of the Revolution. In his absence a change had taken place which put at issue the great question in what kind of government the Revolution would terminate: whether in one vested in a revolutionary character, founded on the principle of the ancient system, or in one which was sought by the friends of liberty. The overthrow of the Directory and the two Councils and establishment of the Consular government made that issue. All prospect of the restoration of the ancient family had then ceased, and the only remaining question was that suggested. In the result of the struggle between the contending parties, he took personally great interest, and endeavored while there to form the best estimate of it that the lights before him could enable him to do. The example which would thereby be furnished of what a people of so great a population and extent of territory, who had so recently escaped from despotism and encountered and surmounted so many difficulties in favor of liberty, were competent to, involved consequences highly interesting to the civilized world. The data on which his estimate would be formed was of a general character, founded on his observations in his first mission, and those to which he had access in the second, without a compromitment of principle, interest, or character. With the enemies of the existing government he had no communications, as has been stated; nor had he with its friends on that subject; they, knowing that he was averse to the change contemplated, had too much delicacy to mention it to him. By what means then was that change brought about; and to what extent was it carried? How far was the power of the people depressed and were they put down? What their acquiescence under it, and what the indication of the public mind respecting it? There were data open to his inspection, without a communication with the leaders of either party. The existing constitution and the means by which it was established furnished the material data in the first instance, and these were to be found in public documents, accessible to all. The state of the interior, whether tranquil or otherwise, furnished those which were most important in the second, and of those every day's experience gave strong proof.

The whole proceeding showed that it was a regularly concerted plan to overthrow the existing system and to establish a government founded on the opposite principle: that it was accomplished by force, in violation of the rights of the people, and that those who were in office exercised the power vested in them by the existing Constitution for its subversion. The people had no agency in it otherwise than as those who acted were used as instruments in subversion of their rights. The plan was formed by a combination of persons who had been friendly to and had supported the Revolution, many of whom had taken the lead in it, were then in high stations, and had acquired great popularity with the nation.

The first ostensible measure was taken by a party composed of members of the two Councils, in concert with General Bonaparte and his friends. The first meeting of those members took place on the 16th of Brumaire at the house of Lemercier, the President of the Council of Ancients, when the plans and the means by which they should be accomplished were decided on. It was agreed at this meeting that the two Councils and Directory should be transferred to St. Cloud and that the Commission of the two Councils should propose the measure to the Council of Ancients, in an extraordinary assembly, to be convened for the purpose on the 18th at seven o'clock in the morning. The arrangement being made, those members parted under a pledge that each should endeavor to draw over the deputies of his acquaintance to its support by exciting a belief that a great crisis had arrived, of the insurgent character, and that the measure proposed was indispensable to the safety of the state. The Commission of Inspectors sent letters to those members of the Council of Ancients who they knew would favor the plan, to meet on the 18th at the hour appointed, withholding the summons from those who they knew were opposed to it.

The meeting took place. The members who were not in the secret expressed their alarm, as they entered the halls, at the extraordinary session, and inquired into the cause which had produced it. They were informed by the others that the anarchists from all parts of France had collected in Paris with intention to overthrow the existing government, restore the National Convention with a Committee of Public Safety, and that the first act of the Mountain party would be the proscription of General Bonaparte, the director Sieyès, and Roger Ducos, and of all the members of the two Councils who were considered by them as aristocrats. The Council of Ancients passed a decree at this meeting, the 18th, by which the legislative corps was transferred to St. Cloud, to meet on the 19th, and General Bonaparte was charged with its execution and invested with ample powers for the purpose. The National Guard and all the troops in and near Paris were put under his command and the citizens were enjoined to obey his summons and execute his orders, should he have occasion for their services. He attended the Council, accepted the trust, and pledged himself by oath to execute it with fidelity. Guards were in consequence immediately posted at the Tuileries and St. Cloud to protect the two Councils from assault or interruption, by insurrection or otherwise, should the measures contemplated and in train produce that effect; and likewise to impose awe on that portion of the people of Paris by whom such movement in other instances had been made. In the Council of Ancients, the affairs had been so well arranged, and such was the advantage gained in the commencement, that little difficulty was experienced there in any stage of the proceeding. In the Council of Five Hundred the struggle was violent. Lucien Bonaparte, who presided, was insulted and driven from the chair, and the General was struck at with a dagger, which was warded off by a grenadier. It was understood, and plainly to be inferred, that there was a decided majority on that Council against the change, but such was the imposing attitude assumed by the advantage gained in the other house by the popularity of the General, who took the lead, and by the force arranged on his side and under his banner, that those opposed to it gradually desponded and yielded the rule to the other party.

As soon as it was known that the Council of Ancients had held an extraordinary session, a meeting of the Directory was called. Three members only attended, Barras, Bohier and Moulin. Sieyès and

Roger Ducos joined the Commission of Inspection, of the Council of Ancients, and supported the projected change. The three members who met sent for the ministry of the government and the commandant of the military force at Paris, and inquired of them what had produced the movement reported. The General stated that the command had been transferred to General Bonaparte and that he was a subaltern under him. These members found that their power was gone and made no effort to recover it. Barras sent his resignation, or dismission, as it was called, to General Bonaparte, who accepted it. No other meeting was held or attempted.

The Directory being thus overwhelmed and all opposition in the two Councils having ceased, a decree was passed by the two Councils by which a provisional government was instituted and endowed with all the powers belonging to the existing government, and with the power also to prepare amendments to it in all the parts which were thought to require them. This government consisted of an Executive composed of three members, entitled Consuls, and of a Legislature with two branches, each consisting of 25 members, one of which was taken from the Council of Five Hundred and the other from the Council of Ancients. The right of originating laws was given to the first, and of approving or rejecting them to the other. In preparing amendments to the Constitution, the two legislative commissions were to act in concert and harmony with the Consuls. In the Consular department, Sieyès, Roger Ducos and General Bonaparte were placed. Affairs being thus arranged, the two Councils adjourned to meet on the first of Nivose, about six weeks afterwards, with the power they then held. Thus the existing government was essentially overthrown and the fortune of the Revolution and the destiny of France were put under the control, so far as the two Councils would accomplish it, of those whose object it was to subvert the existing system and establish a government founded on opposite principles and with a view to their own advancement.

The report which was made of a change in the government, by the three Consuls, and the legislative commissions of the two Councils, corresponded with what might have been, and doubtless was, anticipated from what had preceded. The sovereignty of the people was acknowledged, but all power was essentially taken from them. An Executive was instituted consisting of three Consuls who were to hold their offices for ten years and be reeligible. The principal authority was given to the First Consul. He had the power to appoint and remove Ministers of the government, Ambassadors to foreign powers, Generals of the armies, and Councillors of State. A Legislative Corps

was also instituted, consisting of two branches, one composed of 100
members, called the Tribunate, the other of 300. Neither could origi-
nate any act. The Consuls had the right to submit every proposition
to their consideration, commencing with the Tribunate, and which,
if approved by it, was sent to the other branch. The members of neither
branch were elected by the people. A Corps called the Conservative
Senate, consisting of from 60 to 80 members, was instituted, who
appointed the members to each branch. When a vacancy occurred
in the Senate, the First Consul nominated a person to fill it, as did
each of the legislative commissions, and the Senate chose between
them, and thus preserved their own Corps by appointing themselves.
The Senators held their office for life. They likewise chose the Consuls, members of the Tribunal of Cessation, and commissions, who
were charged with the care of the public treasury. The First Consul
appointed all the other officers in the administration and judiciary.
Thus the power was taken completely away from the people. The
sovereignty was acknowledged to be in them, but as to its exercise it
was so nominally only. Those who filled the different departments
of the government had the means of preserving the power in their
hands without reference to the people; nor were they responsible to
them, in the mode, to give affect to the sovereign authority in the
ordinary administration, nor otherwise, than by insurrection and revolution. The Conservative Senate had the elective and appointive power
without the right to supervise or call to account for misconduct those
elected and appointed. They occupied the place of the people, in those
respects, who were put down; but in performing the service, they
were mere instruments of a controlling power. The whole power of
the government was committed to the First Consul, and who, by the
dependence of every department on him, was in effect the sovereign
of the nation, of which other and the strongest proofs were afforded.
On the 8th of May, 1802, the Senate prolonged his term of service
for ten years, and three months afterwards appointed him for life,
with power to appoint his successor.

The first of these changes, by the institution of the Consular
government, took place in 1799, under which, with those which
followed, the government had been in operation about four years
when Mr. Monroe returned to France in 1803. Would the government, in its then state, be preserved, fluctuating and unsettled as it
was, or would the power be wrested completely from the people and
they be reduced to slavery by making it permanent and hereditary; or
would the people assert their rights, revolt to the principles of the

Revolution, and establish a well-organized representative government
in accord therewith? To this object Mr. Monroe's attention was drawn,
and respecting which he had then formed no decided opinion, but was
inclined to think that the progress would be in a direction unfriendly
to liberty. The Republic of Rome was overthrown by an armed
force. There were different orders in the State, a Senate and the
people, who contrived against each other. Their armies were composed,
at an advanced period, of foreign mercenaries. They were commanded
by Consuls, who by their victories gained popularity, and in the progress of time, as the principles of liberty were undermined, aspired to
the sovereignty, involved the country in civil war, and thus over-
threw the system. But in France the case was different. There was
but one order in the State, that of the people. Her armies were composed of native citizens attached to their country and friendly to
liberty. They had fought gallantly for it and triumphed over the surrounding nations, and would not fight against it nor against each
other. If a revolution took place and despotism should be established,
it must proceed from internal causes and the aid and instrumentality of
the civil authority. The best propositions of the people and of the
armies might be practiced on and embarked in its support, or at
least silenced. The internal disorders which had existed in the course
of the Revolution; the exhaustion which had been produced by so
long a war; the fall of the paper money and the want of a circulating
medium, with the general distress of the people, would favor the
change. All these circumstances, many of which were inseparable
from such a revolution, might be urged as proof of the incapacity
and misconduct of those who had had the rule of public affairs, and
inspire a hope that by placing in power revolutionary characters who
had given proof by their past conduct of their devotion to liberty and
were thought more competent, they should be relieved from their
distress. The overthrow of those they denounced, with the benefits
promised by the change, would be the ostensible objects, and the
great mass might not look to the consequences contemplated and sure
to follow. As the two Councils had taken the lead in the commencement and the responsibility of the change as far as it had gone, and
General Bonaparte was the person who had been placed at the head
of affairs and in whose favor any further change would operate, it
would be difficult to raise an opposition that might be proposed. He
had acquired great glory as a military commander and was very
popular with the armies and the nation. Those who had been put
down, who had before taken the lead, would not dare to stir. The

armies, it was probable, would not move against him from their attachment to and confidence in him personally, and as the civil authority had brought him forward apparently in its support, internal movement of the people would be equally improbable, as they might be considered and punished as insurrections. On this view of the subject, Mr. Monroe was inclined to think that the Revolution would fail in its great object and the ancient system be restored in the person who then held the power and stood so high with the nation. Having witnessed through the whole of his first mission the great zeal which had been displayed by the people of France in favor of liberty; the exertions they had made; the difficulties they had encountered; and the sufferings they had borne in support of that great cause, it was natural that the impression which was then made on him of the probable result should give him great pain.

The motive for the order to General Bernadotte to leave Paris on the day in which it was expected that Mr. Monroe would arrive there was no longer involved in mystery. He was one of those popular generals of whom the First Consul was jealous. Military chiefs were the only competitors whose standing with the nation could give him any inquietude. Pichegru had sunk in the public estimation; Hoche was dead; Bernadotte and Moreau were still in his way. To get rid of the first, the government of Louisiana had been offered to him, which he was willing to accept on certain conditions, which were refused. He was then offered the mission to the United States, with power to adjust all the differences with that rising Republic, and to which other inducements were added of a personal nature of a very alluring character. This offer he accepted and was commissioned accordingly. The object of the First Consul was to settle those differences in Paris and to turn the accommodation with the only well-founded Republic in the world to his own account in promoting the great object of personal aggrandizement which he then had in view. In settling those differences in a manner to attract the public attention and excite the public feeling, his conduct would form an interesting contrast with that of the Directory, who had by the want of self-command and a sound and correct policy, involved France in hostility with the United States. Had General Bernadotte remained a few days only in Paris after the arrival of Mr. Monroe, he would have seen that his mission, whatever might have been the prospects held out to him, would have proved as to fame an empty phantom. He was ordered on the day specified to Rochelle, the port at which a frigate was preparing for him and to which he promptly repaired. By mere accident, that frigate was sent on another service to the Isle of

France, and in consequence his departure was prevented until the treaties were concluded, on hearing of which he returned to Paris, indignant at what had occurred. This information was given to Mr. Monroe at the time and by authority entitled to unlimited confidence.

Silver tray made in London, 1794–1795, by Peter and Ann
Bateman, silversmiths, and inscribed "To the
Honorable James Monroe, Esquire, from His
Friends and Admirers Associated, London,
1803," presented to him while he was
Minister to England.

6

At the Court of St. James

Mr. Monroe left Paris on the 12th of July, 1803, and taking the route of Amiens and Calais, arrived in London on the 18th. He immediately apprised the Secretary of Foreign Affairs of his arrival and requested him to appoint a time when he might wait on and present him a copy of his letter of credence as Minister Plenipotentiary of the United States to his Britannic Majesty. His Lordship appointed the next day, with which Mr. Monroe complied, delivered to him a copy of the document referred to, and expressed his desire to be presented to his Majesty as soon as it might be convenient. Lord Hawkesbury regretted that Mr. Monroe had not arrived a few days sooner, as in that case he might have been presented at the last levee. He assured him, however, that he should be presented without delay, and as he inferred, at the next levee, which would occur a fortnight afterwards. On the day preceding that alluded to, Mr. Hammond, who had been Minister Plenipotentiary to the United States and was then Under Secretary in the Department of Foreign Affairs, called on Mr. Monroe and informed him that the death of Lord Bristol, the father of Lady Hawkesbury, of which an account had been received the night before, would render it impossible for his Lordship to attend the Court the next day; that he hoped it might be agreeable to him to wait another fortnight, at which time he would attend in person and present him; but if he had any objection to the delay, he would request one of his colleagues to render the service on the next day. Mr. Monroe assured Mr. Hammond that it was far from his desire to give to Lord Hawkesbury any trouble: that he would wait with pleasure the time when it would be proper and convenient for his Lordship to present him.

In commencing the mission to England, Mr. Monroe was sensible that those in which he had been employed to France might have excited a suspicion in the British government of his partiality for one to the prejudice of the other nation. His reception by the National Convention in his first mission to France had attracted the attention of all the powers at war with her, and of none with more feeling than Great Britain. His late mission, which had terminated in the cession of Louisiana, had a like tendency. On these points he was incapable of making any explanation to the British Ministry himself, but he was resolved so to regulate his conduct by principle as to give no countenance to such suspicion, if he did not remove it. On the day succeeding the last levee, he was engaged to dine with Sir Francis Baring at his seat in the country, with Mr. Hope, whom he accompanied thither. On the passage, Mr. Hope noticed the fact that he had not been presented to the King on the preceding day, and in a manner to invite an explanation of the cause. Mr. Monroe gave him the explanation, as he did to Sir Francis Baring, with a request that they would communicate it to no person whatever. He stated to them that he thought it probable that the fact of his not having been presented might be noticed by others, and attributed to the cause above suggested; that if any explanation was necessary for the public, it must come from the government and not from him. They approved his conduct, and Mr. Hope observed that he knew the fact stated by Mr. Hammond of the death of Lord Bristol to be correct; that he died at home, and of which he had been advised by a letter which he had received the night before.

A few days before the next levee, Sir Stephen Cotterel called on Mr. Monroe and informed him that he should be presented to the King at that levee and that he would attend and conduct him there. It was impossible for Mr. Monroe to be presented to King George III without experiencing sensations of a peculiar character. From his very early youth, impressions had been made on his mind against that monarch. While at the College, he had attended the debates in the General Assembly and Convention, all of which represented him as unfriendly to liberty. He had fought in our revolutionary struggle against his troops and witnessed in many of our states the distress to which our citizens were exposed in that unjust war. Time had essentially diminished these impressions, but it had not entirely removed them.

The King received Ministers on their first presentation in a private room adjoining the public one. He was conducted to it by Sir Stephen Cotterel, received there by Lord Hawkesbury, and presented to the King. His reception was favorable and kind. It is usual for the Minister who presents his letter of credence to accompany it by the communication of the sentiments which are entertained by his government for the sovereign to whom it is addressed, and for the nation at whose head he stands. Mr. Monroe did this in a very respectful and conciliatory manner. He stated to His Majesty that he was instructed by the President to declare to him, in explicit terms, his desire to maintain the most friendly relations between the two countries, as well from sentiment as interest, and that it would be his object, and in the success of which he should take great interest to preserve that relation by a faithful obedience to the orders of his government. His Majesty replied in a frank and candid manner that nothing was more reasonable than the sentiments which Mr. Monroe had expressed; that since our Revolution he took an interest in our welfare and wished our prosperity; that the motives to a sincere and constant friendship were numerous and strong, such as having the same origin, speaking the same language, and great commercial intercourse. He inquired of Mr. Monroe from what state he came; where was he educated. Mr. Monroe replied that Virginia was his native state, and that he was educated in William and Mary College. The King spoke with interest of that institution and its early establishment. He then adverted to some incidents of Mr. Monroe's public life which had attracted his attention: "You have been in France?" Mr. Monroe replied that he had and at a very interesting epoch in his first mission. "You know those people. You will now become acquainted with those of this country and be able to judge between them. They have no religion, have they?" Mr. Monroe was somewhat embarrassed at this interrogatory, having just left France, where he had many friends and [had] been a party to a transaction of great interest to his country, which was yet unfinished; but after a moment's pause he remarked, with a smile, that there were many people there who, he believed, had none. The King appeared to be satisfied with the answer, and added, he believed there were few who had any. The reception was apparently intended as a favorable one and was, as Mr. Monroe inferred, owing in part, at least, to his not having been presented at the preceding levee, and the desire of Lord Hawkesbury that it might bear that character, in consequence of some criticisms that had been made on the delay. Mr. Monroe left the King with impressions much more favorable to him than he had ever entertained before.

Mr. Monroe felt sensibly the delicacy of his situation in the very important trusts confided to him by his government. His mission to England imposed on him very interesting duties, Great Britain being one of the principal powers of Europe at war with France, and with high pretensions as to maritime rights. The arrangement with France was still unsettled and claiming his attention in many views, on which much might depend. His mission to Spain was still in force, to be acted on when his government should think the moment favorable, and in performing that service, it would be incumbent on him to pass through France to demand the aid of her government which had been pledged in the negotiation with Spain. When he left home he expected to have returned in a year or eighteen months at furtherest, but he was detained in those missions about five years, during which it cannot be said that he enjoyed a moment of respite.

The duties which Mr. Monroe had to perform with the British government were principally from the preponderance of Great Britain at sea and the interfering claims of the two countries respecting neutral and maritime rights. The law of nations was the only standard by which these claims could be settled, and that was viewed in some very important points in a different light by the two governments. France and Great Britain were again at war, and Great Britain had no means of oppressing her adversary other than by the ruin of her commerce. In pursuit of this object she came into conflict with the neutral powers, and with none more seriously than with the United States, whose commerce was extensive and who were then not felt or regarded as a maritime power. Great Britain carried her pretensions still further in regard to us. She boarded our vessels, annoyed our commerce, and violated our rights, not for goods only, but likewise for seamen. Having the same origin and speaking the same language, the sailors of one country resembled those of the other, and the commanders of her vessels of war, in pursuit of their own men, often took by force the native citizens of our country.

Lord Hawkesbury observed to Mr. Monroe, in their first interview, that all the points of variance between the two countries were then happily adjusted, specifying the debts due to British subjects, spoliations on our commerce, and their interfering claims respecting boundaries, the latter of which he had arranged with Mr. King a short time before his departure. Mr. Monroe expressed in reply the same sentiment which he afterwards did to the King when he was presented to him for recognition. To preserve that state—the war then raging between France and Great Britain and the First Consul menacing an invasion of England, and the latter striking at France in every point in which she was vulnerable—although the principles which ought to guide in every instance that might occur were simple and obvious, was nevertheless an object, the attainment of which, if practicable, regarding men and nations as they are, was fraught with difficulty. The incidents attending this very important epoch furnish examples which are very instructive and ought always to be held in view. If one belligerent violates the rights of a neutral power and that power does not resent and repel the aggression with becoming firmness, it is urged in justification of a like violation by the other, which is sure to follow, and thus the neutral power, however great its resources and adequate its means, becomes by its acquiescence the victim of the unjust policy and conduct of both. The more extensive the commerce of the neutral power is, the stronger the temptation to such aggression, especially with the belligerent whose force preponderates at sea, since there is a double motive for it, that of greater gain to the captors and greater annoyance to the enemy. Of the losses which the United States sustained by such aggression in the preceding war, called the War of the French Revolution, notice has been taken in the sketch which has been given of the occurrences of Mr. Monroe's first mission to France. Of his efforts to prevent the adoption of a similar policy by the British government in the war which then existed, notice will be taken in the sketch which we shall give of the incidents attending this, his mission to England. In every step which he took, it was necessary that he should have in view the arrangement which had been made with France, which was still unfinished in every important circumstance, and likewise his mission to Spain, so as to prevent any injury arising from it to the important concerns of his country depending with each of those three powers.

An incident occurred shortly after Mr. Monroe's arrival in England, relating to the treaties with France, which gave him great concern. By the joint letter of Mr. Livingston and himself to the Secretary of State, of the 7th of June, it was shown that after the treaties had been concluded and were ratified by the First Consul, a difficulty occurred by a claim on his part to annex a condition, as to the execution by the United States, which might defeat the whole arrangement. This difficulty related to the payment of the sixty millions of francs to France, the first installment of which it was stipulated by the 2d article of the first convention, should be made within three months after the ratifications should be exchanged and possession of the territory be delivered to the United States. The motive assigned for the proposed condition to the ratification of the treaties was to secure the payment by the United States of the sum stipulated, within the terms specified, although the possession of the territory might not be delivered to them within that term. Mr. Marbois's note stated this to be the object, and which was explicitly declared by Mr. Talleyrand in a conference which our Ministers had with him on the subject. In every view, they deemed the annexation of the proposed condition unreasonable and improper, because there was a reciprocity in the stipulation which would be defeated if the payment should be required before the territory was surrendered. The anxiety of our Ministers was increased by intimations that were given them by persons in whom they confided, that if the treaties had not been concluded, the negotiation would fail, the First Consul having declared that he considered the compact very disadvantageous to France. These persons thought it probable that the measure proposed was intended as an expedient to extricate himself from the compact, in the expectation that our government would furnish him with a justifiable pretext for it. Mr. Talleyrand, in his explanation, gave a different view of the motive. He stated contingencies over which the First Consul could have no control, which might create delay in the delivery of the territory. Spain might fail to surrender it within the term specified, or the British might seize it, and which were probably the real cause. But such was the excitement of the moment at Paris, the war with England pressing and important changes in the government in contemplation, and so inflexible was known to be the character of the First Consul in any measure of compromitment which he had adopted, that our Ministers felt it incumbent on them to avert, so far as they might be able, such a result to an arrangement which they deemed of such high importance to their country. On full consideration, they gave an answer to Mr. Marbois's letter which was satisfactory, and under which impression his letter was recalled and that of our Ministers restored, and an instruction given to Mr. Pichon, chargé d'affaires of France, substituted for them. The instruction to Mr. Pichon was read by Mr. Marbois to Mr. Livingston in an interview between them, with which Mr. Livingston was satisfied, and through him a message was sent to Mr. Monroe to request his attendance at Mr. Talleyrand's office, that it might be shown to him and with which he complied. Of the communication between Mr. Talleyrand and Mr. Monroe, in the presence of Mr. Marbois full notice has already been taken. It is therefore necessary to advert here to that part only which relates to the intimation which Mr. Monroe then gave, that so far as the Ministers had any power to promote the payment, and which he thought extended to the first installment, such was his confidence in the good faith of the French government that he would, under a conviction that the treaties would be ratified by his government, give his sanction to the advance in that amount by the two great houses who had bought the stock, even before the treaties were ratified, and in which he thought that his colleague would unite.

Although the presumption was strong from the communication of

Mr. Talleyrand and likewise from the letter of Mr. Marbois, that the command of the money independent of any contingency, was the sole object and had produced the difficulty, yet other impressions were not entirely effaced. As however, that only was assigned, it might fairly be concluded, if it was removed by the payment of a small portion only, that none other could ever be urged, and that although a delay might occur in the ratification of the treaties and creation of the stock by our government, the First Consul would be so completely bound in honor, as well as good faith, to carry the treaties into effect, that no further difficulty could ever be raised on his part. It was on this principle that Mr. Monroe gave the intimation which has been stated, in his interview with Mr. Talleyrand and Mr. Marbois, in full confidence that the treaties would be ratified and his conduct approved by his government. In any event, such was his anxiety to relieve his government from the embarrassment to which the suppression of the deposit at New Orleans had subjected it, and to relieve likewise his fellow citizens to the west from the losses incident thereto by a comprehensive and permanent arrangement in the spirit of his instructions, that he did not hesitate to take the responsibility of the measure on himself.

It was at this period and under these circumstances that an application was made to Mr. Monroe by the Houses of Hope and Baring, to guarantee to them ten millions of francs, which they had engaged to pay at that time to the French government, on account of the stock stipulated by the late treaties, to be paid to France by the United States for the purchase of Louisiana, and which those houses had bought of that government. Their application was supported by a letter from Mr. Marbois, who adverted to the offer which Mr. Monroe had made, to sanction an advance to that amount before the treaties were ratified by his government under the power which he thought had been given to our Ministers by their original instructions. Mr. Monroe did not hesitate to comply with this application, under the belief that the Ministers had the power, and that by the exercise of it they would promote most essentially the best interests of their country. He considered himself bound also, after what had passed, to act with promptitude and to invite the cooperation of his colleague with him, by urging in the strongest manner that he was able the reasons by which he was governed. It was not the responsibility which he thereby incurred which gave him inquietude, considering it his duty to do it, be the consequences as to himself what they might. He fearlessly met that danger.

It was a difference in opinion on that very important point with his colleague which gave him concern. Mr. Livingston thought they had no power over the two millions of dollars which were voted by Congress and subjected to their control, after the treaties were formed, and that the application or pledge of any portion of the money thus appropriated for the purpose and in the mode suggested was not only unauthorized, but could produce no good effect. Their correspondence on the subject was voluminous and interesting. Mr. Marbois, in his pressure for the guarantee, acted with great delicacy toward both our Ministers. The two houses at length agreed to take [the word] of Mr. Monroe alone, which they assured him would accomplish their object, and which he promptly gave. The instrument being then presented to Mr. Livingston he signed it, but with reluctance. As they had agreed in the extent of the acquisition and in the consideration to be given for it, and in the subsequent measures relating to it, this incident gave to Mr. Monroe pain, especially as the difference of opinion was with a person with whom he had long harmonized in political sentiments, and a friendly relation existed. A copy of the correspondence between our Ministers, and likewise of that between Mr. Monroe and Mr. Marbois on the interesting subject, was transmitted by Mr. Monroe to our government.

To the danger which the execution of the treaties, and accomplishment of the great object provided for by them, was exposed, by France and Spain, Mr. Monroe's attention was increasingly drawn, and respecting which, with the means of averting it, he communicated fully his sentiments in several letters to the Secretary of State. His position afforded him opportunities of acquiring information which he thought might be useful, and which he hastened to communicate to his government in the most minute detail. He was satisfied that the British government was gratified that France had ceded the territory. That government must have heard of the project which was entertained by the Directory, of acquiring and connecting it with Canada, and have apprehended that the acquisition of it by the First Consul was a part of the same system. By ceding it to the United States that danger ceased, and no new one was added in reference to the latter power. On the contrary, there was good cause to presume that an extension of territory to the south would diminish the motive for it to the north. Free governments, even of the confederated kind, are incapable of an extension beyond certain limits. He knew that Spain was dissatisfied with and had complained to the French government of the cession, and he was apprehensive that she would not surrender it within the term stipulated, whereby she would create embarrassments of a very serious character. The First Consul had intimated to Mr. Monroe, in the audience he gave him on taking leave, that Spain had complained of the cession, which he urged as a reason for his declining his visit to Madrid at that period. For the dissatisfaction of the Spanish government there were obvious reasons. While France retained the province, the power of that great nation formed a barrier against the United States in favor of all the Spanish provinces to the south of it. By the cession that barrier was removed, and the people approaching and having intercourse with each other, and the spirit of liberty extending, it was probable that the power of Spain would be immediately shaken and the whole territory be soon wrested from her by the people themselves. He was decidedly of the opinion that it would be advisable for his government to move, in taking possession of the province after the ratifications were exchanged, as if an objection on the part of Spain was not even suspected. The territory had belonged to France by a fair title. She had ceded it to us, and we had a right to the prompt possession of it. By acting on that principle, she would be forced to acquiesce, since by a different course she would not only assume a hostile attitude towards the United States, but likewise against France, who would be bound by good faith and honor to compel her to acquiesce, especially as the French government was in the receipt of the consideration stipulated for it, a part of which had already been paid before the treaties were ratified. Mr. Monroe was persuaded that his government would take the course suggested without any intimation from him, but he deemed it incumbent on him to share with it the responsibility, in case it should, and any injury result from it.

For the war in which Great Britain and France were engaged, it is believed that no justifiable cause can be assigned by either party when tested by sound principles. The pretext on the part of France was the refusal of the British government to give up the Island of Malta, which she was bound to do by the treaty of Amiens. That on the part of England was the aggrandizement of France on the continent, and particularly in Italy. Neither complained of a direct or positive injury to itself. Rivalry and passion contributed much to that result on both sides. The discussion which took place in the two houses of Parliament in the session of 1802–3 which excited in so high a degree the resentment of the First Consul, gave the first ostensible spring to it. Incidents afterwards occurred which increased the irritation on each side. His abrupt and harsh notice of the unfriendly temper manifested by the British government, in his address to Lord Whitworth, the British Ambassador, at a public audience, in presence of the whole diplomatic corps, excited great indignation on the other side of the Channel. War followed immediately afterwards. So far as any reasonable cause can be assigned on the part of England, it was the dread of the maritime aggrandizement of France, under the auspices of the soldier then at her head, and a desire to prevent it. France had by her revolutionary efforts gained in a great measure the ascendancy on the continent, and to which in the latter stages, he had much contributed. Leave her in a state of peace for a long time and he might elevate her naval force to a height to compete with Great Britain for the dominion of the seas, and in which if he succeeded, he might reduce her to a subaltern grade among nations. On the part of France no motive could be assigned of a public nature. The height to which she was already raised left her nothing to ask of the powers on the continent, and by temperate councils, cherishing peace rather than provoking war, she might form such an augmentation of her navy as would put her, on the other element, on equal ground with her rival.

If any motive could be traced, it was a personal rather than a public one. A change in the government was intended, and a state of war, especially with Great Britain, might favor that object. The First Consul held essentially all the power of the nation, and as the passions of the whole community would be raised and embarked on his side in support of such a war, the opportunity would be favorable for the confirmation of it in him and his descendants. Those were, we presume, strong motives on each side. To tranquilize the United States by a friendly accommodation of all differences with them had doubtless its weight, for the reasons stated, in the cession made by the First Consul of Louisiana to the United States. To prevent the aggrandizement of France on this continent and the control it would give her over the colonies, with the means of augmenting her naval force, it cannot be doubted were the motives which reconciled the British government to the cession and induced it, before apprised of it, to make the offer through Mr. King to take New Orleans and cede it to the United States at the peace. With the cause or motives to the war the United States had no concern. It was their duty and their object to maintain their rights and to preserve friendly relations with each power, so far as it might be done on just and honorable conditions. While the danger of invasion menaced Great Britain, her government cultivated the friendship of the United States. While the advancement of Bonaparte to the Imperial dignity was depending, he pursued the same policy.

Warned by the example of the preceding war of the aggressions which had been committed on the rights of the United States and of the injuries they had suffered by spoliations on their commerce and impressment of their seamen, Mr. Monroe was instructed, in the commencement of his mission to England, to use his best efforts to prevent the commission of like injuries in the existing war. The apprehension of such aggressions had been a strong motive with the President in appointing him to England, on the resignation of Mr. King, to take effect provided the affair with France should have been adjusted. In the first interview with Lord Hawkesbury, the subject was adverted to by his Lordship in a conciliatory manner, which was met in a like spirit by Mr. Monroe. In several subsequent interviews their conversation was resumed on the subject generally, in which his Lordship invariably manifested a disposition to accommodate. By agreement between them, Mr. Monroe presented on the 29th of November a note on impressment, founded on a report of Mr. Erving, who was then our Consul for the City of London and agent for the protection of our seamen, a citizen of merit, who was afterwards appointed our Minister to Spain. This aggression was more simple in its nature, was pressed by practice, and therefore demanded immediate attention. The object was to arrest this practice and to prepare by friendly communication the British government for an arrangement which should extend to every aggression, as exemplified by the practice of the proceeding war, as soon as he should receive from his government its views on each point, in a digested plan. In that stage of the war, no invasion had been made of our neutral rights by blockades and spoliations on our commerce, and it was hoped that none would be. It was the duty of Mr. Monroe, under the power which he possessed, to complain of abuses when committed, to prevent the repetition of them, and to use his best efforts to protect our citizens in full enjoyment of all their rights—by treaty, if authorized to make one.

When Mr. Monroe accepted the mission to France and Spain, he expected to have been absent not more than eighteen months at most, but he was employed abroad nearly five years. In that to France, from the time of his appointment, about six months had been devoted. In that to England, there was an interval, formed by his mission to Spain, which, including his visit and detention at Paris, occupied about ten months. Before that mission he was employed fourteen months in England, and after its termination, the residue of his term until his departure thence for the United States in November, 1807. As the epoch was highly important and the trust committed to him with each power very interesting to his country, it is proper to give a concise sketch of his conduct with each government, in every stage.

Of that with the government of France in what regarded the great object of the mission, a full view has already been presented. To do justice to the subject, attention is due to the state of the country with whose government he had to treat at each period, and likewise to those with whom he had to treat. The changes in the ministry of England during his mission there were frequent and numerous. Mr. Addington was the Chief Minister, or Premier, on his arrival in July, 1803, and he remained in power until May, 1804, when he yielded the place to Mr. Pitt, who held it till his death in January, 1806. During the Ministry of Mr. Addington, Lord Hawkesbury was Secretary of State for the Department of Foreign Affairs, as has been observed. On the accession of Mr. Pitt, Lord Harrowby was appointed to that office and Lord Hawkesbury transferred to the Home Department. With these persons Mr. Monroe had to treat before his departure for Spain, and with the latter, sometimes after his return. Of the subsequent changes, notice will be taken when we reach the periods at which they occurred.

To the note on the impressment of our seamen which had been presented to Lord Hawkesbury in November, some months had elapsed and no answer was received. Interviews were obtained of the Secretary of Foreign Affairs, who intimated that the note had been sent to the Admiralty, the head of which was Lord St. Vincent, and from whom no report had been received. The indisposition of the thing, the unsettled state of the Ministry, the two great parties of Mr. Fox and Mr. Pitt uniting in its overthrow, with the delicate nature of the subject, formed serious obstacles to any decision on it. The existing Ministry was unwilling on principle, as Mr. Monroe believed, to promote a rupture with the United States by aggressions on their rights, but it was equally unwilling to make accommodations which might be viewed, regarding the former practice, in the light of concessions.

On the 18th of March, Mr. Monroe received a letter from the Secretary of State, of the 5th of January, authorizing him to make a treaty with the British government for the protection of our seamen and of our maritime rights, in the instances that were most pressing, leaving others for future arrangement. For a full illustration of the President's views, the Secretary transmitted a project containing the objects contemplated, with the conditions on which the adjustment might be made. In compliance with this instruction, Mr. Monroe presented a project to Lord Hawkesbury early in the next month, in conformity with that sent to him, with a few omissions in less important instances, which if urged, he was satisfied would embarrass, if not defeat the others.

[Two sheets (500 words) are missing at this point. They must have dealt with the politics of Pitt's return to power.]

[Mr. Pitt] assumed a different attitude. His attacks bore on the talent of those in power, on their capacity to repel, by a proper application of the force and resources of the nation, the menaced invasion, and which he did in a tone of regret, whereby he took the ground more effectually from under them than he could have done by unqualified hostile assaults. We do not urge this as an imputation on the candor of Mr. Pitt. We think, on the contrary, that he could not have made an attack in any other mode consistent with his own principles and policy. It was understood that he had retired from the Ministry before, in accommodation with the public feeling, to leave the door open for peace under other auspices, to which he would not give his sanction. War being again restored, it was natural that he should wish to resume the direction of it.

As soon as Lord Harrowby was installed in the Department of Foreign Affairs, Mr. Monroe invited his attention to the various subjects which he had submitted to the consideration of his predecessor. His Lordship expressed his willingness to examine them with attention, but intimated that some time must elapse before he could act on them, owing to the great mass of business with which he had been so recently charged and the urgency of a large portion of it at that critical period. Mr. Monroe assured him that although he considered the subjects referred to as very interesting to his country, and as he presumed they likewise were to Great Britain, he should most willingly afford to him all the accommodation in his power. Some weeks had elapsed and no communication was received from Lord Harrowby, which gave to Mr. Monroe concern. The affairs of the United States were, in all instances, pressing. The change of ministry, with the restoration to head of the new one of the person who had held that trust in the preceding war, during which so much injury had been done to the United States, menaced a change of policy corresponding with that which had before prevailed, especially if the danger of invasion should cease and the war assume a more favorable aspect. It was important, therefore, to settle amicably all differences relating to impressment and neutral rights, at that period, if it could be accomplished on fair conditions. An arrangement of another concern, which had recently occurred, had become equally urgent. The treaty which had been concluded by Mr. King with Lord Hawkesbury for the settlement of boundaries had been ratified by our government, with the exception of the 5th article, which had been omitted in consequence of the acquisition of Louisiana, to prevent any difference which might arise under that treaty from the previous unsettled boundary, by a claim of the British government to any portion of that territory. Of this omission Mr. Monroe was advised by the Secretary of State and instructed to explain to the British government the reasons for it. He was also instructed to proceed to Spain, if the state of affairs with England would permit it. The board of commissioners, under the treaty of 1794, had concluded their business, and Mr. Pinkney,[71] who had been charged by our government with the settlement of a claim with the British government by the state of Maryland to some bank stock, and which had been nearly concluded with the preceding Ministry, was desirous of returning home. These considerations made occasional interviews with Lord Harrowby necessary, to arrange in the best manner possible every interest which could be arranged, and in any event, to prepare the British government for his departure for Spain, as soon as it might be done without injury to his country.

An interview was obtained on the 30th of May, which Mr. Pinkney attended, and who opened the subject respecting the claim of Maryland to some bank stock with an explanation of the ground on which it stood and of the state in which it was left by the preceding Ministry. Lord Harrowby promised that it should be promptly attended to and settled as soon as possible, on which Mr. Pinkney withdrew. Mr. Monroe then adverted to the other important concerns of his country, which were depending before the British government. He asked Lord Harrowby if he had examined the project respecting impressment and neutral rights which he had mentioned in their former interview. He had not; the other concerns which pressed on him had rendered it impossible. Had he examined the ratification of the treaty respecting boundaries? He had not, and for the same reason. He censured, however, in strong terms, the omission of the 5th article, or of any article from the ratification, which he considered a new practice that ought not to be sanctioned. He asked on what ground that article had been omitted? He was informed that it had been omitted on consequence of the cession to the United States of Louisiana, to prevent any dispute which the ratification might give birth to of a claim in the British government to any portion of the territory thus ceded; that the treaty in question was concluded without the knowledge of their respective governments that such a cession had been made, being, in fact, concluded almost at the same time with that by which cession was made; and, of course, that the territory thus acquired ought not to be affected by it; that the subject was still open for consideration and amicable arrangement, it being the object of the omission not to gain anything but to prevent a dispute by furnishing no cause for it. He still censured the omission with great severity, and which he thought gave to his government just cause of complaint. Mr. Monroe offered to leave the ratification with him but he declined taking it, observing that it was then impossible for him to act on it. From all that had passed in this interview, Mr. Monroe drew a very unfavorable inference of the prospect of arranging with the existing ministry any of the important points of his country that were depending with the British government.[72]

Other interviews soon afterwards ensued of a nature more conciliatory, but not of a character to authorize the presumption that an adjustment could be obtained on the points in question, or to justify Mr. Monroe's departure for Spain, or even to touch on that subject in his communications with the British Minister. Early in August he attended at the Foreign Office, at the request of Lord Harrowby, who asked him in what light our treaty of 1794 was viewed by our government. Did we consider it as having expired, under the article which stipulated that it should expire at the end of two years after the signature of the preliminary articles of the treaty which should terminate the then existing war between Great Britain and France? Mr. Monroe replied that he presumed there could be but one opinion on that point respecting the commercial part of the treaty, which was that it had expired: that the first articles were made permanent: that the others had been executed, but that those being limited to a definite period, which had passed, must be considered as having expired with it. He thought the case not so clear as had been stated: that the stipulation must have had in view a positive peace which [had] not existed, nor been preserved even in form.

Mr. Monroe observed that the distinction had never occurred to us, but if his government relied on it, it could certainly be duly [relied on] by that of the United States. His Lordship admitted that his construction was rather a forced one. What then, said he, is the existing relation between the two countries? Are we in the state in which we were at the close of your Revolution? By what rule shall our intercourse be governed as to imports, tonnage, and so forth. Mr. Monroe replied that those were interests which each country must regulate for itself. He asked whether our government would be willing that the treaty of 1794 should remain in force for two years after the conclusion of the existing war. Mr. Monroe observed that he had no power to agree to such an arrangement. Lord Harrowby then added that his government would probably adopt the treaty of 1794 as the rule of its conduct toward the United States, which he presumed would be approved and reciprocated by our government. Mr. Monroe repeated that he was not authorized to express any opinion on that point, but assured him that he would communicate to his government the proposal, and by whom it would be duly weighed. The intimation which Lord Harrowby gave as to the adoption of the treaty of 1794 by his government, as its rule of conduct towards the United States, was so general that it was inferred that he meant to apply it to the whole treaty, to neutral rights, as well as to commerce. Mr. Monroe deemed it incumbent on him to preclude the idea that he understood it in that sense, or would for a moment suspend the negotiation on the project which he had presented to Lord Hawkesbury, and was then depending before his government. To give any sanction to that inference would argue an indifference on those points, which was altogether incompatible with the views of his government and with his instructions. He attended, therefore, to that project and to the several objects which it embraced, and expressed a hope that his Lordship would soon be able to act on it. He declined entering into them for reasons he had before given, but in a manner more conciliatory. These subjects were then held on the distinct ground on which they had been before placed, and with a manifestation of the high importance which his government attached to a just and amicable arrangement of them at that time.[73]

On the 9th of August, Lord Harrowby gave notice that his government had blockaded the ports of St. Vallier, Dieppe, the Somme, Etaples, Boulogne, Calais, Gravelines, Ostend, Dunkirk, Nieuport, and others, and that the blockade would be enforced in the most rigorous manner. Mr. Monroe assured him that he would immediately communicate it to his government and to all the Consuls of the United States within the British dominions.

Several weeks having elapsed without hearing anything from Lord Harrowby respecting the decision of his government on the subjects submitted to it, Mr. Monroe concluded that it was its fixed purpose to make no arrangement of those points at that time. He deemed it, therefore, useless to press it. He thought it more advisable to meet its views in a conciliatory manner, on the presumption that he should thereby promote more effectually the interest of his own country in the immediate objects depending, and likewise favor his departure for Spain, which he was anxious to do in obedience to his instructions. With this view, he asked an interview with Lord Harrowby in a note of the 21st of August, for the special purpose, as he stated, of ascertaining the decision of his government on the points submitted to it.

By stating that to be the object of the interview, the negotiation would be brought to a point, and if the British government had resolved either to maintain its former practice or to accommodate, such declaration in either instance would terminate the negotiation. If, on the contrary, it had resolved to suspend the negotiation, to leave the subject open for future arrangement, dependent on events, the indication of that disposition would furnish a favorable opportunity to agree to and propose the suspension for the purposes and in the manner stated. The interview desired took place on the 1st of September, in which the whole subject of impressment, neutral rights, commerce, and the treaty concluded by Mr. King with Lord Hawkesbury respecting boundaries was entered into and discussed in the most amicable manner. As a motive for an early decision, Mr. Monroe took occasion to suggest the instruction which he had received from his government to proceed to Spain for the adjustment of affairs with that power as soon as it should be obtained. The communication was well received by Lord Harrowby, who assured Mr. Monroe that to favor his departure would be a motive with him to obtain of his government as early a decision on the points before it as he might be able. Fearing that the cause of the omission from the ratification of the 5th article of the Convention respecting boundaries might not be well understood by the Cabinet, Mr. Monroe addressed a note to Lord Harrowby a few days after this interview, in which he gave a full explanation of it.

Further delays and other circumstances occurred which satisfied Mr. Monroe that it was the intention of the British government to suspend the negotiation without making a declaration of its views or subjecting itself to a restraint of any kind, and, in consequence, he addressed a note to Lord Harrowby on the 29th of September in which he expressed his willingness to meet the object of the British government by the suspension of the negotiation, to give it full time to decide on the subjects involved in it. He intimated his intention to depart for Spain at an early day, leaving Mr. Purviance, Secretary of the Legation, in charge of the affairs of the United States, in obedience to the orders of his government. He added that his absence would be of short duration and that he would resume the negotiation on his return, when he hoped that his Lordship might find it convenient to act in it. Lord Harrowby's reply, which was on the same day, was of a very conciliatory character. He assured Mr. Monroe that he hoped to be able, after the delay suggested, to enter into a full discussion of every proposition which he had submitted to him, which were then before the Cabinet, but which from their importance required a longer time for their decision, that would be consistent with his duties at Madrid. A day was appointed for the reception of Mr. Purviance, in the character stated, on which day Mr. Monroe attended at the Foreign Office and presented him to Lord Harrowby in that character.

The negotiation was thus suspended by mutual consent in accord with the views of the British government. Had nothing more occurred in the negotiation, it might fairly have been inferred from the manner in which it was suspended that the British government would have pursued the same conduct in the instances embraced by it, during the suspension, and until it was resumed and concluded, by accommodation or otherwise, that it had done pending the negotiation and at the time of the suspension. It is due to candor, in regard to government and also to the character of Mr. Monroe, to add that he informed his government that Lord Harrowby assured him that his government would adhere to its principles during the suspension, but would act with moderation in the practice of them towards our country. The conduct of the British government, from the commencement of the war, had been moderate and friendly towards the United States in regard to neutral rights, and had been so represented by Mr. Monroe in strong and explicit terms in several letters to the Secretary of State.

At the period adverted to only one of their vessels had been condemned on any principle whatever, and on which decision an appeal had been taken. Another engaged in a trade between Batavia and Holland had been seized, and although the judge maintained the British doctrine, which the cause was in hearing before him, as to the trade of a neutral with an enemy's colony in war, which was not allowed in peace, yet it was not certain, should that trade fall under that description, that she would finally be condemned as others engaged in the same trade, which had been stopped and examined at the mouth of the Texel by the cruisers. The only restraint to which Mr. Monroe thought that the British government had in strict and rigorous construction subjected itself, was to make no change in its practice for some months after his departure, nor until due notice had been given to his government that such change was intended. The moderation which had been observed, it would not be doubted, had arisen from the difficult and embarrassed state of the country, menaced with invasion and standing alone as Great Britain did, without an ally to support her, and averse to throw[ing] the United States into the scale of her enemies. Under such circumstances the friendly conduct of the United States towards Great Britain gave them a stronger claim to the delay and previous notice suggested, before a change of policy should be adopted.

Silverware owned by James Monroe: Pair of Sheffield candlesticks,
circa 1795, bearing family crest; Sheffield punch bowl,
probably presented to him while he was Minister to
England during the period 1803 to 1807; silver
ladle, initialed "M," made in Edinburgh,
Scotland, in 1806.

7

Minister to Spain: A Diplomat Concludes His Education

The mission to Spain formed a new epoch in Mr. Monroe's second mission to Europe. It was connected by his appointment with that to France, and in this present stage its success depended essentially on the part the French government might take in it. In the negotiation for the cession of Louisiana, that government had pledged itself to afford its support to the United States in the negotiation which was contemplated with the government of Spain for the acquisition of the territory which remained to her on the eastern side of the Mississippi. To obtain that aid, Mr. Monroe was instructed to pass through Paris and to require it in the extent to which it had been pledged. In execution of this duty, he left London on the 8th of October, 1804, and passing circuitously through Holland, which became necessary on account of the existing war, he arrived in Paris on the 20th of that month. His reception by the First Consul, by his old friends, and by those in power generally, corresponded with that which had been given to him on his arrival there the year before.

The object of his visit was well known to the French government, as it was that his detention in Paris, regarding his duties elsewhere, ought to be of short duration. It had been proposed, as has been observed, to commence the negotiation with Spain immediately after the conclusion of that with France for the cession of Louisiana, and it was delayed at the instance of the French government. It was now thought, on an intimation from Mr. Livingston, that that government had then no objection to its commencement and was prepared to afford the aid which it had promised. Mr. Monroe expected, therefore, to be detained at Paris a few days only. Such, however, was the state of affairs at that period and the views manifested respecting the mission to Madrid, that an early departure, in accord with the French government, was found to be impracticable. A complete revolution, by the abandonment of those free principles for which the people of France had so long contended and shed so much blood, was about to take effect. The coronation of Napoleon Bonaparte as the Emperor of France had been decided, and the day on which it should be performed was not distant. Many in power pressed Mr. Monroe to remain and attend the solemnity. It did not accord with his principles or feelings to be present at such an event, but he saw distinctly, if he should depart before it occurred, that it would produce such an excitement as might defeat the mission to Spain. He saw also, to his great mortification, that such views were taken of the relative rights of the United States and Spain, that |unless| a change could be produced, it would be difficult if not impossible to form a treaty with the Spanish government which should comport with his instructions or the honor and interest of his country.

Mr. Livingston informed him on the night of his arrival that the prospect of success in the mission to Spain had of late become unfavorable: that Admiral Gravina, the Spanish Ambassador at Paris, had presented a memorial to the French government in which he had protested against our claim to West Florida and insisted that the province was restricted to a very limited boundary on the western side of the Mississippi, and that the French government had answered or prepared an answer to it, by which it was admitted that pretensions of Spain were well founded. Mr. Livingston stated also to Mr. Monroe that he had written a note to Mr. Talleyrand on the subject, to which he understood he had prepared an unfavorable answer, but which he begged him not to send to him, as his successor, General Armstrong, had arrived at the port and was daily expected in Paris. He stated also to Mr. Monroe that he had a plan for the settlement of our differences with Spain, which was that she should put us in possession of the disputed territory and that we should create a stock of seventy millions of livres and lend them to Spain, reimbursable in seven years, in equal annual installments, with a provision that the boundary should be settled in the interval by amicable negotiation. To this plan Mr. Monroe objected. He remarked that it was not authorized by their instructions and might terminate in our paying twice for the same territory, especially as it did not comprise East Florida, the only portion to which we had not a just claim. Mr. Livingston added that that might likewise be provided for.

The mission to Spain had three objects in view: the first, the settlement of the boundaries of Louisiana; the second, the acquisition of the territory remaining to Spain eastward of the Mississippi; the third, the indemnity for injuries by spoliation on our commerce and by the suppression of the deposit at New Orleans. Mr. Monroe was satisfied that the French government took part against us on every point, and from motives of a peculiar character. He was assured by authority entitled to confidence that the government of Spain was indebted to that of France a considerable sum under certain stipulations relating to the existing war, and that the French government expected to receive whatever sum the United States might engage to give for the territory which might be ceded. This view was confirmed by informed communications with some in power with whom he had daily intercourse, and who had the best means of information, and to which it was added that the French government thought that Spain was entitled for the whole of the territory which she held eastward of the Mississippi, should she make the cession, to a sum nearly equal to that which had been given for Louisiana. From these communications Mr. Monroe was satisfied that the cause of Spain had become that of France, and that it would be impossible to form a treaty with the Spanish government consistent with his instructions and on just principles unless an impression should be made on it that the failure would produce consequences fatal to Spain; that in looking to her welfare, it might be separated from or be induced to act so powerfully on the French government as to produce a change of policy in it.[74]

Knowing the connection which existed between the two governments and the dependence of that of Spain on that of France, he hesitated whether he ought to proceed in the mission or abandon it and return to England, but on mature consideration he concluded that it would be most advisable to proceed although it should fail. Should he abandon it in that stage, Spain might think herself slighted and degraded, and France be equally offended. The cause of its failure might likewise be desired. By pushing it to its natural result in the course it had taken, the conduct of every party would appear in its true light. If the French government failed to perform its duty, according to the pledge it had given as to the contemplated cession and the existing relation between the two countries, in other respects, that would be seen, and obtain its merited censure from the American government and people. Should Spain refuse to render justice to the United States, a like view would be taken of her conduct. By pursuing the negotiation to a regular termination, nothing could be lost and much might be gained. His government would have the whole subject before it and might pursue the course which a just sense of its rights and interests might dictate

A question occurred in this stage, whether he should leave France in silence after all that he had heard of the views of the French government, or make an effort to produce a change in its policy by a fair and candid appeal to its good sense, its good faith, and the interest of the nation. Should he proceed in the mission without making such an effort, some sanction might be given to those views, as he was satisfied they had been communicated to him with the knowledge and at the instance of the government, to reconcile him to them. In every instance in which they were communicated, he repelled them with decision, which he presumed had been reported to the government; but he thought that it neither comported with the character of his government, with his own, or the interest of his country to withdraw without taking a more decisive attitude against them.

By a full development of all the objects of the mission to Spain, it would be shown, if the rights of the United States were secured in the points specified, that not one cent could come to Spain, although the territory sought should be ceded. Such a development would prove that West Florida formed a part of Louisiana and had been ceded to the United States by France, and that our claims to indemnity for spoliation on our commerce, and that suppression of the deposit at New Orleans, if settled on just principles, would exceed the sum which could be given for East Florida, if valued by any fair standard. All hope of gain and every motive of interest would thus be extinguished in the French government, whereby the prospect of obtaining its aid in the negotiation would be improved, or at least its interference to the prejudice of the United States, if not already compromitted to that effect, be prevented.

That he had a right to make this communication to the French government and that it was imperatively his duty to do it, regarding the trust which he then held, the object of his visit to Paris, and his previous relation to that government, cannot be doubted. As Envoy Extraordinary to Spain, authorized to treat with her government jointly with our Minister there on several important principles, and particularly for the cession of Florida, on which all the others would essentially depend, he had been ordered to pass through France to obtain the aid of her government in the negotiation for that cession, which had been pledged in the preceding negotiation for the cession of Louisiana. This circumstance alone formed an official relation between him and the French government, especially as it was known to it that he had such orders, would make the visit, and the object of it. There were others of a still more decisive character. He had been Envoy Extraordinary to France in the mission which had obtained the cession of Louisiana, and to him jointly with Mr. Livingston, the pledge to render that aid had been given, and to him afterwards, before his departure for England, when he was about to prosecute the mission to Spain, it had been renewed. It will be recollected that the postponement of the mission to Spain was at the instance and in accommodation with the views of the French government, and that the promise then made of affording that aid was in the expectation that he would return and prosecute the mission at a period more suitable to that government. By his original appointment the mission to France and Spain had been united, because the cause which produced them was so, and the subsequent incidents adverted to tended to unite them more closely. Thus his official character to the French government could scarcely be said to have ceased. The relation to it was evidently such as to authorize a direct communication with it, and which, under existing circumstances, it would have been highly reprehensible in him to have neglected. It might fairly be presumed also that such a communication from him would not be disregarded. He alone knew the conditions on which a treaty could be formed. His declaration to that effect would be entitled to respect, as he would be bound by good faith and a respect to his own character to state the truth. The communication would, of course, be respectful and confidential, and on the points which applied to the information he had received of the views of the French government, such as would throw light on the rights and views of his own government without any imputation or reference to those of that of France.

Mr. Monroe addressed a note to this effect to Mr. Talleyrand on the 8th of November, 1804, in which he gave a full development of every subject on which he had to treat with the government of Spain, and particularly of the opinion which his government entertained of the extent of the territory which had been ceded to the United States by France, with the ground on which it was founded.[75] The province when held by France in its original state extended, as was believed, on the right of the Mississippi to the Rio Bravo, and on the left, or eastern side, to the Perdido. In 1762, France ceded the Island of New Orleans and all the portion lying to the right to Spain, and that part lying to the east, extending as above stated to the Perdido, to England. While Great Britain held territory in that quarter, she divided it into two provinces. The portion which she had previously held she called East Florida, and that which she had thus acquired of France, she called West Florida. In 1783, she ceded both provinces to Spain, and then Spain became possessed of the province of Louisiana in the full extent that France had held it. By

the treaty of St. Ildephonso Spain ceded it to France in 1800 in exchange for Tuscany, in the same extent that it had in her hands, and
that it had when France possessed it, and such as it should have after
the treaties entered into between Spain and other powers. If it had
been intended that this cession should have comprised the province
in its dismembered state, it would have been easy to have given it that
limitation. But when it was seen that care was taken to preclude that
idea, and that the most guarded terms were adopted to secure to it
its original form, and to which Spain was fully competent, there was
not the slightest foundation for such a construction. It was obvious,
therefore, that the territory which Spain would have a right to cede
would be of little value, that it would comprise East Florida only,
which estimated by any correct standard, would not more than indem-
nify the United States for the injuries of which they so justly complained. In this note he pressed with great earnestness the pledge which
had been given by the French government, pending the negotiation
with it, to support that contemplated with Spain, to obtain the cession
of Florida. He sent to him also a copy of the view he had taken at
that period of the extent of the territory ceded on both sides of the
river, bounded on the right, as already observed, by the Rio Bravo,
and on the left, by the Perdido.

It is painful to remark that Mr. Livingston was seriously opposed
to this measure, considering it, as he informed Mr. Monroe, an interference with his rights and duties as Resident Minister there. His
opposition involved much discussion between them, but the impression
being decisive on Mr. Monroe that he ought to take the step, Mr.
Livingston at length acceded to it and communicated Mr. Monroe's
note with the paper referred to in it to Mr. Talleyrand. Mr. Monroe
inferred that Mr. Livingston's opposition arose from the plan he had
adopted for the settlement of differences with Spain, which he intimated he had communicated to his government and to which he had
received no answer. As that plan differed altogether from Mr.
Monroe's instructions, by which he was bound, it furnished an
additional motive for making the proposed communication to the
French government, especially as it was favorable, that government was acquainted with it. General Armstrong, the successor to
Mr. Livingston, arrived at that period, and being consulted on the
whole subject, approved the measure, as Mr. Monroe understood, the
note which was finally communicated to Mr. Talleyrand.[76]

Mr. Monroe had been pressed on his arrival at Paris, with great
solicitude, to remain and attend the coronation, which he wished to
avoid if he should be able to do it without attracting attention by

his departure and exciting an unpleasant feeling to the injury of his
mission to Spain. This would depend altogether on his obtaining a
prompt arrangement for the support of that mission in the instance
in which it had been pledged. It has been shown that in accomplishment of that object he had been disappointed. In seeking it he had
been detained while he entertained the hope for a short period before
that event occurred and, as he was apprehensive if he departed then
it might operate to his prejudice, he resolved to wait and attend it,
which he accordingly did. The solicitude for his attendance had
diminished, and by the government itself no invitation was given to
him. Being apprehensive that the cause of his failure to attend, should
that occur, might be misrepresented, General Armstrong, at his instance, informed the Minister of Foreign Affairs that he would remain
and attend the solemnity, with a request that a suitable place might
be assigned to him. On the day preceding the event he dined with
Mr. Marbois, who expressed an earnest hope that he might meet him
on that important occurrence the next day. Mr. Monroe informed
him that no invitation had been given to him. Mr. Marbois expressed
his astonishment at the neglect, arose from the table, and wrote a
note to the master of ceremonies requesting that he would immediately
invite Mr. Monroe and his family to attend the solemnity and assign
to him and them the proper stations in the Church of Notre Dame, in
which it was to be performed. At a late hour in the night two sets
of cards were received, one at the instance of General Armstrong,
the other of Mr. Marbois. He was placed in the gallery, in a great
measure out of sight, and not with those in his grade, the Foreign
Ministers. His inference was that this inattention proceeded from the
difference which existed between him and the government as to the
object of the mission to Spain, and a knowledge that he would look
solely to the infraction of his government and the interest of his
country. Mr. Talleyrand had likewise a seat in the gallery, on the
opposite side, and being within view and observing each other, a
salutation passed between them, so that his attendance was known to
the government.

By those who communicated to Mr. Monroe the views of the
French government respecting the relative claims of the United States
and Spain, and the support which was given by it to those of the
latter, and in whose representation he had full confidence, he was
assured that the difference of sentiment between Mr. Talleyrand and
him had not excited any unfriendly feeling towards him. Mr. Talleyrand's conduct towards Mr. Monroe during his mission to France the
year before and on his present visit corresponded with that representa-

tion. Mr. Monroe had formed an acquaintance with him in the United States in 1794 on the introduction of Colonel Hamilton, and while in France on his first mission an opportunity occurred in which he was enabled to render him an essential service. At the moment when the Convention was about to transfer power to the Directory and the two Councils, some of his friends were desirous to repeal the decree which prohibited his return to France. This was opposed. It was known that he had been in the United States and, in consequence, several of the popular members, and among them Louvet and Tallien, applied to Mr. Monroe for information respecting his conduct there. Inquiry was made, did he indicate hostility to France and a support of the allied powers against the Revolution? Mr. Monroe assured them that he saw no proof of that feeling, that his conduct, so far as he was acquainted with it, was calm and friendly to his country. Of his disposition in regard to the Revolution he knew nothing. The decree was repealed, and permission granted to him to return, which Mr. Monroe had good cause to conclude was promoted by the representation received from him. He does not know that this fact was known to Mr. Talleyrand, but he thinks it probable that it was, and that it produced the kind feeling suggested.

Although those latter details are of minor importance, yet as they tend to place in a true light the conduct of each government with its motives, and of those who acted under them in those very interesting concerns, it is thought proper to give them a place in this narrative.

More than a month elapsed and no answer was received, when it was inferred that none would be given. In this interval the coronation took effect, which Mr. Monroe attended with his family. Having thus done everything in his power to secure the good offices of the French government in negotiation with Spain, there seemed to be no motive for him to remain longer in Paris, and in consequence he departed for Madrid on the 9th of December, 1804. We state with pleasure that Mr. Marbois gave him a letter to General Beurnonville, the French Ambassador to Spain, requesting his good offices in the negotiation with the Spanish government, and acquainted him fully in all respects of the engagements he had entered into.

Under these circumstances Mr. Monroe left Paris on the 9th of December, and taking the route of Bordeaux and Bayonne through France, and of Victoria Burgos and Levona through Spain, arrived at Madrid on the 2d of January, 1805.

In entering Spain and treating with the Spanish government, very different sensations were excited from those which arose in the mission to France, in either instance, or in that to Great Britain. In all governments in which the people hold exclusively the sovereignty, in whatever state they may be, or in which they participate with other orders, the spectacle which they exhibit in their movement is interesting and instructive. All the great passions of man are in operation and, moving to the same result, show to the intelligent observer how far one modification, either of principle or organization, is better calculated to preserve liberty and promote the happiness of the community, than another. In those of the first class, at a period of revolution and convulsion, although the government which may be formed is that with which you have to treat, yet as the people in that state move in mass and form in reality the government, a course of conduct may be necessary to gain their good will, to prevent the most serious injury. In well-organized governments of this class, where the people are competent and confine themselves within their appropriate sphere, the movement is simple and the Executive is the sole object to which Foreign ministers meet and must look. The Directory of France, notwithstanding all its difficulties, reached this state. In mixed governments, although the Executive power is vested exclusively in the monarch, yet as public measures depend essentially on the other branches, and especially the popular one in which the contest for power between the opposition and the Ministry, which is often violent, takes place, it is incumbent on Foreign Ministers to be guarded in their intercourse with the leaders of the opposition, although respect be due to them lest it might impair their standing with the Ministry and the monarch himself to the injury of their respective countries. But in a government which is perfectly despotic, in which the people count for nothing, there is but one object that demands attention, which is the ruling power of the state. On the government, a few words might give its character, but that is so well known that none are necessary. The view which may be taken of the people of the country; of its agriculture, commerce, and the state of the arts and sciences, is descriptive only. Of man, you have an inanimate painting before you. His passions are hidden and the human character is lost. A like decline is visible on almost every other object. We shall confine our remarks here to that of the mission, the negotiation with the government of Spain, and its result in all its bearings. To others, some attention may be shown hereafter.

On Mr. Monroe's arrival at Madrid he appraised Mr. Pinckney[77] of it, who immediately called and communicated his arrival to Mr. Cevallos, the Minister of Foreign Affairs, who was then at Aranjuez, to which place the King with his family and Ministers were then moving, it being the residence of the Court during the winter. Mr.

Cevallos, in his reply, invited our Ministers to Aranjuez, that Mr. Monroe might be presented without delay to the King. With this invitation they promptly complied and had an interview immediately after their arrival with the Minister. Some excitement having occurred between Mr. Pinckney and the Minister before Mr. Monroe's arrival, Mr. Pinckney offered in the interview to leave the negotiation altogether to Mr. Monroe and to sign whatever they might agree on. The Minister observed that he should treat with pleasure with any Ministers whom the President might appoint. On the 13th Mr. Monroe was presented to the King, who received him with kindness and attention. Immediately after his presentation, he received a letter from Mr. Madison of the 25th of October, with a commission authorizing him to treat singly with the Spanish government, provided he should deem it expedient so to do. This measure was adopted in consequence of the disagreement suggested between Mr. Pinckney and the Spanish Minister, with which the President had become acquainted. Mr. Monroe thought that Mr. Pinckney's aid in the negotiation might be useful, and that the disinterestedness with which he had offered to withdraw from it before the latter commission was received gave him a strong claim to his continuance, which he intimated to him, and with which he complied.

As the points involved in the negotiation were of a distinct and definite character, and the part which the French government might act in it was a contingency on which the result might depend, our Ministers were desirous of placing each point on its merits, in the most explicit and intelligible form, to do justice to the subject and to the character of the governments of France and Spain in an occurrence which was highly interesting to the United States. They assumed also that in this mode they should hasten the negotiation to an early termination, and if it should fail, in a manner the most honorable and advantageous to their government and country. With this view they addressed their first note to Mr. Cevallos on the 28th of January, 1805, in which they gave a full development of every subject on which they proposed to treat. They sent to him at the same time the project of a treaty which corresponded with the note.[78]

The project comprised four objects: first, an indemnity for spoliations on our commerce; second, a like indemnity for the injuries sustained by the suppression of the deposit at New Orleans; third, the settlement of the boundaries of Louisiana; fourth, the acquisition of East Florida. The project contained seven articles, commencing with the confirmation of the cession made by France of Louisiana, with an extent eastward of the Mississippi to the Perdido; and with the cession of the territory remaining to Spain on that side, placing the inhabitants on the same ground in which those of Louisiana were placed by the treaty with France. The second article proposed that the River Colorado, from its mouth to its source, with other specified limits, and the Rio Bravo should remain vacant for . . . years. The third, that the boundaries of Louisiana should be traced and established within the term specified in the second. The fourth proposed that a board of commissioners should be formed with power to adjust the claims for injuries committed in the late war by individuals of either nation, or by others within the jurisdiction of the other nation, contrary to the law of nations, the treaty existing between them on the principles of justice, and to grant awards for the same. By the fifth, the board was authorized to adjust the claims for the injuries sustained by the suppression of the deposit at New Orleans. The sixth contained a stipulation that the United States should pay all sums due by Spain to their citizens for the seizures specified in the two preceding articles, not exceeding . . . dollars, with a provision that if those sums should exceed that which might be agreed on, the balance should be paid by Spain, and if less, that the United States should pay the surplus to Spain. The object of this stipulation was to fix the price of Florida. The seventh fixed the periods within which the treaty should be ratified and exchanged. The note and project were both drawn in the most liberal terms in respect to any claims of Spain, and most conciliatory to the Catholic King that could be used.

On the subject of boundaries, our Ministers sent to Mr. Cevallos with their note and project a copy of the view which had been taken by Mr. Monroe on the conclusion of the treaty with France, which proved, as they presumed, that they extended to the Rio Bravo on the right and to the Perdido on the left, or east, of the Mississippi.

In reply to this note and project, Mr. Cevallos proposed, in his of the 31st of January, to examine each point separately, to take up one at a time and to postpone the others until that should be decided. He adverted to three subjects which had been submitted to his consideration: first, damages by spoliation on our commerce; second, [damages] by the suppression of the deposit at New Orleans; and third, the demarcation of the boundaries of Louisiana. Respecting the cession by Spain of her right to territory eastward of the Mississippi he said nothing. To damages for the suppression of the deposit he denied our right, it being, as he said, the unauthorized act of the Intendant. Respecting the boundary, he observed that the King had appointed for their demarcation in the commencement of 1804 an agent, who was then at New Orleans, invested with the necessary power. The only subject on which he proposed to enter was that of the claim to damages for spoliations on our commerce, which he said had been essentially adjusted by the Convention of August, 1802, which had been ratified by our government and would be by his when certain obstacles were removed. He did not even allude to the spoliations which had been committed by French cruisers within the jurisdiction of Spain, but seemed rather to preclude the idea of bringing them into view. It was obvious from Mr. Cevallos' reply that it was the intention of his government to accommodate on no point, to protract the negotiation as long as possible with a view to interpose the government of France between those of the United States and Spain, for the relief of Spain.

At this period Mr. Monroe received a letter from General Armstrong, our Minister at Paris, of January 6th, with a copy of one to him from Mr. Talleyrand, of December 21st, which was intended as a reply to that of Mr. Monroe, of the 8th of that month.

Mr. Talleyrand confined himself to one point only, the extent of Louisiana on the east of the Mississippi, which he affirmed was bounded by that river, by the Iberville, and the Lake Pontchartrain, and that it did not include West Florida or any portion of it. He dwelt on the term "retrocession" in the treaty of San Ildephonso, to which he gave the most rigorous construction, confining it to the portion which had been conveyed by France to Spain by the treaty of 1762 and excluding that which had been ceded by her to England at the same time, and afterwards by England to Spain. He spoke of a correspondence which had taken place in the negotiation of the treaty of San Ildephonso, by which the province had been ceded to France, and an understanding to that effect which grew out of it. He considered the divisions which had been made on that side and the changes of sovereignty which each part had undergone as precluding the possibility of any portion of the territory, between the bounds specified and the Mobile, as belonging to Louisiana, or being comprised in the cession of it by Spain to France, or by France to the United States.

This note of Mr. Talleyrand confirmed the representation which had been given to Mr. Monroe at Paris of the views of the French government relative to the points to be adjusted between the United States and Spain, as it did of the probable issue of the negotiation. We shall not dwell on the merits of the question here. We cannot, however, withhold the remarks which are applicable to the conduct of the French government in this important occurrence. France had ceded to the United States the province of Louisiana in the full extent that it had been ceded to her by Spain, and to make the title complete in that extent, had inserted in the treaty with the United States the third article of the treaty of San Ildephonso, by which the cession was made to her.

The right of the United States was, therefore, to be tested by the fair import of that article, according to the well-established rules of construction. There was nothing in the treaty to impair it, and every circumstance that occurred in the negotiation tended to increase its force. It would have been more agreeable to our Ministers had the boundaries of the province been defined, since to such limits the consideration would, of course, be adopted. When the object in all its parts, is known, the value may be more easily ascertained, since in that case there could be no difference with Spain respecting them— whereas, if left unsettled, such difference might arise, which she wished to avoid. Their view was communicated to the First Consul by Mr. Marbois, who reported to them his remark on it, which was that if the boundaries were not obscure, they ought to wish to make them so. No stronger proof could be afforded that the boundaries were obscure and that it was the intention of the French government to give to the article the most liberal construction that it could bear pending the negotiation, to enhance the value and price. How far it might comport with propriety to take the opposite ground after- wards, and to give it, in support of Spain, the most contracted, under the change of circumstances and the different state in which the parties were, the impartial will decide. That it had been communi- cated to the Spanish government in reply to the note of Admiral Gravina at the time suggested by Mr. Livingston could not be doubted.

To this note of Mr. Talleyrand no reply could be given by Mr. Monroe. It was not addressed to him nor intended to produce a dis- cussion with him. The sole object of it evidently was to throw the weight of France into the scale of Spain against the United States in the negotiation depending between them. It remained for our Ministers to pursue the negotiation on the principle heretofore suggested, look- ing, in the spirit of their instructions, to both powers in the prosecu- tion of it.

In prosecuting the negotiation with the Spanish Minister, his reply to their note would naturally form the basis of their next communica- tion. As all the subjects contemplated by the negotiation had been presented in their note, with a full development of each claim, with the conditions on which they were willing to adjust them, with [as] his reply had neither accepted nor proposed anything, the negotiation seemed to be essentially at a stand. In denying the right to the well-founded claim arising from the suppression of the deposit at New Orleans, resting it on the unauthorized act of the Intendant, and for which his government was not responsible, after their discussion, that point seemed to be useless. And by stating that his government had appointed an agent and given him full authority to make the boundaries of Louisiana according to the cession made by France to the United States, their right to set up any opposite pretensions seemed to be precluded. In regard to spoliations in the preceding war, so far as they respected an important branch, those committed by French cruisers within the jurisdiction of Spain, that claim likewise seemed to be rejected. The only subject on which he seemed to think we had a right to complain and on which he showed a disposition to treat was that relating to spoliations committed by the subjects and citizens of each power within the jurisdiction of the other, respecting which a treaty had been concluded and ratified by our government but not by his. On this he was willing to proceed, with a view to obtain certain accommodations in favor of Spain, which were specified. He professed, however, a willingness to examine every subject which had been brought forward and to conclude a treaty on conditions on which they could agree for the adjustment of every difference existing between the two countries. Our Ministers saw no prospect of obtaining a satisfactory arrangement, especially after receipt of Mr. Talleyrand's letter. Painful, however, and unprofitable as the discussion might be, they resolved to proceed in it until every subject should be placed in its true light.

In performing this duty they resolved to do it, so far as it might comport with a just sense of what was due to the rights and honor of their government and country, in accord with the plan which had been sketched by Mr. Cevallos, which was to take up one subject at a time and to commence with their respective claims. In a note of the 5th of February, 1805, they gave a full development of these claims, and particularly of that respecting the aggression by French cruisers within the jurisdiction and under the sanction of the Spanish government, which had not been provided for by the treaty of 1802, and likewise of that arising from the suppression of the deposit. They considered Spain as equally responsible for the one class of spoliations as for the other, on the principle that every independent power was answerable for whatever occurred under its jurisdiction, whether committed by its own people or those of another power, if acquiesced in by it. A contrary doctrine could not fail to make the power to which it applied an instrument in the hands of the other and to deprive it completely of its sovereignty. With respect to the suppression of the deposit, they considered the Spanish government responsible for the act of the Intendant, whether committed by its order or not, although in a spirit of conciliation they were willing to admit that it was his unauthorized act and not that of the government. In either instance it was a violation of our treaty with Spain by which we had sustained great injury, and for which, as her government was bound to execute it, she was responsible.

As Mr. Cevallos had intimated that His Catholic Majesty had appointed an officer and given him powers to mark the limits of Louisiana, he seemed to invite a notice of that subject also, and in consequence it was observed that that officer could not perform that duty until the principle by which those limits should be defined should be settled by the two governments. This afforded an opportunity to refer to their former note on that subject with the proof it afforded that the province extended on the right of the Mississippi to the Rio Bravo and on the left to the Perdido. This was deemed the more necessary as it apprised his government that the opinion expressed by that of France was not binding on the United States. In noticing the claim to indemnity for spoliations on their commerce, our Ministers observed that they could make no stipulation respecting it, unless those committed by French cruisers and condemned in Spanish ports were provided for in like manner with the others, [they] having recently received a special order to that effect from their government.

In concluding their note, they remarked that as they had given the explanations on the particular point on which he had asked them, and the whole subject was then before his government, both in detail and in a general view, and had been long under its consideration, they presumed that he would give them a corresponding answer. They added that it would be in the power of his sovereign to fix the relations which should exist between the two countries, and as the United States had exerted their best efforts to place and preserve them on a more friendly footing, they indulged a strong hope that His Catholic Majesty would meet them in a like spirit. (They were induced to make these remarks from a belief that should the negotiation fail, as they were satisfied it would, the sooner it was brought to that result the better the effect would be on the future relations between the two countries. They thought also that an independent tone was best calculated to obtain success.)

Mr. Cevallos, by his reply on the 10th to this note, confirmed the impression which our Ministers had before taken of the result of the negotiation. He expressed his willingness to treat of claims, but confined himself to spoliations on our commerce and to those only which were committed by the citizens and subjects of each power on the property of the other, within its own jurisdiction, which were provided for by the treaty of 1802, the ratification of which had been suspended by his government. He explicitly rejected those which were committed on our commerce by French cruisers within the jurisdiction of Spain by demanding that the article by which the rights of the parties were reserved, by the treaty, should be expunged from it, or that his government should be authorized to make such exceptions and declarations respecting it as would destroy its effect. He likewise brought the subject of boundaries into view, though unconnected with claims, and in a manner to assert the right of Spain to West Florida and to treat any pretension to it by the United States as an outrage on her government. As the limits of Louisiana were undefined, and our government was satisfied that they extended on the east of the river to the Perdido, it had as much right to occupy any vacant territory in that quarter to that extent as Spain. The act of Congress which authorized the taking possession of Louisiana was founded on that principle, but the President, in a spirit of great moderation and conciliation, suspended its execution until the boundary should be settled by amicable arrangement. The act was censured in the harshest manner, and the President's proclamation termed equivocal. No disposition was shown to cede the territory in that quarter, nor was the proposal to establish a vacant territory on the western side of the river, within, as was thought, the limits of Louisiana, with a view to the tranquility of the Spanish provinces, even noticed.

Under these circumstances our Ministers thought it improper to proceed further on the subject of spoliations, and doubted whether they ought not to consider the negotiation as terminated. As, however, he had proposed to discuss one point at a time and had selected that of claims, one branch of which, that of spoliations only, he had entered on—a large portion of which he had rejected—yet as he had brought the others into view incidentally, although in treating on them he precluded all prospect of accommodation, they thought proper to consider that point alone as disposed of, and called on him for the decision of his government on the others. These consisted of the injuries arising from the suppression of the deposit at New Orleans; of the adjustment of the boundaries of Louisiana; of the proposition they had made of the cession by Spain of her territory eastward of the river; and of the establishment of a neutral territory between Louisiana and the Spanish provinces to the west. Their note to this effect bore date on the 12th of February.

Mr. Cevallos' reply of the 16th corresponded with his previous notes. He complained of the unwillingness of our Ministers to proceed in the discussion on the subject of spoliations although as they presumed, the subject had already been settled; they having informed him that unless both classes were provided for, no stipulation could be agreed on, and he having decisively rejected one. He communicated an extract from a note of the Minister of Foreign Affairs of 27th of July, 1804, to the Minister of Spain, which stated that France had by treaty extinguished those claims, and that Spain, by countenancing them in any manner, had made an improper condescension, which his government highly disapproved.

The claim to an indemnity for injuries arising from the suppression of the deposit, he treated with like disrespect. The grant on which it was founded, he said, was gratuitous, and for three years only, and had been prolonged in a like spirit four years beyond that term. [He added] that the suspension had been owing to the abuse of the privileges by smuggling, to the great injury of the revenue of Spain, and that the injury was trifling, as our merchants had loaded and unloaded their vessels in the stream. He complained of misrepresentation and abuse in our papers of his government, and intimated that our government, instead of listening to such falsehoods, should have solicited in a respectful manner the renewal of the grant with the privileges attending it at some other point less injurious and more agreeable to his government. He added that he would then proceed to discuss the limits of Louisiana. Our Ministers thought that this note indicated great disrespect for their government, and concluded that his object was to reject every claim, in the expectation that they would finally abandon them and offer a sum for the territory eastward of the Mississippi which should correspond with the views and wishes of the French government.

To this calculation they were resolved to give no countenance, and in consequence a note of the 18th of February asked an interview before they gave a reply to it. They observed that they considered his note as tending to terminate the negotiation in an unfriendly manner, which they wished to avoid, and sought the interview in the hope that it might yet be possible to arrange amicably all the differences existing between the two countries. The note from Mr. Talleyrand formed no obstacle to this measure. On the contrary, it increased the motive to it, as they wished it to be understood that their government stood on independent ground and would judge for itself in all questions touching its rights and honor.

In Mr. Cevallos' note of the 16th, he intimated his intention to proceed in the discussion of the boundaries of Louisiana. His note on that subject was received by our Ministers before they had sent to him their note demanding an interview. They nevertheless resolved to communicate it to him, but to do it with their reply to his on the boundaries. They deemed it improper to suffer his arguments on that subject to pass unanswered, or to make it dependent on the explanations he might give respecting his offensive note of the 16th. Should his argument respecting the boundaries not be answered, it might be inferred that it was irresistible and that the interview was demanded to avoid giving one. They thought it proper, however, in reply to his note on the boundaries, to state their objections to that of the 16th and to his management of the negotiation in every preceding stage. Their note to this effect bears date of the 26th of February. They announced it to him in a short one of the same date, in which they informed him that, having prepared it with intention to have communicated it before, they had sent to him both, that the whole subject might be before him at the same time.

In a review of the negotiation from its origin, the offensive note formed an incident which grew out of what had previously passed in it. Our Ministers thought it advisable to notice that note when by a regular progress they should reach that stage. Much had occurred to show the moderation, spirit of conciliation, and candor which had animated them, and the indecision, evasion, and procrastination which he had practiced in every stage. By presenting this contrast in a clear light, as might be done by reference to the documents, it was presumed that a more favorable result might be obtained, and in any event, if his government had resolved not to accommodate, that it would bring the negotiation to a more speedy termination.

Our Ministers reminded Mr. Cevallos, in the note which had been specified, that in their first interview after Mr. Monroe had been presented to the King all the objects of his mission had been fully communicated, and that it was agreed that they should present to him a project for the adjustment of every point, and to which he would give an early and explicit answer. They stated that they had presented to him a project in accord with the agreement, with a note illustrative of the rights and views of their government on each point, in the expectation that he would have given an answer equally full and explicit on the whole subject. They observed that his answer differed in all respects from that which they had expected. To the very important points contained in the project respecting the boundaries of Louisiana, the cession by Spain of East Florida, and an arrangement, by the establishment of a neutral territory between our southern states and the Spanish provinces, to secure their peace and tranquility, no answer was given. The only proposition which he did make was to discuss each point separately and to commence with that on the spoliations committed by the cruisers of each country on the commerce of the other, respecting which a Convention had been formed, which had been ratified by our government but not by his. By confining the proposed discussion to such spoliations, those which had been committed on our commerce by French cruisers in the ports of Spain were by strong implication rejected; the claims to an indemnity for the injuries arising from the suppression of the deposit at New Orleans were rejected in explicit terms.

Our Ministers predicted from this note of Mr. Cevallos the failure of the negotiations, because they inferred from his silence on the important points, and the procrastination which would arise from the manner of the proposed discussion, that his object was to profit of the aid of France on those points, and in every instance in which it would be given. They knew also that the French government would afford that aid in regard to West Florida by declaring that it had not been included in the cession made by France to the United States of Louisiana, and that our claim for spoliations committed by French cruisers in Spanish ports had been provided for by their treaty with the United States. The alternative thus presented to them was either to demand an explicit answer on every point, with the project of a treaty which the Spanish government was willing to form, or to proceed in the discussion in the manner he had proposed. On full consideration they concluded that the latter course was the best adapted to the circumstances of their country and views of their government, and adopted it. They were the more decided in favor of this policy from its accord with the view they had taken before the negotiation commenced, of its probable failure, and the propriety of tracing the cause to its proper source by showing the part which each government had taken in it. [There are two remaining sheets of manuscript, about 500 words, which are omitted here because they are recastings of the preceding.]

Notes

1. Monroe wrote to Sir John Sinclair, 17 November, 1817: "My family was from the Highland of Scotland, a place called Fowlis, lately owned by Sir H. Monro. My ancestor emigrated about the year 1645, having been an adherent to the house of Stuart, and induc'd to leave the country, in consequence of its misfortunes. He settled on the Potowmack in Virginia, where I was born. Tho' young, at the commencement of our revolution, I took part in it, and its principles have invariably guided me since. Nothing can be more deeply fixed, in the judgment and heart of anyone, than are the principles of our free system of government, in mine. Tho' so many years have elapsed, since my family emigrated to this country, as to make us in a great measure, a distinct race, I have nevertheless always looked to Scotland, and to those of the same origin there, with peculiar interest. To be in any degree connected, or allied with you, cannot fail to afford me much satisfaction." This previously unpublished letter belongs to Mr. and Mrs. Philip Lang of Lake Forest, Illinois, and is quoted with their kind permission.

2. In 1774, Monroe's last year with Parson Campbell, his companion on the long walk to school was John Marshall. See W. P. Cresson, *Monroe*, p. 7.

3. Monroe's recollection of this night was far more vivid than he chose to indicate here. At a White House dinner, as President, he gave the following account to Lewis Coryell: "After crossing the river, I was sent with my command (a piece of artillery) to the intersection of the Pennytown (now Pennington) and Maiden Head (now Lawrenceville) roads, with strict orders to let no one pass until I was ordered forward. Whilst occupying the position, the resident of a dwelling some distance up the lane, had his attention directed to some unusual commotion by the barking of dogs. He came out in the dark to learn the cause, and encountered my command, and supposing we were from the British camp, ordered us off. He was violent and determined in his manner and very profane, and

wanted to know what we were doing there such a stormy night. I advised
him to go to his home and be quiet or I would arrest him. When he discovered that we were American soldiers, he insisted that we should go to
his house, and not stay out in the storm, and he would give us something to
eat. I told him my orders were strict and we could not leave, when he
returned to the house and brought us some victuals. He said to me, 'I
know something is to be done, and I am going with you. I am a doctor,
and I may help some poor fellow.' When orders came for us to hasten to
Trenton, the doctor went with me." See W. W. H. Davis, "Washington on
the West Bank of the Delaware, 1776," *Pennsylvania Magazine of History
and Biography*, IV, 148.

4. While the foregoing paragraph interrupts the narrative and was certainly intended to be used elsewhere, it is left here, as Monroe left it, since
it suggests his concern not to overplay his youthful revolutionary exploits.

5. In May, 1779, Washington wrote the following letter to Archibald
Cary in Virginia: "Dear Sir: I very sincerely lament that the situation of
our service will not permit us to do justice to the merits of Major Monroe,
who will deliver you this, by placing him in the army upon some satisfactory
footing. But as he is on the point of leaving us and expresses an intention of
going to the Southward where a new scene has opened, it is with pleasure
I take occasion to express to you the high opinion I have of his worth. The
zeal he discovered by entering the service at an early period, the character
he supported in his regiment, and the manner in which he distinguished
himself at Trenton, where he received a wound, induced me to appoint him
to a captaincy in one of the additional regiments. This regiment failing from
the difficulty of recruiting, he entered into Lord Stirling's family and has
served two campaigns as a volunteer aid to his lordship. He has in every instance maintained the reputation of a brave, active, and sensible officer.
As we cannot introduce him into the Continental line, it were to be wished
the State could do something for him, to enable him to follow the bent of
his military inclination and render service to his country. If an event of this
kind could take place it would give me particular pleasure, as the esteem I
have for him, and a regard to merit conspire to make me earnestly wish to
see him provided for in some handsome way." (*Writings of George Washington*, ed. Fitzpatrick, Vol. 15, 198–199.)

6. Something of the problem Monroe faced at the time in deciding
whether to remain in Williamsburg with Wythe, or go to Richmond with
Jefferson when the capitol was moved, can be felt in a letter from his
fatherly uncle, Joseph Jones: "Charles Lewis' going down to the College
gives me an opportunity of answering by him your inquiry respecting your
removal with the Governor or attending Mr. Wythe's lectures. If Mr.
Wythe means to pursue Blackstone's method I should think you ought to
attend him from the commencement of his course if at all. . . . The
Governor need not fear the favor of the community as to his future appointment while he continues to make the common good his study. I have

no intimate acquaintance with Mr. Jefferson but from the knowledge I have of him, he is in my opinion as proper a man as can be put into the office, having the requirement of ability, firmness, and diligence. You do well to cultivate his friendship and cannot fail to entertain a grateful sense of the favors he has conferred upon you, and while you continue to deserve his esteem he will not withdraw his countenance. If, therefore, upon conferring with him upon the subject he wishes or shows a desire that you go with him, I would gratify him. Should you remain to attend Mr. Wythe, do it with his approbation and under the expectation that when you come to Richmond, you shall hope for the continuance of his friendship and assistance." (Hoes Collection, Library of Congress microfilm.)

7. See Monroe, *Writings* (ed. Hamilton) I, 3–8, for a long report to Governor Jefferson written during this mission. (Hereafter cited as *Writings*.)

8. Once in the legislature Monroe was careful to keep his political fences well·mended. On August 15, 1782 he wrote a long letter to Washington containing such passages as this: "Having gone through that course which in the opinion of Mr. Jefferson, to whom I submitted the direction of my studies, was sufficient to qualify me in some degree for public business, in my application to my country in the first instance, and in the subsequent appointment of the Assembly to the Executive Council of the State, I have had the pleasure to experience your friendly letter in my favor of essential service to me." And this: "If in the line of my present appointment fortune should put it in my power to pay attention to or obey in any instance your Excellency's commands, believe me she could not confer a favor on me I should receive with greater pleasure from her hands." (*Writings* I, 19–22.)

9. Monroe had assisted Jefferson in drafting the famous "Ordinance of 1784." This document was actually a committee report without force of law. See *Journals of the Continental Congress,* ed. Fitzpatrick, XXVI, 275 ff. Monroe gave his support to Jefferson's clause, defeated by Congress, "that after the year 1800 there shall be neither slavery nor involuntary servitude in any of the said states."

10. Fort Stanwix. For Monroe's views on the treaty see *Writings,* I, 46 ff.

11. In a letter to Jefferson after his return to Trenton Monroe wrote that "my excursion hath been attended with great personal exposure and hardship and much greater expense than I had expected." (*Writings,* I, 41.) This long letter gives a contemporary account of the trip richer both in color and interpretation than his recollections after forty-odd years. Monroe says nothing here of his purchase, jointly with Madison, of some 8,000 acres in New York. The land came into their hands in 1785, but they could not afford to hold it as absentee owners and were never able to take up residence on it. See Irving Brant, *Madison,* II, 324 ff.

12. In his letter to Jefferson covering a copy of the pamphlet (*Some Observations on the Constitution, etc.*) Monroe wrote: "From the first view I had of the report from Philadelphia I had some strong objections to it. But as I had no inclination to enlist myself on either side, made no communication or positive declaration of my sentiments until after the Convention met. Being however desirous to communicate them to my constituents, I address'd the enclos'd letter to them, with intention of giving them a view thereof eight or ten days before it met, but the impression was delayed so long, and so incorrectly made, and the whole performance upon reexamination so loosely drawn that I thought it best to suppress it." (*Writings*, I, 187–188.)

13. The house, "Ashlawn" near Jefferson's "Monticello," was partly designed for Monroe by Jefferson, and is now a museum.

14. Jefferson, Washington's Secretary of State, had been Minister to France from 1784 to 1789.

15. Monroe's memory was faulty. He wished very much, in 1788, to move from the Virginia Assembly to the U. S. House of Representatives, ran for a seat against Madison, and was defeated.

16. Again Monroe's memory betrays him. His correspondence with Jefferson in October, 1790 shows that he was, in fact, making every effort to get Grayson's seat in the Senate. For example, "After the most mature reflection I have at length yielded to my inclinations to suffer my name to be mention'd for a publick appointment." Again, "Mr. Harvie, Mann Page, Walker, and Governor Harrison are in or rather will be in the nomination, and as some of them are active in their own behalf it is extremely doubtful how it will terminate." Finally, "I have determined in great measure in case of my election to abandon my profession." See *Writings*, I, 217–220. The election actually took place in November and Monroe arrived at Philadelphia to take his seat on December 6, 1790.

17. Monroe's contemporary correspondence gives no hint of any such considerations.

18. The text of Monroe's unprecedented address was as follows: "Citizens, President and Representatives of the French People:—My admission into this Assembly, in the presence of the French Nation (for all the citizens of France are represented here) to be recognized as the Representative of the American Republic, impresses me with a degree of sensibility which I cannot express. I consider it as a new proof of that friendship and regard which the French Nation has always shewn to their ally, the United States of America.

"Republics should approach near to each other. In many respects they all have the same interest. But this is more especially the case with the American and French Republics:—their governments are similar; they both cherish the same principles and rest on the same basis, the equal and unalienable rights of men. The recollection too of common dangers and difficulties will increase their harmony, and cement their union. America had her day of oppression, difficulty and war, but her sons were virtuous and brave and the storm which long clouded her political horizon has passed and left them in the enjoyment of peace, liberty and independence. France, our ally and our friend, and who aided in the contest, has now embarked in the same noble career; and I am happy to add that whilst the fortitude, magnanimity and heroic valor of her troops, command the admiration and applause of the astonished world, the wisdom and firmness of her councils unite equally in securing the happiest result.

"America is not an unfeeling spectator of your affairs in the present crisis. I lay before you in the declarations of every department of our Government, declarations which are founded in the affection of the citizens at large, the most decided proof of her sincere attachment to the liberty, prosperity and happiness of the French Republic. Each branch of Congress, according to the course of proceedings there, has requested the president to make this known to you in its behalf; and in fulfilling the desires of those branches I am instructed to declare to you that he has expressed his own.

"In discharging the duties of the office which I am now called on to execute, I promise myself the highest satisfaction; because I well know that whilst I pursue the dictates of my own heart in wishing the liberty and happiness of the French nation, and which I most sincerely do, I speak the sentiments of my own Country; and that by doing everything in my power to preserve and perpetuate the harmony so happily subsisting at present between the two Republics, I shall promote the interest of both. To this great object, therefore, all my efforts will be directed. If I shall be so fortunate as to succeed in such manner as to merit the approbation of both Republics I shall deem it the happiest event of my life, and return hereafter with a consolation, which those who mean well and have served the cause of liberty alone can feel."

19. Monroe here refers his reader to his *View of the Conduct of the Executive, etc.*, which he published in 1797 after his return, for the text of the letter. I have omitted his footnote references to this pamphlet. The *View* may be found in Volume III of *Writings*. For the letter to Randolph see *Writings*, II, 16 ff. This was Edmund Randolph (1753–1813), Secretary of State 1793–1795.

20. See *Writings*, II, 31 ff.

21. The Paine episode was one of the most interesting, and annoying, of his mission. It is curious that Monroe does not make more of it here. Paine violated Monroe's hospitality and betrayed his friendship by writing vicious attacks on the American administration and on Washington personally, while Monroe's guest. Monroe was fearful that he would be assumed to share Paine's sentiments and to have conspired in their publication. In fact he had asked Paine's word not to participate in politics while living in his house. See Monroe's letters to Madison, January 20 and July 5, 1796. (*Writings*,

II, 440 ff. and III, 20 ff.) He reported Paine's release to Secretary Randolph on November 7, 1794. See *Writings*, II, 98 ff.

22. Text of the note is in *Writings*, II, 41 ff.

23. Text in *Writings*, II, 88 ff.

24. See letter to Randolph, January 13, 1795, *Writings*, II, 167 ff.

25. See Monroe's letters to Randolph, January 13, and Jay, January 17, *Writings*, II, 167, 180 ff.

26. See *Writings*, II, 182 ff.

27. See *Writings*, III, 407–408.

28. *Writings*, II, 193 ff.

29. *Ibid.*, 206 ff.

30. *Ibid.*, 217 ff. "Thomas Pinckney (1750–1828), Minister in London, negotiated the Treaty of San Ildephonso with Spain in 1795."

31. *Ibid.*, 238 ff.

32. *Ibid.*, 229 ff.

33. *Ibid.*, 238 ff.

34. *Ibid.*, 272 ff.

35. *Ibid.*, 304 ff.

36. *Ibid.*, 339 ff.

37. *Writings*, III, 415 ff.

38. *Ibid.*, 424 ff. Randolph resigned 19 August 1795 under charges that he had conspired to prevent ratification of the Jay Treaty and was paid by the French. His public career was ruined, but he was never tried, and returned to Virginia to become one of the leading lawyers of his generation. He was succeeded as Secretary of State by Timothy Pickering. Randolph's conduct is "vindicated" by the modern scholarship of Irving Brant. See his *Madison*, III, 425 ff.

39. *Writings*, II, 368 ff.

40. *Ibid.*, 379 ff.

41. *Ibid.*, 407 ff.

42. *Ibid.*, 454 ff.

43. *Ibid.*, 460 ff.

44. *Ibid.*, 463 ff.

45. *Ibid.*, 484 ff.

46. Monroe's long letter, here summarized, is in *Writings*, II, 467–483.

47. *Ibid.*, 489 ff.

48. See *Writings*, III, 439.

49. *Ibid.*, 1 ff.

50. *Ibid.*, 4 ff.

51. See *Writings*, III, 8 ff. and 440.

52. *Ibid.*, 27 ff.

53. *Ibid.*, 48 ff.

54. *Ibid.*, 51 n.

55. *Ibid.*

56. *Ibid.*, 54 ff.

57. *Ibid.*, 62.

58. It is interesting, at this point, to go back to Monroe's private correspondence during the years of this mission. But see especially letters to Jefferson, July 30, 1796, and to Madison, September 1, 1796. The contemporary private record shows that while Monroe made every honest effort to carry out the policy of his government, he had no respect for it and every sympathy with the French. He also failed to confine his reports to the State Department. On August 1, 1796, for example, he wrote to Madison as follows: "I find by a paper from Tazewell that insinuations are made that (and perhaps I am meant) a party of Americans here are provoking the French to acts of hostility against us. Of all infamous calumnies this is the most infamous. This shows how necessary it is for me to put in the hands of the house organs of the public . . . a copy of every thing I do, as a guarantee against the attacks of those who are not with this view. Therefore I send you a copy of my correspondence with the minister of foreign affairs upon this subject. . . ." (Rives Collection, unpublished letter, Library of Congress.)

59. *A View of the Conduct of the Executive, etc.*, 1797.

60. This remarkably generous apology for Washington's policy and decision has no model in Monroe's reactions at the time of his recall. It is an ex-President, full of experience of the heavy responsibilities of that office, who speaks here.

61. But as early as June, 1798 he was consulting with Jefferson as to how best to return to public life. The U. S. House and Senate and possibly the governorship of Virginia were under consideration. See *Writings*, III, 128 ff.

62. There is reason to think, however, that Washington was angered by the news of Monroe's election. See P. L. Ford (ed.), *Writings of Washington*, XIV, 246 ff.

63. Monroe was governor from 1799 to 1802.
64. Madison.

65. Monroe's cordial, if reserved, treatment of Robert R. Livingston in these passages shows how the ex-President had mellowed since twenty-five

years before. See, for example, his private letter to Madison, April 15, 1803:
"I was informed on my arrival here by Mr. Skipwith that Mr. Livingston,
mortified at my appointment, had done everything in his power to turn the
occurrences in America, and even my mission, to his account, by pressing
the Government on every point with a view to show that he had accomplished what was wished without my aid. . . ." (*Writings*, IV, 9 ff.) At the
end of the mission he wrote as follows in a private letter to Madison: "I
enclose you a letter open addressed to Gen'l Mason, W. C. Nicholas, and
Mr. Breckenridge containing a statement of facts relative to what has occurred here which I have thought proper to put under your control. You
may either deliver it or retain it to be returned to me when I get back to
America. Circumstances may occur to make a knowledge of those facts
necessary, in which case it is possible there may be an advantage in their
being known, without it being supposed they came from you. Of this you
will judge and dispose of the enclosed as you think best. You will readily
concur how much to be avoided everything like a discussion of the kind
referred to is to be. I sincerely wish my colleague to derive all the advantage
and credit which his good exertions and intentions entitle him to, but the
transaction ought to rest on its own grounds, as a memorable incident of
our history tending to prove the wisdom of the measures of the last session.
I am of opinion that it imports the credit of the administration to treat him
with friendship and attention." June 8, 1803 (Rives Collection, Library of
Congress). By August the never-to-be-ended dispute over credit for the
Louisiana Purchase was on in earnest. See "private" letters from Monroe to
Madison, August 11, 23, 1803 (Rives Collection, Library of Congress).

66. See *Writings*, IV, 8, for an indication of the importance Monroe attached to his status as Minister Plenipotentiary.

67. For Monroe's contemporary view of this whole matter see his letters
to Madison May 14, 1803 (Rives Collection, Library of Congress) and July
26, 1803 (*Writings*, IV, 53–59).

68. See letter to Madison, June 8, 1803 (*Writings*, IV, 34 ff.).

69. *Ibid.*

70. Monroe takes his account of this conversation with Napoleon directly,
sometimes verbatim, from his letter to Madison of July 20, 1803 (*Writings*,
IV, 48–50).

71. William Pinkney (1764–1822), then attorney general of Maryland.

72. See letter to Madison, June 3, 1804 (*Writings*, IV, 191 ff.).

73. See letter to Madison, August 7, 1804 (*Writings*, IV, 228 ff.). The
Rives Collection in the Library of Congress contains many private letters
from Monroe to Madison during this period. In particular, they deal at
length with Robert R. Livingston's self-appointed mission to London, in
which he tried to act as a peace emissary on behalf of France.

74. For Monroe's contemporary analysis of the situation see *Writings*, IV, 266–298.

75. *Writings*, IV, 266–274.

76. See letters to Livingston and Madison, November 13 and December 16, 1804 (*Writings*, IV, 274–297). General John Armstrong (1758–1843) was the new American minister in Paris.

77. Charles Pinckney (1757–1824), Republican supporter of Jefferson, not to be confused with his cousin, General Charles C. Pinckney, Federalist leader who succeeded Monroe at Paris in 1797.

78. Two long letters to Madison dealing with these matters, January 27 and May 26, 1805, are in the Rives Collection, Library of Congress.

Index